T0199217

JOHN
MILTON

JOHN MILTON

A HERO *of* OUR TIME

DAVID HAWKES

COUNTERPOINT
BERKELEY

Library of Congress Cataloging-in-Publication Data is available.

ISBN: 978-1-58243-713-2

Cover design by Roxanna Aliaga
Interior design by Megan Jones Design
Printed in the United States of America

COUNTERPOINT
2560 Ninth Street, Suite 318
Berkeley, CA 94710

www.counterpointpress.com

for Simten Gurac

Rouze up O Young Men of the New Age! set your foreheads against the ignorant Hirelings! For we have Hirelings in the Camp, the Court, & the University: who would if they could, for ever depress Mental & prolong Corporeal War. Painters! on you I call! Sculptors! Architects! Suffer not the fashonable Fools to depress your powers by the prices they pretend to give for contemptible works or the expensive advertizing boasts that they make of such works; believe Christ & his Apostles that there is a Class of Men whose whole delight is in Destroying.

WILLIAM BLAKE, *Milton*[1]

We did not fall because of moral error; we fell because of an intellectual error: that of taking the phenomenal world as real.

PHILIP K. DICK, *VALIS*[2]

PREFACE

THERE ARE MANY brilliant and exhaustive biographies of Milton already. What is different about this meager essay? Most previous works on the subject have conscientiously attempted to place Milton in the context of his time. That is of course a prerequisite of a successful biography, and I hope that this one does not neglect it. The debt I owe to the historical insights provided by earlier biographies is obviously incalculable. But I have tried to make my emphasis slightly different, insofar as I concentrate on what Milton has to tell us about our own time: the "postmodern" era of the twenty-first century. I hope that I may be acquitted from the charge of anachronism on the grounds that Milton considered himself a prophet and that he often explicitly states that he is speaking to the people of the future, to us.

Most of the interpretations of Milton's work found here have been made before by others, and my intellectual obligations are so great as to render any invoice risibly inadequate. But I would mention in particular the work of Victoria Silver, who first taught me about Milton in graduate school, and whose book *Imperfect Sense: The Predicament of Milton's Irony* has influenced my ideas in ways so profound that I am doubtless unaware of many of them. The original idea for this book came from my astonishingly generous colleague Ayanna Thompson, who was also kind enough to read and comment on portions of the work in progress. Kathy Romack, Rebecca Steinberger and Barbara Traister were especially inspiring conversationalists, and I learned a great deal from them. Obviously, however, no one but myself bears any responsibility for my hermeneutical and historical blunders.

I wish to thank the English department at Jadavpur University, Kolkata, which provided me with a very useful Humanities fellowship just as I was finishing this project. The intellectual and personal generosity of Swapan Chakrovorty, Supriya and Sukanta Chaudhuri, Amlan Das Gupta, and Malabika Sarkar was truly overwhelming. The entire department of English at Arizona State University also deserves my thanks, and I've benefited in particular from the conversation and collegiality of Cora Fox, Joe Lockard, Richard Newhauser and Brad Ryner. Phillip Karagas, Risha Sharma and Karen Silva have been unbelievably patient and helpful, and Neal Lester has unfailingly provided every aid and support I either asked or hoped for. I am extremely grateful to Eileen Cope for her initial faith in this project and her encouragement as I worked to complete it. Jack Shoemaker and Laura Mazer have been everything an author could possibly desire in a publisher. My friends and family have been staunch in their support as always, and this project could never have been conceived, let alone completed, without the unfailing loving kindness of Simten Gurac.

INTRODUCTION:

PROPHETIC STRAIN

I

Although he has been dead more than 300 years, John Milton should be judged by the standards of the twenty-first century. We ought to evaluate his work by its relevance to our situation today. Other authors of the past do not invite this demanding kind of scrutiny, but Milton insists on it. Throughout his life, Milton claimed to be a prophet. He frequently declared that he was speaking primarily not to his contemporaries (whom he thought hopelessly ill-equipped to understand him) but to the people of the future, to us. He believed himself divinely ordained to announce truths that might be ridiculed by his own era but that would be resoundingly vindicated by succeeding ages. He thought he was ahead of his time. He arrived early at this belief, and he never wavered from it. At the age of twenty-two he envisioned for himself a life of study and contemplation "[t]ill old experience do attain / To something like Prophetic strain."[1] His later pronouncements on the subject dispense with the qualifier. We are his intended audience; we are the ones who can judge the accuracy of his predictions. Does Milton explain the nature of our own predicament, does he indicate how it came about, does he offer a way out of it? Was he a prophet?

Prophets are not honored in their own countries, and Milton's opinions were not highly esteemed by most of his contemporaries. His views on matters ranging from monarchy to divorce were considered wildly outlandish by all but the extreme avant-garde, and the books in which he expressed them were received with furious outrage and ribald laughter. Many writers would have concluded that there was something eccentric or incoherent about their own opinions, but Milton concluded that it was everyone else who was wrong. He was, he thought, battling against the spirit of the age itself, the zeitgeist:

I did but prompt the age to quit their clogs
By the known rules of ancient liberty,
When straight a barbarous noise environs me
Of owls and cuckoos, asses, apes and dogs.[2]

To "quit their clogs" means to "leave their shackles," and Milton spent his life trying to break what his admirer William Blake was to call the "mind-forg'd manacles" in which, he believed, his countrymen had imprisoned themselves. His battles were largely lost and his life ended with all of his causes defeated, but rather than question the virtue of those causes, he blamed the servile mentality of his fellow Englishmen. Attempting to liberate willing slaves was merely "casting pearl to hogs." The people loved their shackles.

Milton believed that most people are natural slaves. He got this idea from Aristotle, who used it to rationalize ancient Greek society's dependence on slave labor. In Aristotle, a slave is a person whose actions serve the purposes of somebody else: a person whose own activity is alien to him, because it belongs to another. By serving the purposes of another he ceases to belong to himself—he becomes an attribute, a "property," of the other person. Serving alien purposes is unnatural, because it is human nature to pursue one's own purposes, but many, perhaps most, people are attracted to this unnatural way of life. These people would rather be slaves than be free.

It is easy to dismiss the concept of natural slavery as a piece of self-interested fiction. Of course the ruling class in a slave-owning society will need to believe that slaves are naturally suited to their condition. But Milton was well aware that legally enslaved people are not necessarily natural slaves and that many natural slaves are not legally enslaved. The Aristotelian argument describes the nature of servility, not the empirical characteristics of slaves. Milton believed that every individual was naturally inclined toward mental slavery. Not everyone acted on his or her natural inclinations, however, and in fact a virtuous life should be a continuous act of resistance to slavish temptations. For Milton, virtue was not innate but had to be actively produced, manufactured through the battle against vice, just as good is created by the fight against evil, and freedom is won only through incessant internal and external war against our natural tendencies to slavery.

Milton presupposed that, in general, it is servile to focus one's desires and attentions on the empirical world, the world that we experience through the senses. For Milton, the natural goal of empirical experience was to serve the purposes of a more profound reality. Properly understood, the physical world consists of images, of signs that designate metaphysical referents. But a natural slave will forget or ignore this and assume that the physical world is the proper end (in every sense) of his life. He will be unable to interpret signs, because he does not understand that it is the nature of signs to point to something beyond themselves. A natural slave will be unable to distinguish between appearance and reality, between sign and thing. He will assume that signs are all there is; he will believe that the world of appearances is the real world. He will live in a kind of hyper-reality, in which simulacra are all that exist. In other words, he will enter into what twenty-first century philosophers call "the postmodern condition."

A natural slave will also be a literalist. Because he does not grasp the relation between signs and their referents, he will not read beneath the surface meaning of a text; he will not be able to perceive figurative, symbolic or metaphorical kinds of meaning. Milton argued that this leads to serious errors in religion. He protested against what he called "servile," literalist interpretations of the Bible. The religious fundamentalists of the twenty-first century would, by Milton's standards, exhibit a slavish mentality. But the same would be true of most secular inhabitants of the liberal, relativist, pragmatic Western world, with its postmodernist philosophers who celebrate the plethora of depthless simulacra that distinguishes our era. He would have judged these two modes of thought, which seem polar opposites to us, as different versions of the same underlying slave mentality, different ways of fetishizing images.

According to Milton the primary characteristic of the slave mentality is idolatry. We tend to think of idolatry as mainly a religious matter, and this explains why, during the secularizing nineteenth and twentieth centuries, the relevance of Milton's iconoclasm was frequently obscured. That relevance will surely become more evident in the post-secular environment of the twenty-first century, but in any case the question of whether icons and images should be part of religious worship was a major issue in seventeenth-century English politics, and especially in the revolution of the 1640s. Milton and his fellow Puritans strongly opposed such ecclesiastical ornaments because they believed that many of the congregation would follow the slavish tendency to worship the material signs of divinity rather than God himself. And because religion was of such central significance to people's lives, religious idolatry had clear implications for other areas of experience. Thus Milton believed that idolatry caused people to form their political opinions on the basis of image and rhetoric rather than logic. The English monarchy survived by fostering the King's image and cultivating his aura. Milton opposed monarchy because he believed that most people automatically tended to idolize their king, making him into an earthly divinity and willingly serving his purposes instead of their own.

At one stage in his life, Milton imagined that the English revolution, in which he was a prominent participant, was divinely destined to abolish all forms of idolatry. Its failure to do so convinced him that natural slavery was the general, if not quite the universal, human condition. However, he also believed that it was an unnatural, perverted condition. Human beings were naturally free, although they were everywhere in chains. The servile mindset shared by the majority of the human race must therefore be the result of some universal perversion, some general distortion of human nature, and this is what Milton called "the Fall." Following the defeat of his political aspirations, he devoted his best efforts to analyzing the consequences of the Fall, in the hope that by doing so he might enable later ages to escape them. He wanted to teach the people of the future how to escape from slavery. He wanted us to break the shackles that he could not.

Milton assumed that the first step toward the abolition of natural slavery was the reform of religion. It was in church that people were trained and habituated to the adoration of images. Images and icons do not appeal to the mind by way of reason or logic; they appeal to the emotions by means of the senses. By worshipping religious icons people learned a slavish reverence for signs in general—they learned to accept appearances as real, and to serve the fleshly ends of the body above the spiritual purposes of the mind. So liberation from slavery meant, first of all, smashing the physical icons that tempt us to worship them. Milton was an iconoclast; he believed that the worship of images was the root of all evil. But the destruction of physical images was only the precursor to a far broader, deeper iconoclasm that would transform the condition of the entire world and the nature of everybody's daily experience. Milton tried to imagine a world completely free of idols. He even tried to bring such a world into existence, in his revolutionary political career. He applied the principle of iconoclasm to everything: to religion but also to politics, to law, to marriage, gender and sexuality, to the most intimate feelings and experiences. He practiced iconoclasm everywhere: in church, in the Council of State, in the law courts and, one suspects, in bed. He made iconoclasm his way of life.

And it is here that we find Milton's relevance to the present day, for ours is the era of the image. Capitalist society is idolatrous to a degree surpassing the worst nightmares of seventeenth-century iconoclasts. It is a cliché of postmodernist philosophy that the distinction between sign and referent has collapsed and with it our ability to distinguish an essential, objective reality beneath the hyper-real world of simulacra that constitutes everyday experience. For example, the concern of today's politics with style over substance, with perception rather than reality, is obvious and undisguised. The rise of the image has often been linked to a relativist, pragmatist morality that can conceive of no absolute, ultimate truth underlying rhetorical signification, and to the spread of popular materialism: the widespread assumption that the world of appearances is the only reality. Its causes have been traced to the growth of the market economy, which depends upon the manipulation of images, and to a change in the nature of money, which has mutated into a non-material, purely imaginary or symbolic form. Images rule our world, and a world ruled by images needs an iconoclast.

Since Milton believed that idolatry was slavery, he would not be surprised to find that virtually everyone in capitalist society is enslaved. Traditional forms of slavery are of course illegal, but slavery in the Aristotelian sense, the sense that Milton connected to idolatry, is almost universal. Aristotle defines a slave as one who serves the ends of another. A slave's activity is not his own. The slave does not belong to himself—he has become alienated from himself and made a "property" of his master. We might think that this almost never happens in today's Western societies, but in fact anyone who works for a salary enters into this condition. Any wage-worker sells his life piecemeal, serving the purposes of his employer for a given amount of time. Wage-labor is not necessarily unpleasant, and it can often be highly lucrative, but it is nevertheless piecemeal slavery, because it involves the alienation of our activity, albeit on a temporary and voluntary basis.

Voluntary for some at least. The independently wealthy can refuse to sell their time for money, but the best most of us can hope for is to find a benign master to serve. If we do not sell forty or fifty hours of our lives each week, we will find it difficult to survive. Wage-workers, even those with shining white collars, are not at liberty, they are not free, when they are at work: their time is not their own, and their time is their life. In capitalist society, for the first time in human history, people who live by selling their time for money have very nearly become the universal class. Almost everyone gives up a portion of his or her freedom every day. We live in a slave society, and such societies produce a slavish mentality in their inhabitants. Not everyone shares that mentality, and those who do exhibit it to widely varying degrees. But it is fair to say that the psychological tendencies that Milton considered servile and idolatrous are much more powerful and widespread today than they were when he wrote. It is theoretically possible for an enslaved person to live and think in a free manner. But the habits of thought developed by slavery are easily formed and hard to break. They are readily reinforced by indulgence in sensual appetite and consolidated by superstitious fascination with images. These were the habits that Milton set out to break, first within himself and then in the English people as a whole.

If it is still thought desirable to alter such habits, we might do worse than consider Milton's suggestions about how this might be achieved. His ideas on the subject are worth considering in depth, because he actually tried to put them into practice, not just in his personal life but also through a political revolution. Milton was that rarest of beasts, otherwise virtually unknown in the modern Western world: a supremely talented artist who also exercised significant political power. The author of *Paradise Lost* was also Secretary for Foreign Tongues to the revolutionary Council of State. The poet who gave us "Lycidas" was also the government propagandist commissioned to produce the official defense of the King's execution. Few Europeans since Cicero had played such exalted aesthetic and political roles in one lifetime, and none has done so since Milton. Milton provides an example, almost unique in the history of capitalist society, of an artistic intellectual's attempt to put his theories into practice. Most of those attempts were unsuccessful, but it is worth considering the possibility that Milton was right about the reasons for this. Perhaps he really was ahead of his time. Perhaps the shackles he tried to break have not yet been broken. In that case, Milton's efforts to break them may yet bear fruit.

Some of them already have. On the issue of divorce, in which Milton had a strong personal interest, the ideas that seemed so shockingly radical when he expressed them in the 1640s are commonplace today. Milton was the first Englishman, and one of the first people anywhere, to argue that divorce on the sole grounds of psychological incompatibility ought to be legal. Today, in the West, his aim has largely been achieved. Milton was also among the earliest advocates for the freedom of the press, and today this principle, if not its practice, is widely established. He was in the vanguard of those who argued for the separation of church and state, and for the abolition of the monarchy, and although these reforms have not been implemented in his native country, they have gained widespread success throughout the world. In many ways his claims to be a prophet have been vindicated.

But on the issue of idolatry, Milton's teachings fall on very stony ground today. Most people today never think about idolatry and would probably see nothing wrong with it if they did. Our widespread ignorance and apathy over this matter would surprise and dismay Milton. Idolatry was the issue about which he felt most strongly, because he thought that it both encapsulated and explained all the other problems that beset the human race. To understand its significance for him, we must abandon our modern assumption that idolatry is a specifically religious issue. In essence, idolatry is the tendency to misconstrue the relation between images and reality, between signs and what the signs represent. If we find that tendency prevalent today, if we find ourselves attracted to images at the expense of reality, if our rulers address us through the media of rhetoric rather than logic, if we notice that sexuality is increasingly filtered through pornographic imagery, then we need to read Milton. For Milton is the greatest iconoclast in the history of thought. His iconoclasm is unremitting and thoroughgoing, and it extends into the deepest crannies and recesses of the psyche, into justification of political revolution, and into startling interrogations of sex and gender. Milton prescribes iconoclasm as life's most basic principle, an attitude and a practice to be implemented in politics, sexuality, law and above all in the psyche. That is why we need him today, for we are ruled by images, and their rule is by no means benign. It might even be called tyrannical.

II

FROM AN EARLY age, Milton determined to live his life on iconoclastic principles. Predictably, this resulted in a tragic, violent, frenetic and heroic biography. The sheer drama of his trajectory, the brutal severity of the ordeals he endured, the seminal significance of the political revolution in which he participated, the unsurpassed glory of his poetic achievements, might have made him into England's national hero. And there was a time when many people thought him exactly that. The Romantic poets worshipped him; Byron, Keats and Shelley were restrained from making him a god only by his own stern injunctions against idolatry. Wordsworth called for a Miltonic response to the industrial age: "Milton! Thou shouldst be living at this hour: / England hath need of thee...."[3] William Blake wrote an epic poem entitled *Milton*, which argued forcefully, if eccentrically, for the earlier poet's prophetic role. The founding fathers of America saw themselves as completing the Miltonic reforms that had been thwarted in England. Karl Marx cited him as the ultimate exemplar of unalienated human activity. Today, however, his reputation is rather less exalted. Milton is now read mostly by reluctant undergraduates and studied in detail only by their tutors. He retains a precarious position on university curriculums, but the popular audience he enjoyed for centuries has largely evaporated.

The decline in Milton's posthumous fortunes is often attributed to a critical campaign waged in the early twentieth century by T.S. Eliot and F.R. Leavis, who thought that Milton epitomized, or even caused, a destructive "dissociation of sensibility" from which England has never recovered. They had a point, in the sense that Milton's thought, as well as his political activities, represents a fundamental break with the concepts and attitudes of the Middle Ages. For English conservatives the seventeenth-century revolution is the definitive historical disaster, almost a fall from grace, and Milton not only fanned its flames with polemic but carried out its most dubious pragmatic necessities. He was a practical revolutionary, revolutions bring radical change, and the critics who attacked Milton were nostalgic for the world he helped to destroy. But there are surely deeper reasons for the decline in Milton's readership. Perhaps that decline is one of quality as well as of quantity. Perhaps we are no longer equipped to understand him.

This might be because Milton's religious references and concerns are unfamiliar to many people today. But that should not be an obstacle to understanding his work, any more than the obsolescence of the Greek Pantheon should be an obstacle to understanding *The Iliad*. We do not have to believe in Zeus to grasp Homer's meanings, and we do not need to believe in God to appreciate Milton's ideas. We do not need to believe in the historical reality of King Oedipus to take Freud seriously, nor do we have to believe in the actual existence of Adam and Eve to give Milton's opinions their due consideration. His commentaries on the Bible are also commentaries on the human condition as a whole. The adventures of characters like Satan, Beelzebub and Gabriel do not purport to provide an account of real, historical events: Milton consistently opposed literalistic interpretations of scripture. Such figures are personified concepts, ideas, psychological states and experiences. As soon as we understand Milton's religious terminology as a network of tropes and metaphors, a mythologized mode of expressing philosophical, political, even sexual positions, then their implications for our own situation will become clear. Milton wrote at the very end of the era in which philosophical and psychological issues were discussed in religious terminology. To understand him, we must abandon our tendency to concentrate on the literal meanings of religious terms; we must refuse to be distracted by our knowledge that Satan "does not exist." We must take the ideas of the past seriously.

Consider the issue of magic. Most citizens of the modern West do not believe in it, while Milton did. But we would be foolish to allow our skepticism to prevent us from giving his ideas due consideration. Milton believed that magic was made possible by idolatry: it worked only when people believed in the objective, practical power of signs and images. This was the basis of his society's identification of magic as a Satanic force. Magic is the practical deployment of the efficacious, autonomous power of signs and images; a magician attempts to achieve objective effects by the manipulation of symbols. Magic does not use signs for their natural purpose, which is to refer to things. Rather, magic bestows independent power on the symbols it utilizes: it makes fetishes of them, using signs to do things, not to mean things.

The precise nature of magic was of course much debated, but in Milton's day the conventional position was that although signs and images do not naturally have effects in the real world, they can *appear* to have such effects, and this illusion is the work of magic. The unreal but apparent effects of the signs must be produced by some power other than the signs themselves, since signs cannot naturally do anything, or even pretend to do anything. Because they are unnatural and illusory, these effects cannot be caused by any benign power; they must in fact be produced by a perverse and deceitful power, one that enters into and perverts the human mind. The people of Milton's time called that power "Satan." They believed that all magicians, witches and sorcerers were, at least implicitly, guilty of a pact with Satan, and so deserving of execution.

If this logic seems strange or barbaric to us it is because we find nothing amiss in the power of signs and images; it has become second nature
to us, and we are generally happy to allow this second nature to override
the first. We do not "believe in" witchcraft. But if we are to take the ideas
of the past seriously, we must imagine the logic by which Milton and
many other highly intelligent, learned people of his day concluded that
the autonomous power of representation is Satanic. That is not easy, in
large part because of our literalist habits of interpretation. If Satan does
not literally exist, we assume, then he does not exist at all—he is a mere
fantasy, a non-entity, unworthy of serious consideration. But for Milton,
literalism in interpretation was itself a satanic tendency and the direct
result of Satan's influence within the mind. It has often been said that
Satan's success is complete when people cease to believe in him. We easily
lapse into the assumption that human life is always and inevitably ruled
by images; we see no means to end that rule, and so it is hard for us to
see what is evil about it. The sense that the rule of images is normal and
enjoyable pervades academic discourse as well as popular culture, and
perhaps this is the primary difference between the seventeenth-century
mind and the postmodern one.

In one sense it is true that human experience always and inevitably
consists of images. Most people could probably agree that what we call
"reality" is a construction, a set of images that we have made in our
minds. Of course there is an objective, physical world outside our minds,
and of course we experience that world through our senses. But unlike
animals, human beings naturally and inevitably interpret that world in
the act of experiencing it. Human beings cannot help but impose concepts upon our sensory experience. That is the difference between us
and animals: where a dog sees only a black, cold, inedible object, we
see a computer. We experience the computer with our senses, but that

experience is influenced by our knowledge that the object of experience is a particular instance of a general concept. This does not mean that there is no reality outside human experience, but it does mean that human beings do not have unmediated access to that reality. We do not see things as they really are, we see things as we conceptualize them, as we construct them—we see their images. Images are the very stuff of human experience; they cannot be avoided or destroyed.

So a true iconoclast does not destroy images. We might even say that an iconoclast *creates* images, in the sense that he draws attention to their existence and explains their nature. For it is very easy—it is in fact the definitive temptation of human nature—to forget that we are experiencing the world via humanly constructed images. It is easy to believe that we are experiencing the world directly, as it really is, rather than merely as it appears to be. It comes naturally to us, and because it comes naturally it is tempting. It has become much more tempting since Milton's time; indeed, it is arguably more tempting today than ever before. One reason for this is the sheer ubiquity of visual images that our technology has created. This is a new situation; previous generations did not have access to the same plethora of images that we do. It seems reasonable to assume that this explosion of images has affected the way we think about images in general.

Another reason for the rise to power of images is economic. Over the last three centuries, in a process that Milton was among the first to witness and exploit, money has come to rule over economic activity. The prerequisite for this growth in the power of money was the relaxation, and eventually the abolition, of laws against "usury." This precondition was being established in Milton's time, and as we shall see, he was fully conscious of its significance. His response to it was necessarily complicated and ambivalent: he was himself a professional usurer, but he acknowledged the coherence of the ethical case against usury. He saw that once money is permitted to reproduce autonomously, to "breed," it moves beyond human control. It attains a life of its own; it develops its own needs and makes its own demands, which often conflict with those of the human beings who have brought it into existence. Furthermore, the rise to power of money has revealed its true nature. When Milton was born, most people still innocently equated financial value with physical precious stones and metals. And until quite recently most people continued to assume that financial value had some physical existence, if only in the form of paper banknotes. Today, however, our use of credit cards and electronic banking has made everyone aware that financial value exists only in symbolic form. Despite being a purely symbolic phenomenon, however, it has extremely powerful objective effects. Indeed, it rules the world. Financial value, in short, is an image with practical power, an idol.

All this is widely understood today. Our problem today is not ignorance of the power of images. Our problem is in seeing anything wrong with that power. To return to the example of magic, when we say that we do not "believe in" it, we do not mean that signs cannot be manipulated in order to achieve objective effects. We all know that they can—we all demonstrate this power of signs whenever we use a credit card. Such attribution of efficacious power to signs is the very definition of magic. But when we say that there is nothing "magical" about the power of financial value, we really mean that there is nothing wrong with it. We mean that it is not evil. We sometimes still pay lip service to the idea that politics ought to be about substantive issues rather than images; we may disapprove of individuals who are overly concerned with their images, or who judge others by appearances. Some people still raise objections to the total economic domination of money; some people are uncomfortable with the fact that the most powerful force in the world has no physical existence. Most people harbor a vague unease regarding the rule of images. But we lack a thoroughgoing ethical theory that would allow us to understand why the rule of images is evil. We acknowledge their power, we feel that there is something wrong with that power, but we seem unable to say exactly what it is. That is the great ideological deficiency of our time.

It is true that there are plenty of iconoclasts at work in the world. Islamic fundamentalists undoubtedly hate images and destroy them wherever they can. The Taliban's explosion of the Buddhas of Bamiyan and the attack on the World Trade Center were arguably the most dramatic acts of iconoclasm in history. But such literalistic, facile attacks on physical images do nothing to impair their true power, which is not physical but psychological. An object becomes an image, and an image becomes an idol, only within the human psyche. Since idols have no power outside the human mind, it is impossible to abolish idolatry by destroying the objects on which it is focused. To try to do so is actually to encourage idolatry, by denying its true nature. If we really want to undermine the power of images, we will need a more sophisticated kind of iconoclasm, one that attacks images where they live: in the human mind. That is what Milton has left us, and that is why he matters today. His iconoclasm is his prophecy.

III

MILTON'S IDEAS CANNOT be understood apart from his biography, and he made sure posterity knew it. He continually reminded his readers of his personal history and circumstances, often discussing them explicitly, and alluding to them in virtually everything he wrote. This is not mere vanity but also a deliberate strategy to demonstrate the close connections between the individual mind and the political nation. No one was ever more convinced than Milton that the personal is political. His shockingly original, idiosyncratic ideas were made possible by the astonishing, unprecedented personal and political events through which he lived. He argued that good government is impossible unless the people are mentally healthy, and he blamed the English revolution's defeat on the English people's diseased psychology. He traced the dilemmas of his personal life to their socioeconomic roots, and he suggested that the solutions he found to his own personal problems might be replicated on the larger scale of national politics. This habit is unusual enough today to seem comic to modern readers; it is amusing when Milton's *Second Defense of the English People* develops into a defense of the author's personal courage, his sexual chastity, even his youthful good looks. It is titillating to read Milton denouncing his opponent's seduction of chambermaids in a pamphlet ostensibly devoted to justifying the execution of a monarch.

Such tactics have led many modern readers to convict Milton of the ad hominem fallacy. They note, correctly, that he often attacks his adversary's personality rather than his opinions. But Milton believed that personality and opinions were inseparable. To him it simply made no sense to evaluate ideas without also considering the characters of the people who held them. This was a common belief in seventeenth-century England, and the political conflict between King and parliament was also played out within the minds of individuals. The battle lines were not only drawn between republicans and royalists but also between "Puritan" and "Cavalier" personality types. The English revolution was won, and eventually lost, in the English psyche. That is why Milton's official political work is packed with autobiographical anecdotes, personal allusions, domestic digressions. From his earliest juvenilia he consciously constructs a public persona, informing the reader who he is, pointing out the links between his life and work, promising and describing greater works to come. His is the work of a man utterly confident that he will be read with care and attention for hundreds of years after his death. Milton always wrote for posterity.

He wanted posterity to understand him, because he felt no one else did. In life he was personally and intellectually lonely, but he took comfort in the company of his future audience. He tells us a great deal about himself, both deliberately and unconsciously, when he offers his own character as an object of study. In doing so he also raises questions about the nature of character itself. The modern world insists loudly on its individualism. We follow a cult of personality; not of individual personalities but of personality in general, personality as such. Newspaper stories always begin by focusing on a single individual, for that is how to get the reader's attention. Television programs sell themselves through the personalities of their presenters. A cast of bizarre celebrities provides dramatic entertainment in our public sphere. Economic theories extrapolate the behavior of individuals into rules for entire societies. Political democracy and the free-market economy represent themselves as promoting the virtues of individual choice, and politics mimics advertising, addressing itself to the subjective whims of the individual voter/consumer. Popular discourse is devoted as never before to the self: self-fulfillment, self-esteem, self-expression, self-help and self-image are the stuff of most people's aspirations. But what kind of self is being fulfilled, esteemed, expressed, helped and imagined?

Milton would have described the modern self as servile, and he would interpret its nature as the posthumous victory of his political opponents. But he has left us the weapons to subvert that victory. His diagnoses of natural slavery are matched by numerous and detailed descriptions of the free self, the liberated, heroic personality. His work provides several models of heroes, such as Jesus of Nazareth or Oliver Cromwell, and critiques of false heroes, such as Satan and Charles I. His political writing makes personal heroism the criterion by which leaders should be chosen: he propagandized for the heroic status of Cromwell and other leaders of the revolution, and he mercilessly mocked the attempts of Charles I's spin doctors to fashion a hero from the King's gauche and maudlin figure. Above all, however, Milton made a hero of himself. He made a concerted, conscious attempt to live a heroic life, which he believed a necessary pre-requisite of producing great art:

> [H]e who would not be frustrate of his hope to write well hereafter in laudable things, ought him selfe to bee a true Poem, that is, a composition, and patterne of the best and honourablest things; not presuming to sing high praises of heroick men, or famous cities, unless he have in himselfe the experience and the practice of all that which is praise-worthy.[4]

What would it mean to "be" a poem, as Milton aspires to be? To a far greater extent than prose, poetry assumes, and even produces, an awareness of imagery in the reader. It uses language symbolically, drawing attention to the symbolic nature of experience in general. It makes it impossible to forget that we are experiencing images rather than reality. In this sense, poetry can be considered the antithesis of idolatry. It can also be used as the antidote to idolatry. That is certainly how Milton used it. He intended his life, as well as his work, to be a poem and to provide a "patterne" for the consideration of future generations. He wanted us to read his biography alongside his writing, and to interpret his private thoughts and actions as we interpret his words. He wanted us to find the *meaning* of his life. This book attempts to do so.

1

THE FRUIT OF USURY

I

THERE IS A sense in which Milton was his own biographer. His work constantly reflects on his life and, like most other biographies, it begins by mentioning his recent forbears. The very first line of his earliest surviving poem, written at the age of fifteen, is pointedly autobiographical. The poem is "A [free] Paraphrase of Psalm 114," and it opens with a striking departure from the scriptural text. The biblical line refers to the Israelites as "the house of Jacob," but Milton alters this to "the blest seed of Terah's faithful son" (1). Terah was Abraham's father, and he is condemned by the Bible as an idolater, whose false religion contrasts with his son's worship of the true God. Milton introduces him here as an allusion to his own paternal grandfather, a yeoman farmer of Oxfordshire named Richard. Richard Milton was a Roman Catholic in the reign of Elizabeth and thus by Protestant standards an idolater. He refused to attend the compulsory services of the Anglican church and was prosecuted and fined for his defiance. But his son John, who would become the poet's father, was a Protestant, as Richard discovered when he found an English Bible in the youth's bedroom. Outraged, the patriarch expelled his son from the family home and disinherited him, forcing him to seek his own fortune in London, where he met and married Sarah Jeffreys, who became the mother of his children.

John Milton the poet was thus literally born out of the conflict between idolatry and iconoclasm, and he signals the seminal importance of this fact by invoking it in the earliest line of verse he preserved for posterity. There is a notable immodesty about the allusion, for Abraham became the father of God's chosen people, whom the psalm calls "the house of Jacob." Jacob was Abraham's son and thus, in the terms of the allusion, Milton himself. He is himself the "blest seed" of which he writes. It seems that the fifteen-year-old Milton was already claiming prophetic status, already imagining himself the patriarch of an elect race of spiritual descendents. The rest of the psalm recounts the flight of the Israelites from servitude in Egypt. Milton was already preoccupied with the theme of escape from slavery, which would remain his prime concern throughout his life. There is only one other poem that survives from this early date: a loose translation of Psalm 136, which also describes God's assistance of the flight from Egypt: "[I]n despite of Pharoah fell, / He brought from thence his Israel" (41–42). Milton's God is above all a liberator, who "doth the wrathful tyrants quell" (10), and frees his people from oppression. In his mid-teens, Milton had already established liberation from slavery as his life's guiding motive and his religion's primary end.

Cut off from his landed inheritance, John Milton senior had to make his own money from nothing. He had to make money itself bear the fruit that, for him, land could not. This makes him an emblematic figure of his age, which witnessed a shift in power away from traditional, landed property and toward financially based, mercantile wealth. He was a self-made man in the age of self-fashioning, fortunate to be thrust upon his own resources at a time when opportunities for clever, industrious young men were plentiful in the humming metropolis of London. In the late sixteenth century the city was undergoing a population explosion that would bring its inhabitants to almost half a million by 1650. Like the poet's father, most of the new arrivals were refugees from the countryside, but unlike Milton senior, they were usually former peasants who had been driven off their land by the process of mass expropriation euphemistically known as "enclosure."

Peasants produce the means of their own subsistence, and however lowly their lifestyle, they therefore retain a degree of independence. Peasants often live in poor conditions, but they are normally able to sustain their own lives. The daily activities of peasants may be arduous and tedious, but they are generally carried out in freedom from supervision. A peasant is basically a free person. Yet over the course of the sixteenth and seventeenth centuries, most English peasants were driven off their ancestral lands by fraud or force. They found their land "enclosed" within the estates of larger landowners, and they lacked the legal documents or skills to challenge this process, which would be repeated throughout the world in the eighteenth and nineteenth centuries. Many newly wealthy landowners looked to invest their surplus fortunes as capital. Many dispossessed peasants gravitated to London, where the market for labor was liveliest, and they became proletarians: people who lived by exchanging their labor power for money.

The term "enclosure" refers to the long and nefarious process by which England acquired the final preconditions of a capitalist market economy. The ultimate steps on the road to the dominance of the market are the making of saleable objects out of human life itself, and out of the earth by which that life subsists. Land and labor-power must be commodified. But people find it counterintuitive to conceive of land and labor-power as things that can be bought and sold, and it took hundreds of years for them to learn to think in this way. The lengthy, painful process of enclosure shows the efforts this demanded and the price it exacted. Enclosure concentrated wealth in relatively few hands, thus making surplus capital available for investment, a process known to economic historians as "primitive accumulation." It also produced the kind of workforce a capitalist economy demands: a class of people who lack any other way of feeding themselves than selling their labor-power.

A wage-laborer differs from a peasant because he cannot feed himself. Neither a peasant nor a wage laborer can survive without working, but a wage laborer cannot survive without working for someone else. He depends on another for his existence, and unlike the work of peasants, the daily activity of wage-laborers is generally closely supervised by those to whom it belongs. A wage-laborer also differs from an independent craftsman, because he does not own the products of his labor. He therefore cannot sell the products of his labor as an independent craftsman does. Rather, he sells his labor-power, his capacity to labor for a certain amount of time, which effectively means that he sells his life. The condition of a proletarian can accurately be described as piecemeal slavery, and an economy based on proletarian labor-power is a vast slave market that transforms human activity into the representational form of money. Every day a proletarian exchanges his time, his life, his very self, for wages. The money that he earns represents his own activity in external, alien, symbolic form. This is the source of the ethical critique of capitalism as a systematic form of "alienation."

The establishment of a market in labor involves the reduction of labor to a commodity, but it also involves the elevation of the universal commodity to the status of labor: it puts money to work. Labor is translated into financial form so that it can be alienated, separated from the person who performs it, and allowed to reproduce in an apparently independent fashion. This enables some people to survive through the manipulation of money alone, and these people are known as "capitalists." Today, virtually everyone in Western society is a proletarian, but virtually everyone is also a capitalist: they sell time for wages but also receive some income, however small, from capital investments. The class struggle between proletarians and capitalists, which dominated nineteenth- and twentieth-century politics, has become internalized within the individual. Under such circumstances economic and political contradictions are experienced as psychological events, and this should make us look again at the lessons to be learned from Milton's politics, which are ultimately located internally, within the self.

The London that received Milton's father offered ample opportunities for aspirant capitalists. It was already an important center of trade, and the nature of its trade was rapidly changing. The established business conducted with continental Europe was being supplemented by intercourse with the newly discovered or newly accessible territories of the West and East Indies. Over the preceding century an enormous influx of African and American gold and silver had monetized the European economy. Payments that had previously been made in kind, in goods or services, were now made in cash, and what had been direct relations between people were now filtered through money. This situation was complicated by the fact that material cash was often in short supply, so that most financial transactions had to be conducted through the insubstantial medium of credit. Finance was a new science, and very few people understood it; this put those who were prepared to seize the opportunity in an excellent position.

John Milton senior was prepared. He farmed money as his father had farmed land. He manipulated the new, mysterious power of financial value as his son would manipulate the signifying power of words. He set up shop as a scrivener, a profession whose main purpose was to facilitate moneylending, by arranging, witnessing, and enforcing debts. It also gave him ample opportunity to lend money for profit himself: in short, he was a usurer. He steadily prospered at this dubious trade, and by the dawn of the seventeenth century, when he was around forty, he was in a position to marry. His bride was the daughter of a merchant tailor and thus born into the mercantile element of which John Milton senior now formed a prominent part. At some unknown date she bore a daughter, Anne, and on December 9, 1608, she gave birth to a son, John, who was followed by a brother, Christopher, in 1615. These three siblings survived into adulthood; like so many other seventeenth-century children, the Miltons' three other offspring died in infancy.

It is a remarkable fact that both the towering geniuses of early modern English literature, Milton and Shakespeare, were the sons of usurers. Shakespeare's father was twice accused of criminal usury, and Milton's father was constantly being sued by disgruntled debtors. Indeed, both poets were themselves lifelong practitioners of usury. They were capitalists living at the dawn of capitalism, and perhaps this gave them special insight into the nature of the capitalist era. Perhaps they appeal to us more than any of their contemporaries because their involvement with usury gave them a peculiar knowledge of the psychology of the future, in which usury would dominate the world. Perhaps their facility in deploying the reproductive powers of money is connected to their skill in using the semantic power of language. Money and language are both systems of signs, which have over the last 400 years displayed a growing proclivity to occlude or replace their referents. Those who evince particular skill in handling financial signs have frequently been regarded with deep suspicion. It is not easy for us to grasp exactly what it meant to be a

usurer in early sixteenth-century London, but the practice of usury was
certainly held in low esteem. The Miltons were undoubtedly a well-liked
and respectable family, very far from being pariahs, but it is nonetheless
true that many of their neighbors would have looked askance at John
Milton senior's profession.

The first half of the seventeenth century has been called "the age of
debt." Debt litigation exploded between 1575 and 1635, and a considerable amount of it involved the Miltons, both father and son. Extant
records show that both men spent a large proportion of their lives in
court, arguing over money. The incessant haggling and nitpicking involved
in seventeenth-century legal cases surely left their mark on the Miltons'
minds. Due to the ubiquitous necessity of small-scale moneylending, relations between creditors and debtors were extremely complicated in early
modern London. They were also extremely intimate. Creditors and debtors rubbed shoulders daily in the throng of the commercial city, and a
glance at the literature of the age, especially the popular "city comedies"
of Thomas Dekker, John Marston, or Thomas Middleton, shows how
emotional, even sexualized, such connections could become. As we shall
see, Milton's love life, with its intricate, oddly comic interactions between
sex and usury, seems almost to spring from the pages of such drama.
Furthermore, since most people would have simultaneously occupied the
roles of debtor and creditor, the profound ethical and logical questions
surrounding usury would to a great extent have been internalized and
experienced as psychological, or rather spiritual, concerns. It was sinful
to pay interest as well as to receive it, and since it was virtually impossible
to live without sullying one's hands in this way, usury was regarded as a
vice to which all were tempted and in which most indulged. The advice
offered by Shakespeare's Polonius to his son, "neither a borrower nor a
lender be,"[1] was extremely topical but impossible to obey.

But while a degree of involvement in credit and debt was unavoidable, to make one's living by usury was widely regarded as despicably predatory. Preachers and pamphleteers inveighed daily against the taking of interest, and Richard Stock, the minister of Milton's parish church, was prominent among them. Stock, whose sermons Milton presumably attended, inveighed against usury as "the cursed trade" and declared that "an Usurer is a reproach amongst men."[2] Under such circumstances moneylending is more than a simple business matter, and usury easily becomes regarded as an antisocial perversion. John Milton senior was no money-grubbing Philistine. He was an aficionado of the arts, a brilliant musician and composer whose talents won him a considerable reputation. His biographer remarks: "If we listen to his music today, it delivers to us across the centuries an impression of a great personality, at once genial, robust, and touchingly impassioned."[3] Perhaps that personality shielded him from some of the obloquy directed against usurers; certainly he could have expected no such protection from the fact that he styled himself a "scrivener." He was among the most prominent scriveners in London and held the offices of Assistant and Steward in the Scriveners' Company during the poet's childhood. He literally lived under the sign of the scriveners: The spread-eagle, with which he adorned the entrance to his shop, was also the symbol of the profession as a whole. His son would adopt it as his family coat of arms.

Scriveners were, if anything, held in yet greater fear and contempt than outright usurers. Seventeenth-century literature generally portrays them as sinister middlemen, shadowy go-betweens who, mediating the relation of borrower to lender, play the role of pimp in the ubiquitous comparison of usury to prostitution. The anonymous *Character of a London Scrivener* (1667) describes

[a] surreptitious race of men, not of God's Creation, but born (like Vermin) out of the corruption of several Ages, or (like some Afric Monsters) the Amphibious Product of a Heterogeneous Copulation: for when Persons of different Interests and humours met together in a Contract, this Jarring Conjunction begat Scriviners. . . . Sometimes he plays the Baud, prostitutes the same Title to all comers . . . sometimes he solders up a crackt Title, and passes it away for a pure Maiden-head . . .[4]

Scriveners were the fruit of unnatural copulation, emerging out of the unnatural intercourse between credit and debt, and also the procurers, facilitating further illicit liaisons. They were the practical agents of usury, which was often depicted as a quasi-sexual perversion, conceiving offspring from what is naturally barren. The usurer violated nature by making the sterile substance of money "breed." To be a usurer was, in the words of Thomas Dekker, "to keepe a Bawdy house for Lady Pecunia."[5] Usury's mirror-image was held to be "sodomy," which made the act of reproduction into a sterile pleasure.[6] Miles Mosse was typical in calling usury "*Sodomia naturae*, a kind of Sodomie in nature."[7]

But the most pervasive strain of imagery in anti-usury invective was Satanic. The relation between creditor and debtor was seen as fundamentally adversarial. Economic tracts of the period ceaselessly referred to creditors as "adversaries," a term that naturally evoked the devil, since "satan" is the Hebrew word for "adversary." The seventeenth-century credit crisis produced a campaign against the imprisonment of debtors that endlessly employed this image. The treatise *A Supply to a Draught of an Act or System Proposed* appeals for the relief of "poor prisoners against merciless Adversaries," and William Bagwell's *The Merchant*

Distressed addresses a rhyme "To him that betrayed the Prisoner into his Adversaries hands."[8] Phillip Stubbes's *The Anatomie of Abuses* describes usurers as worse than murderers, Jews, Hell, death and the devil before announcing that "there be no men so great doers in this noble facultie and famous science as the Scriveners be."[9] Scriveners are in fact "the Divels agents to set forward Usurie," and "the Scrivener is the instrument whereby the Devill worketh the frame of this wicked woorke of Usury" (ibid. 129). In Thomas Dekker's *News from Hell* (1606), Satan is the "Setter up of Scriveners" (138) and "All the Scriveners ith'town he had at his becke, but they were so set a worke with making bondes between Usurers and Unthriftie heirs, betweene Marchants and Tradesmen . . ." (93). Literature on all sides of the issue refers to scriveners as devils, to debt as damnation and to debtors' prison as Hell. For Wye Salstonall a scrivener was "a Christian cannibal that devours men alive. His life is so black that no ink can paint it forth, he is one of the Devil's engines to ruin others, he is a paper-worm, or a rack for honest men."[10]

The young Milton must have been keenly aware that his father's business was widely considered the work of Satan, and that the luxury of free time to study and write had been purchased for him at some ethical cost. He certainly sounded cognizant of the exploitative character of the family trade when he reminded himself, in 1642, that "ease and leasure was given thee for thy retired thoughts out of the sweat of other men" (1:804). The complicated and subterranean nature of the trade meant that it was often handed down from father to son, and this increased the suspicion with which usurers were viewed. In *The Arraignment and Conviction of Usurie* (1595), Miles Mosse refuted a defense of usury that claimed a usurer's benign son might dispose of his father's ill-gotten gains in a charitable manner: "For commonly such egge such chickin, such syer such childe: the father an vsurer, the sonne vnmercifull" (14). The personality traits of usurers were inherited, like bad genes. Usury was also extremely vulnerable to the charge of idolatry, because it worked by making money, a mere sign, reproduce. Since Aristotle, who declared that usury was "most reasonably hated,"[11] the orthodox position had been that usury was unnatural because money was not a commodity itself but a sign of other commodities, a medium of expression for their symbolic value. In the words of Thomas Aquinas:

> All other things from themselves have some utility; not so, however, money. But it is the measure of utility of other things, as is clear according to [Aristotle] in the *Ethics* V:9. And therefore the use of money does not have its utility from this money itself, but from the things which are measured by money.[12]

Money was not a thing but a sign of other things. To treat money as if it were a thing of value in itself, rather than as the abstract standard of value (thus making the essence of value into an object of value), was to confuse the relation of sign and referent, which was held to be an egregious violation of nature. Usury's opponents claimed that it was a kind of magic or witchcraft, for it granted practical, efficacious power to something that did not exist in nature. To make money breed was to effect a re-creation, to displace God's creation by a human concept, to override nature with the supernatural.

The Milton household must frequently have been filled with the melodious harmony of its patriarch's musical compositions. Just as often, however, it must have been filled with a more discordant noise: the squabbling, haggling and even brawling that accompany the business of small-scale moneylending in any age, and especially at times when the morality of the profession is held in low regard. Milton the scrivener conducted his business from home, and his enemies knew where to find him. Several of his debtors made allegations under oath that he had dealt fraudulently with them. The stakes in such disputes were extremely high, because the creditor had the right to throw defaulting debtors into prison, where conditions were such that death was a real possibility. In 1628 it was estimated that ten thousand people were in debtors' prisons.[13] In 1624 we find one of John Milton's wretched clients begging him: "That if execucion were sued out against him, he should be forced to lye in prison, which would be his utter overthrowe, and undoeing."[14] An example of a far less serious case, the details of which are preserved in court records, will serve to show the kind of business that went on in the poet's childhood home.

In 1626 the senior Milton sought out a widow named Rose Downer, having heard that she had money to invest. She testified that he "advised her to put out the said fifty pounds at interest rather than to employ it any other ways, and used divers persuasions unto [her] that he might have the putting of it forth. . . ."[15] Milton was touting for business, his importuning was successful, and Mrs. Downer allowed him to loan out her money for her. It was practically her entire estate; two years later she desperately needed it back and went to Milton's house to ask for it. According to her testimony in court, Milton's partner Thomas Bower refused to give it to her, saying that he would invest it again instead. At that point Milton himself entered, seemed to be angry, and declared, "What a stir is here about your money! [To Bower] Pay her her money. I will be rid of her, and her money too!" (ibid. 44). Bower demurred, claiming that he had promised to lend the money to another client. At this the widow suspected a trick and told the court that Milton had behaved "with such gesture and subtle carriage as [she] did plainly perceive that it was a mere confederacy and a combination between them to detain her money from her" (ibid. 37).

She did not receive her money on that occasion, nor during her two subsequent visits to the Spread-eagle. Eventually, Milton informed her that the borrower had ceased to pay interest on her loan and advised her to sue for it in court. Rose Downer then became convinced that Milton was exploiting "an ignorant poor old woman" (ibid. 38), and hoping she would die before she could collect. She continued visiting his house, but he fobbed her off with "fair words and promises" (ibid. 39). She tried sending an emissary to plead her case, but Milton dismissed him, saying: "Whatsoever promise I made her at first, yet in regard she has accepted of interest for the said money, I hold myself to be discharged. She may get her money where she can" (ibid. 45). Of course the scrivener disputed her interpretation of events, but he admitted the substantive facts of the case, and the court found against him. Nor was this the only case of this nature brought against the poet's father. There is not enough evidence to conclude that he was a Shylock, but he was certainly no bleeding heart when it came to business.

The traditional image of Milton the poet spending his youth in peaceful, studious contemplation is thus far from the truth. The Spread-eagle stood in Bread Street, at the heart of the city's frenetic commercial center; according to John Stow's *A Survey of London* it was "wholy inhabited by rich Marchants."[16] By the time of the poet's birth his father's trade was thriving, and he eventually amassed a fortune that permanently exempted his son from the necessity of working. Instead, he taught him how to make money work. He made sure to involve young John in his business from an early age, making large loans in his name and spurring him to collect the interest with alacrity. At just fourteen years old the future poet was a legal witness to his sister's marriage settlement, which bestowed the enormous dowry of £800 on her civil servant husband, Edward Phillips.

Milton thus grew up daily witnessing, even practicing, an activity that was widely regarded as Satanic, and it is not surprising that the usury controversy insistently insinuates itself into his mature work. Nor is it surprising that he should develop an unusually sophisticated understanding of idolatry, a profound respect for the power of signs, and a unique personal morality, based on what we might call an ethics of signification. His figurative associations and logical procedures are frequently drawn from the debate around usury, and the formal pattern of that argument stamped itself clearly on his mind. His explicit discussions of moneylending are few and defensive. But the theological and ethical implications of the usury debate reverberate throughout his life and work, informing his opinions and attitudes in ways that the modern reader may find surprising.

II

THE MILTONS EVIDENTLY experienced no contradiction between the sordid business of usury and the exalted pursuits of music and literature. When the young John retired to his chamber to read into the early hours, as he did throughout his childhood, he probably felt that he was not escaping the world of finance but exploring it by other means. Usury is made conceptually possible by the recognition that money is not a substantial thing but a sign. It is however a special kind of sign, one that is "performative" or efficacious. As such it is able to reproduce, to proliferate autonomously, in the same way that the meaning of a word will shift with time and context, acquiring new connotations and significances with each new reader. Milton may have seen his interpretations of literature and his breeding of money as different aspects of the same basic operation and as evidence of the same essential psychological orientation.

In his early thirties the poet recalled that "[m]y father destined me from a child to the pursuits of literature; and my appetite for knowledge was so voracious that, from twelve years of age, I hardly ever left my studies, or went to bed before midnight"(4.i.612). In his early twenties he composed a lengthy Latin poem thanking his father for allowing him to pursue literature to the exclusion of more worldly activities. "Ad Patrem" ("To My Father") draws a deferential distinction between the fecundity of the older man's moneylending and his son's verbal dexterity, announcing that "my greatest gifts could never repay yours, for they cannot be equalled by any barren gratitude of futile words" (11–12). But Milton immediately goes on to insist that his poetry is the moral equivalent of his father's wealth: "[W]hatever wealth I possess I have reckoned up on this paper, for I have nothing except what golden Clio has given me" (14–15).

As the poem acknowledges, John Milton senior had fostered his son's literary as well as his financial acumen. He engaged a series of private tutors for the precocious child, so that Milton's education began long before he started school and continued throughout his life. It is no exaggeration to say that by early middle age he had read everything that his culture considered of any importance. With regard to religion, this meant a deep familiarity with the strain of thought derisively known as "Puritanism." The "Puritans" were so called because they wished to purify the Church of England, to sweep away the residual elements of Catholicism, or "rags of Rome," that had survived the perfunctory reformation introduced by Henry VIII. They were animated by iconoclasm and by the doctrine of *sola scriptura*, "scripture alone," which insisted that the Bible was the sole legitimate basis for theology and church organization. This made them hostile to the Anglican state church, which retained many liturgical and disciplinary features drawn from tradition rather than the Bible, and by the early seventeenth century the Puritans were deserting the Anglican Church in large numbers, preferring to found their own illegal, independent congregations.

One of Milton's childhood tutors, a Scottish Presbyterian named Thomas Young, exerted a particularly profound influence on his charge. In Young's homeland the official state church was Presbyterian, but Presbyterianism was not officially tolerated in England. Like the poet's Catholic grandfather, many English Puritans were technically outlaws, for regular attendance at Anglican services was compulsory, while other forms of observance were forbidden. More seriously, the Puritans' religious convictions logically, though not yet explicitly, placed them in opposition to the English state. The King was the head of the state church, and to disregard that church's teachings was thus to flout royal authority. The logic by which religious Puritans would be made into political revolutionaries would not become evident until the 1640s, but the process was surreptitiously at work far earlier in minds like the young John Milton's. He was born into the progressive vanguard of English society's every sphere. In economics he was raised a capitalist, in religion he was brought up a Puritan, and these tendencies laid the groundwork for the political republicanism he would espouse on his entry into public life.

Thomas Young departed when Milton was eleven, to minister to the English Puritan merchants at Hamburg. In Elegy IV, a verse letter written at the age of eighteen, Milton calls Young "more than the other half of my soul" (22) and compares him to the tutors of Achilles and Alexander the Great, likenesses as flattering to himself as to his teacher. He also likens their relationship to that of Socrates and Alcibiades, who were not only pupil and teacher but also homosexual lovers. Although it would be presumptuous to take this literally, it illustrates the way in which Milton filtered his emotional experience through his reading. His psychological life was

forged out of the contradictions between the austere Hebraic tradition and
Hellenic culture, with its pagan sexual permissiveness. Milton found that
Mediterranean tongues like Latin, Italian and Greek provided a medium
he could use to explore his sensual side. This habit of thought put him at
odds with the repressive morality of his more severe Puritan contemporaries, many of whom recommended ignoring pagan literature altogether.
Better-rounded scholars like Milton expended much effort in finding the
points of connection between the Judeo-Christian and the Greco-Roman
traditions and in forging such connections where they seemed lacking. In
Milton's case this meant recapturing the relaxed hedonism with which the
pre-Christian world had approached sexuality, and he was to become a
sexual revolutionary as well as a political and religious one.

At the age of seven Milton began attending St. Paul's school, a short
stroll from the Spread-eagle, in the shadow of the great cathedral. St.
Paul's churchyard was the hub of London's intellectual life, packed with
the stalls of booksellers, and the venue for regular preaching of various
religious hues. From 1621 the Dean of St. Paul's was John Donne, known
today as the foremost of the "metaphysical" poets, but famous in his
lifetime as the most powerful preacher in England. We can presume that
the young Milton heard some of his sermons. The poet grew up in the
intellectual, as well as the mercantile, center of the city, and he took full
advantage of the opportunities this offered. He was a startlingly academic
child even by the standards of that learned age, and his brother confirms
Milton's own report that "when he was very young he studied very hard
and sate-up very late, commonly till 12 or one aclock at night."[17]

The education Milton received at school was a mere supplement to
this rigorous self-instruction, but it nevertheless far surpasses any conceivable modern humanities curriculum. One of the most important, and
most easily forgotten, differences between modern people and Milton's

contemporaries is the great gulf between their literary learning and our own. We often take the technological advances of our age as an indication that we are more knowledgeable than the people of the past, but in languages, literature, philosophy and humanistic culture in general, a reasonably bright seventeenth-century undergraduate would humble many famous professors of our day. A properly religious education demanded a comprehensive knowledge of scripture, which made necessary the acquisition of Hebrew, Greek and Latin; Milton also learned French, Italian and, later, Dutch. Scholastic exercises placed a premium on translation, and pupils might be asked to render a text from Greek into Latin, then into English, and then back again into Greek. Even by these demanding standards, Milton's linguistic fluency was prodigious. His facility in foreign tongues permanently affected his writing style, which makes such intensive, allusive use of other languages that it often scarcely seems to be English at all. In addition to the Bible he studied ancient, scholastic and Protestant theologians from Augustine through Aquinas to Calvin. But the main focus of his studies was the literature of classical Greece and Rome, and he took more interest in the pagan, permissive elements of ancient culture than in the Puritan theology of the earthly saints.

Perhaps the most important lessons Milton learned at school were emotional rather than academic. It was at St. Paul's that he met the love of his life. A year younger than Milton, Charles Diodati was the scion of an eminent Italian Protestant family. His father was a famous physician, and his uncle Giovanni was a world-renowned Calvinist theologian and the translator of the Bible into Italian. The two boys formed an attachment so passionate that our age is immediately inclined to inquire whether their relations were sexual. After a detailed study of their relationship, John Shawcross reaches the plausible conclusions that

[t]he total view of Diodati seen from the extant evidence certainly points to a homosexual nature; of Milton, to a latent homosexualism which was probably repressed consciously (as well as subconsciously) from becoming overt except with Diodati.[18]

But to lay too much stress on this issue would be anachronistic and naive. The borderline between spiritual and physical love was more porous in the seventeenth century than it is today. Notions of privacy, and of contact between bodies, were very different. It was normal, for example, for people who were not romantically involved to share a bed. Milton's era had no concept of what we call "homosexuality," and people did not perceive their sexual behavior as part of their identity. The physical act of sex between men constituted the sin of "sodomy," but so did non procreative sex acts between men and women. In practice there was little stigma attached to love between men or boys, and such emotions were often conceived as higher, more spiritual, than heterosexual intercourse. The Earl of Rochester, comfortably the most notorious libertine of Milton's day, expressed this attitude succinctly:

Love a woman? You're an ass
'Tis a most insipid passion
To seek out for thy happiness
The silliest part of God's creation . . .
Then give me health, wealth, mirth and wine
And if busy love entrenches
There's a sweet, soft page of mine
Does the trick worth forty wenches.[19]

It might appear odd to compare Milton, whom tradition labels a "Puritan," to an infamous libertine like Rochester. But a contemporary

described Milton as a "libertine" in 1649, and another repeated the
charge in 1660.[20] As Nigel Smith has recently noted, Milton "may best be
described as *libertine,* in the sense of a poet who dares to speculate on the
highest and most perplexing matters in the most challenging of literary
ways."[21] Although his language is always tasteful, and his ideas usually
expressed through learned mythological allusion, he writes about sex as
extensively and radically as any of his more overtly lascivious contemporaries. His conclusions often startle even the liberal morality of our own
age: he wrote in favor of polygamy, for example, and once actually proposed a bigamous marriage. In the Latin and Italian poems addressed to
the men and women he loved, in his tracts on marriage and divorce, and
in his greatest English verse, Milton develops a comprehensive, radically
liberating theory of sexuality.

A portrait of Milton at the age of twenty shows a beautiful young
man with luxuriant, long hair and delicate, feminine features. We can
assume that he was the object of frequent advances. In later life, scurrilous opponents accused Milton of being a confirmed sodomite, even
a homosexual prostitute, and alleged that his lovers included the poet
Andrew Marvell. There are certainly homosexual allusions in several of
his juvenile poems, and Milton's writing from his teens and early twenties
seems to conduct a debate among various kinds of sexuality. In his first
Elegy, a verse letter to Diodati, he addresses his friend as "Adonis," and
in 1629 Diodati wrote to Milton, urging him teasingly to turn away from
his books and enjoy the pleasures of life: "[B]e merry, but not in the manner of Sardanapalus in Soli" (1:337). The Assyrian king Sardanapalus
was an effeminate voluptuary, and although Milton is instructed not to
emulate him, the reader naturally wonders why this injunction was necessary. At the age of twenty-eight Milton was still writing to his friend in
amorous tones:

Know that I cannot help loving people like you. For though I do
not know what else God may have decreed for me, this certainly
is true: He has instilled into me, if into anyone, a vehement love of
the beautiful. Not so diligently is Ceres, according to the Fables,
said to have sought her daughter Prosperina, as I seek for this idea
of the beautiful, as if for some glorious image, throughout all the
shapes and forms of thing. (1:326)

In good Platonic fashion Milton seeks the "idea" of beauty, but this
search requires a close examination of its physical "shapes." The "idea"
is compared to an "image," which is a very different concept, for images
are sensual, and to be found in the "forms of things." Milton is searching
for an idea in the same manner he would if it were an image: physically,
through the senses. He suggests that sensual love is legitimate so long as it
is recognized as the admiration of an image that refers to an idea. A puritanical rejection of physical pleasure and a Cavalier indulgence in concupiscent sexuality are both species of idolatry, which focus on physical sex,
on the "image" which is the body, as an end in itself. But for Milton, sex
is neither good nor bad in itself; the question is whether the image of the
body is interpreted with reference to the idea of the soul. Milton thought
sex should mean something.

Following Charles Diodati's early death in 1638, Milton composed "Damon's Epitaph," a broken-hearted lament for his friend. It
was the last poem he ever wrote in Latin, which was for him the language of love, and no lover was ever mourned with greater passion. At
the poem's climax Milton imagines Diodati in heaven. Addressing his
beloved, Milton declares that "because you never married," Charles is
enjoying sensual pleasures in paradise, where he "will forever take part
in the marriage celebration; where song joined with the harp rage in

blessed dance, and orgies like those of Bacchus under the Thyrsus of Sion."[22] Few Christian visions of heaven find room for Bacchic orgies, and the fact that Charles is evidently being sexually rewarded for having abjured the love of women during his lifetime suggests an exalted opinion of homosexual love. It suggests that "orgies like those of Bacchus" are holy. But we will never know whether Milton and Diodati "had sex," and it really does not matter. What is clear is that they were in love. Such close friendships between boys were not unusual at the time, and although we do not know why Charles left St. Paul's school a year early, A.N. Wilson's speculation that "[p]erhaps the parents felt that the intensity of the friendship between the two boys called for a separation" seems unduly prurient.[23]

Although it certainly does not preclude same-sex desire, the adolescent Milton was highly susceptible to heterosexual lust. He composed a handful of short verses describing the attractions of a dusky Italian girl named Aemilia. Milton's friendship with the Diodatis would have given him access to London's Italian community, and there is no reason to dismiss these verses as fantasy. They may even have been written for the girl they describe, for Milton wrote them in Italian. Their main purpose is to capture the overwhelming, irresistible power of sexual desire. The poem known as Sonnet VI extols the virtues of Stoic morality, which claims to be impervious to the vagaries of fortune, before undercutting its own argument by noting a vital exception: "Only at a single point will you find it less unyielding—the point where Love's dart has pierced incurably" (13–14). The phallic image of Cupid's penetrating arrow dominates Milton's youthful erotic verse. Sonnet II refers to Aemilia's "fair looks and the gifts which are the arrows and the bow of love" (7). Elegy V, composed at the age of twenty, depicts a rampant, rapacious Cupid attempting to conquer all creation with his phallic equipment:

Now wandering Cupid runs at large throughout the whole world
and kindles his dying torch in the flame of the sun. The lethal
horns of his bow are resonant with new strings, and his gleaming
shafts, tipped with new steel, are ominously glittering. And now
he attempts the conquest of even the unconquerable Diana and of
the chaste Vesta, whose seat is the sacred hearth. (97–102)

Translated out of its mythological imagery, the poem declares that
Milton's sexual urges are dominating his entire life. His adolescent verse
reinterprets the figure of Cupid, translating him from a mischievous baby
into a powerful, even Satanic tempter. Milton often places himself in a
passive, feminine role in relation to Cupid. In one of his college prolu-
sions, composed at nineteen, he demands: "have I been violated by some
god, like Caenus of old, and won my manhood as the price of my dis-
honor" (1:283). Caenus was a woman who attained the power of changing sex after being raped by Neptune; here Milton describes his own
attainment of masculinity as the paradoxical consequence of being treated
as a woman. Elegy VII, written in the same year as the prolusion, recalls
how the overconfident poet once "poured scorn on the arrows of Cupid
as childish weapons." In his inexperienced naivete he underestimated the
god's power, and this has provoked Cupid to revenge: "Cupid would not
bear the insult—for no deity is swifter to anger—and the vengeful boy
burned with double heat" (11–13). He fixes the poet with his "sweetly
menacing eyes," and Milton compares him to Ganymede, the beautiful
boy who excited the homosexual desire of "amorous Jove." But Cupid
chooses to assault Milton by heterosexual means. As the poet wandered
among "groups of radiant girls with divinely lovely faces" he "lost all
control of my eyes" and "caught sight of one who was supreme among
the rest. . . . She was thrown in my way by the grudge-harboring rascal,

Cupid" (61, 65). This experience of lust is deeply disturbing to Milton.
Cupid's darts "struck my defenceless breast in a thousand places. In an
instant unfamiliar passions assailed my heart. Inwardly I was consumed
by love and was all on fire" (73–76). Amazed and confused by the strength
of his own desire, Milton makes an astonishing promise. He vows to worship Cupid, to become an idolater:

> Now, O child of the goddess, with your darts no less powerful than
> fire, your bow is beyond all doubt dreadful to me. Your altars shall
> smoke with my sacrifices, and, as far as I am concerned, you shall
> be sole and supreme among the gods. (95–99)

This amounts to a declaration that his life will be devoted to sex. But
he will not be a willing votary. Milton describes sexual desire as a power
that is violently applied to him, a force that is imposed upon him by
supernatural agency in defiance of his own volition, a tyrannical enemy
who threatens to enslave him. His senses, not his reason, are the por-
tals by which this alien power enters him. Sonnet IV describes the erotic
urges stimulated by the Italian lady's voice, and Milton declares himself
defenseless against her appeal: "[S]o potent a fire flashes from her eyes
that it would be of little avail to me to seal up my ears" (13–14). His
early erotic poetry asks how one should respond to this fierce power that
besieges the young man's sensibility. How, the adolescent Milton asks,
should one cope with the fact that one is always horny?

The conventional Puritan response would be to attempt to repress
one's desires. In Milton's view, however, this reveals a servile belief in
the importance of the physical. Throughout his life, Milton's intellectual
insights always sprang from his ability to see the common assumptions
shared by two ostensibly opposing positions, and thus to move beyond
both of them. In philosophical terminology, he always produced an

aufhebung out of a dialectical antithesis. He saw that asceticism and hedonism both bestow an unwarranted ethical priority on the pleasures of the flesh. Although he experienced sexual desire as an irresistible temptation, Milton never describes it as sinful or as an offence against God. In fact the main ethical problem with sex is that it is a distraction from his poetic ambition. In a poem entitled "Canzone" Milton finds himself mocked by a group of "amorous young men and maidens," who accuse him of wasting his talent on erotic verse while more serious tasks call for his attention:

> And thus they make sport of me: Other rivers, other shores and other waters are waiting for you, on whose green banks now, even now, an immortal guerdon of undying leaves is putting forth its shoots to crown your locks. Why the superfluous burden on your shoulders? (7–12)

We may doubt whether Milton's youthful contemporaries actually urged him on thus in his pursuit of the poet's laurel wreath, and we may suspect that his real purpose here is to explain his dalliance in the erotic to the posthumous audience whose existence he never doubted. The answer to the question is the poem itself: "Canzone, I will tell you, and you shall answer for me. My lady, whose words are my very heart, says, 'This is the language of which Love makes his boast.'" Milton acquits himself of neglecting his poetic talents by cordoning off a particular sphere for the erotic. There is a place for love poetry: in Italian, and also in youth. When he came to publish these verses at the age of thirty-seven, Milton appended an editorial note:

> These are the monuments to my wantonness that with a perverse spirit and a trifling purpose I once erected. Obviously, mischievous

error led me astray and my undisciplined youth was a vicious
teacher until the Academy offered its Socratic streams and taught
me how to escape from the yoke to which I had submitted. From
that hour those flames were extinct and thenceforward my breast
has been rigid under a thick case of ice, of which the boy [i.e.
Cupid] himself fears the frost for his arrows, and Venus herself is
afraid of my Diomedean strength. (61)

There is a note of self-mockery in Milton's hyperbolic announcement
of his heroic chastity. But we can take seriously his description of sexual
desire as slavery, a "yoke to which I had submitted." For Milton, sex pursued for its own sake was submission. It was pleasant, but it was a force
beyond rational control, and as such a species of slavery. The temptation
to pursue sexual desire as an end in itself was an element of the natural
slavery that constituted the postlapsarian condition of humanity. To liberate ourselves from slavery it was necessary to resist that temptation, but
in order to resist it, we must first experience it. Temptation is therefore
not to be avoided but actively sought out. The Puritan's flight from temptation revealed a fleshly, "carnal" psychological orientation as surely as
the Cavalier's surrender to it. Much later in life, writing in the service of
Oliver Cromwell's revolutionary government, he applied his ideas about
sexuality to the political sphere:

[I]t usually happens by the appointment, and as it were retributive
justice, of the Deity, that that people which cannot govern themselves, and moderate their passions, but crouch under the slavery of
their lusts, should be delivered up to the sway of those whom they
abhor, and made to submit to an involuntary servitude. (4.i.461)

But Milton was never opposed to sensual pleasure. On the contrary, his argument is that surrender to temptation actually diminishes sensual pleasure. Milton derived considerable erotic pleasure from the experience of unsatisfied temptation. He enjoyed tantalizing himself, frequenting the fields outside London where, as he noted at the age of eighteen, "you may see groups of maidens go dancing past. Ah, how many times have I been struck dumb by the miraculous grace of a form which might make decrepit Jove young again!" (Elegy I, 52–54). Like many a bashful teenage boy, he fails to approach the objects of his lust. But rather than rue his reticence, Milton finds an erotic satisfaction in resisting temptation. He breaks off his rapturous admiration, realizing that the girls' flowing blond locks are "golden nets flung by Cupid, the deceiver" (60). He invokes the assistance of "divine moly," the herb with which Odysseus inoculated himself against sexual desire, to help him "secure the safety of distance from the infamous halls of the deceiver, Circe" (87). Homer's Circe is a witch who exploits Odysseus's sexual urges to delay him on his journey homeward, and a figure who suggests the connection between magic and lust. Both are forces that bypass reason, which Milton regarded as the immortal element within the human soul (our modern use of words like "enchantment" and "glamour" to signify sexual attraction testifies to this connection, for they originally referred to magical illusions). This is conventional Puritan morality, but Milton's treatment of sexual desire emphasizes the need for, and thus the basic goodness of, temptation itself. He deliberately exposes himself to sexual temptation in order to resist it, seeking out girls to lust over for the purpose of strengthening his character by refusing to approach them.

Milton's attitude here anticipates the views of such famous Cavalier poets as Sir John Suckling, whose "Against Fruition" contrasts the pleasure of continually stimulated desire with the *tristesse* produced by satisfaction:

Stay here, fond youth, and ask no more; be wise:
Knowing too much long since lost paradise.
The virtuous joys thou hast, thou wouldst should still
Last in their pride; and wouldst not take it ill,
If rudely from sweet dreams (and for a toy)
Thou wert wak't ? He wakes himself, that does enjoy.[24]

The word "pride" was conventional code for an erection, and
Suckling recommends remaining permanently in the dream state of sexual
excitement, which is destroyed by satisfaction and which he describes
as a "virtuous" form of joy. There is a sensual pleasure in abstention.
Like Suckling, Milton did not advocate virtue out of an especially austere
morality; he advocated it because he believed virtue was more pleasurable
than sensual indulgence. And virtue required temptation, for it was produced by resisting temptation. Milton always needed something to resist.

III

HE FOUND PLENTY to resist at university. In April 1625, at the age of
sixteen, Milton matriculated into Christ's College, Cambridge. There he
encountered a breed of people who must have seemed a race entirely apart
from the urban, Puritan merchants among whom he had been raised: the
English aristocracy. Many of these people would have roundly disliked
Milton for three obvious reasons: he was the son of a usurer, he was
an intellectual, and he seems to have been considered effeminate. They
nicknamed him "The Lady." A formal speech that he delivered to his
undergraduate peers, and which he took the trouble to preserve for posterity, indicates that the distaste was mutual: "Some of late called me 'The
Lady.' But why do I seem to them too little of a man?" He speculates

that it is because he does not enjoy boozing, brawling, or engaging in physical labor, but also because of his apparent lack of sexual interest in women: "because I never showed my virility in the way these brothellers do" (1:283). In another public address to his fellow students he exclaims: "To what distress am I reduced today! . . . [H]ow can I hope for your goodwill when in all this assembly I see only persons who are hostile to me?"[25] He goes on to qualify this, noting the presence of "some who clearly show me by their quiet countenances that they wish me well." Presumably those who did not wish Milton well were demonstrating their feelings in a less quiet manner. Elsewhere he recalls his surprise at finding a favorable reception for his speech "even on the part of those who had previously shown me only hostility and dislike" (1:267). But Milton concludes his critical analysis of his audience with a gesture that will recur throughout his career. He separates them into those few capable of understanding him, and the uncomprehending masses: "The approval of these, however few, I value more than the numberless company of the ignorant" (ibid.). Milton believed that only a few people were able to liberate themselves from the naturally servile condition of fallen humanity, and it was to them alone that he addressed himself.

It seems that Milton found college intellectually and socially uncongenial. He was acutely conscious of his precocious learning and innate intelligence, which he scorned to hide. An early biography records that at Cambridge Milton "was esteemed to be a virtuous and sober person, yet not to be ignorant of his own parts."[26] This may explain why, according to a note appended by his brother to an early biography, his tutor William Chappel "whipt him." Chappel was a formidable character who was famous for having made one debating opponent faint by the sheer force of his argument. Milton was a ferocious debater himself, and he was later to boast of actually having killed a polemical adversary. Presumably the discussions between pupil and teacher grew heated, possibly even physical. Formal corporal punishment was not often applied to undergraduates, and it is tempting to imagine that Milton and Chappel, who was still a young man himself, simply came to blows during an especially fierce disagreement over Aristotle or Plato. Whatever the nature of the encounter, Milton got the worst of it. In early 1627, two years into his course of study, Milton was suspended, or "rusticated," from the university and forced to return to London.

In his first Elegy to Diodati, composed during this hiatus, Milton mentions the "threats of a rough tutor" among the "indignities which my spirit cannot endure" that he has suffered at Cambridge and proudly declares that "I feel no concern about returning to the sedgy Cam" (11). He presents university life as a distraction from study and claims that only in London can he "devote my leisure hours to the mild Muses" (25). Continuing his lifelong tendency to interpret his biography with reference to classical precedents, he compares himself to Ovid, exiled by Augustus ostensibly for writing obscene verse but actually for political dissidence. The allusion permits him to slip in a remarkable, albeit implicit statement of poetic ambition. If only Ovid "had never had to bear anything worse! Then he would have yielded nothing to Ionian Homer and you, O Maro [i.e. Virgil], would have been conquered and stripped of your prime honors" (23–24). The clear implication is that Milton himself aspires to surpass the epic poets of the classical world.

Undisguised hubris can be irksome in the very young, and perhaps this accounts for the social and academic difficulties Milton encountered at Cambridge. When he eventually returned to the university he was transferred to a different tutor. This arrangement proved more satisfactory, and he proceeded to get his bachelor's degree in 1629 and his master's degree in 1632. He was supposed to be training for the priesthood, but the conduct of the future priests around him fermented doubts about the profession's value. Ten years later Milton recalled attending college theatricals in which students in training for the priesthood performed. He found their antics unbecoming:

> In the Colleges [they] . . . have bin seene so oft upon the Stage writhing and unboning their Clergie limes to all the antick and dishonest gestures of Trinculos, Buffons, and Bawds; . . . they thought themselves gallant men, and I thought them fools, they made sport, and I laught, they mispronounc't, and I mislik't, and to make up the *atticisme*, they were out, and I hist. (1:887–8)

This wording is not necessarily metaphorical; it is easy to envision Milton literally hissing from the audience of a tasteless and inept student production. This would not have endeared him to his colleagues. But it was not just the undignified behavior of theology students that turned Milton away from a clerical career. During his undergraduate years the Anglican state church took a direction diametrically opposed to the Puritan principles with which he had been brought up. As graduation approached and Milton found himself about to encounter the wider world as an independent adult, that world's numerous and weighty problems began to prey on his mind. As Milton prepared himself for maturity, England was taking its first tottering, then lurching, steps toward revolution.

2

TYRANT SPELLS

I

OVER THE COURSE of his Cambridge years, Milton gradually came to feel excluded from the Anglican priesthood, an experience he was later to describe as being "church-outed by the prelates" (1:823). It was a purely psychological process. As far as we know there were no material impediments to Milton's taking holy orders, as he and his family seem to have assumed he would. But Milton's mind was changing and developing in response to changes and developments in the political nation. King Charles I inherited the throne in 1625 and soon developed a serious image problem. Early modern monarchs did not keep standing armies or police forces; rather, their power was internalized within their subjects. Their authority was maintained not by physical coercion but by the awe and reverence in which the people held them. This demanded the projection of a particular kind of image. Charles's predecessors Elizabeth I and James I had deployed the pomp of regality in a skillful, sparing manner that secured the respect, and often the devotion, of their subjects. Charles lacked their skill in public relations. He used his image as a blunt instrument, attempting to overpower his subjects' sensibilities by the glitzy ostentation of his court.

We have seen in our own time how easy it is for royalty to lose the respect of their subjects by developing an inappropriate image. Charles I's tactics might have worked on a gullible peasantry, but England was no longer a nation of gullible peasants. The sophisticated, cultured, increasingly puritanical merchants and lawyers of London found Charles's aesthetic taste vulgar and foreign. They associated it with the ornate vestments and liturgy of Catholicism, and they blamed it on the excessive influence of Charles's French Catholic queen, Henrietta Maria. They particularly resented Charles's continual requests for more taxes to pay for the banquets, costume balls, and masques that the monarch deemed necessary to the maintenance of political power. An ominous concoction of Puritan iconoclasm and mercantile self-interest was brewing in the minds of many Londoners.

It might never have reached the boiling point if Charles had matched his father's shrewd instinct for compromise, but this he singularly lacked. The first fractures appeared in the church. When William Laud was ordained Bishop of London in 1628, then Archbishop of Canterbury in 1633, the Church of England embarked on a concerted campaign to reintroduce "the beauty of holiness" into religious observance. This meant reviving the use of sensory aids to worship, reintroducing altar rails, priestly vestments, icons, and incense to the services from which the enthusiasts of the early Reformation had expelled them. Puritans believed that such objects invited idolatry. They argued that, because of the fallen human tendency to mistake an image for what it represented, it was inevitable that many among the congregation would forget that a statue of Christ was merely a block of wood and worship it as if it were Christ himself.

So what? The question comes naturally to a modern reader: Why should it be a fighting matter, why should it matter at all, if people want to look at images in churches? After all, we look at images all the time, and we do not think doing so harms us. But Milton and most of his contemporaries believed that one's attitude to representation, which was fostered by and developed through habitual church attendance, had profound consequences for one's ethical and political beliefs. They did not see issues of interpretation, of hermeneutics, as ethically or politically neutral. To people of Milton's liturgical bent, the introduction of icons into churches seemed almost designed to sink the population in idolatrous habits of thought. The King's undisguised investment in religious iconography was effectively an admission that his own political power depended on fostering idolatry in his subjects. As the conservative Anglican bishop Gardiner admitted:

> The destruction of images, containeth an enterprise to subvert religion, and the state of the world with it. . . . If this opinion should proceed, when the king's majesty hereafter should show his person, his lively image, the honour due by God's law among such might continue; but as for the king's standards, his banners, his arms, they could hardly continue in their due reverence.[1]

Idolatry, whether their own or that of others, was the one thing that people of Milton's mind could never tolerate. Strange as it seems to us, they would die first, and that is the primary reason for the English Revolution. Furthermore, the liturgical practices Laud sought to propagate were exacerbated by the disciplinary measures by which he enforced them. With the encouragement of the King he worked to centralize religious authority, expelling Puritan ministers from their livings and insisting on theological uniformity despite the wishes of congregations. To join the Anglican Church during the 1630s would have been to subjugate one's private opinions to the coercive authority of the state, and this Milton was quite unable to do. In fact his mind was working in reaction against the state, growing more iconoclastic as the King tried to encourage iconography. Naturally Milton abandoned the prospect of a secure clerical career with some reluctance. In 1629 and again in 1632, as preconditions for receiving his degrees, he swore oaths upholding the royal supremacy and the liturgical authority of the Anglican prayerbook. But he refrained from taking orders until events had made the prospect intolerable. In one of his earliest pamphlets he described Anglicanism as slavery:

> The Church, to whose service, by the intentions of my parents and friends, I was destined of a child, and in my own resolutions till, coming to some maturity of years, and perceiving what tyranny had invaded the Church, that he who would take orders must subscribe slave, and take an oath withal, which unless he took with a conscience that would retch, he must either straight perjure or split his faith,—I thought it better to prefer a blameless silence before the sacred office of speaking bought and begun with servitude and foreswearing. (1:882–3)

Idolatry transforms "service" into "servitude." To alienate one's religion to an external power, to subjugate private beliefs to the dictates of the state, as an Anglican priest had to do, was for Milton an even more disgraceful slavery than that involved in alienated physical labor. Reason was the definitive characteristic of humanity and the immortal element of the soul; to alienate it was to commit the sin of Faustus. The lengthy process of thought that preceded Milton's refusal to submit to the servile condition of idolatry confirmed his lifelong understanding of iconoclasm as liberation from slavery.

The centrality of that understanding to Milton's religion was already clear in the six poems that he composed, while still a teenager, on the

Gunpowder Plot: the Catholic conspiracy to blow up King James I and both houses of Parliament that had been narrowly foiled in 1605. Its impact on seventeenth-century English people was akin to the effect of the destruction of the World Trade Center on modern Americans, and the phrase "the 5th of November" evoked the same kind of emotions that "9/11" does today. In "On the Same," Milton traces the conspiracy to its source in the "beast in ambush on the Seven Hills" (2) and describes how "the Latin monster with its triple crown gnashed its teeth and wagged its ten horns with menace horrid" (3–4). This is Antichrist, universally identified by seventeenth-century Protestants with the Pope. Milton's mockery focuses on the material trappings of Catholic observance, and he challenges the Pope to "[b]low your detestable cowls, rather, up to the skies, and all the idol gods that profane Rome contains" (7–8).

The identification of Antichrist with the Pope brought a special virulence and violence to religious disputes, and this led many of Milton's contemporaries to conclude that they were living in the last days. The international struggle between Catholic and Protestant, which reached its height during the pan-continental Thirty Years' War of 1618–48, was widely viewed as the harbinger of imminent Apocalypse. Milton's early political poems meditate on this possibility by presenting earthly events as the consequences of superhuman spiritual warfare. The opening lines of "On the Fifth of November" mention the accession of King James to the English throne, but then the scene suddenly shifts to the supernatural, and for the first time, we are introduced to the monstrous figure who will dominate Milton's mature thought. That shadowy personage is here described as "the cruel tyrant who governs the fiery streams of Acheron, the father of the Eumenides, the wandering outcast from the celestial Olympus" (7–8). He is ranging through the world, counting "his faithful slaves" and attempting "to corrupt even the heart that is locked against sin" (18).

It would be misleading to call him "Satan." That is a Hebrew word, but the appellations Milton gives him here are drawn from the morally complex Greek tradition. The Eumenides were the offspring of Pluto, the King of Hades, but their function was, like that of the Furies, to avenge crimes committed by mortals. They were among the guarantors of morality in the universe, not its opponents. Even at this early stage, Milton's portrayal of evil is nuanced and sophisticated, demonstrating a learned knowledge of the various mythological traditions that have attempted to define it. For Milton, cosmic conflicts are replicated in psychology and also in politics. "On the Fifth of November" presents the worldly eminence of Antichrist as the result of baleful supernatural influence, but Antichrist has a vital role to play in God's providential plan. Enraged at the piety and prosperity of the British people under James I, the ruler of the underworld makes his way to Rome, where he finds the Pope being borne around the city in a triumphal litter, "carrying with him his gods made of bread" (56). The scornful allusion here is to the Catholic Mass, in which the ritualistic actions of the priest are supposed to transform the wafer-bread into the body of Christ.

For Protestants this constituted a form of magic, because it assumed a literalistic interpretation of Jesus's words at the last supper: "[T]his is my body." As Milton saw it, Catholics committed the basic idolatrous error of taking a sign for the referent it signified. Properly understood, the bread was merely a sign of Christ (although that did not preclude its having a real, objective effect in the mind of the believing communicant). Jesus had been speaking metaphorically, as he usually did, precisely in order to expose and exclude the idolatrous literalists among his audience. Like Milton, he sought a "fit audience, though few," allowing only those who "have ears" able to interpret his parables correctly. In his second prolusion, Milton approvingly notes "the example of the poets, or (what is almost the same thing) of the divine oracles, who never display before the eyes of the vulgar any holy or secret mystery unless it be in some way cloaked or veiled" (1:235–6).

Milton's biblical exegesis, like his politics, assumed that truth can be recognized only by the light of its contrast with falsehood. We can discover the nature of Christ only by analyzing the nature of Antichrist, and Milton's poem describes Antichrist in great detail. There follows a lurid description of depraved Roman rites, in which the chanting of monks is likened to the shrieking "followers of Bacchus when they chant their orgies" (64–65). Milton conceived of Catholicism as a sensual religion and thus as the modern inheritor of the orgiastic cult of Bacchus. He likened the more austere observances of Protestantism to the ancient Orphic religion, and he saw the resurgence of counterreformation Catholicism as a recapitulation of Orpheus's dismemberment by Bacchus's frenzied female followers, the Maenads. Milton's reluctance to assume the responsibilities of an Anglican priest must be seen in this context: he believed that the Anglican Church's burgeoning sympathy for Romanesque liturgy was the latest, and perhaps the last, phase of a conflict stretching back far beyond the Christian era to the misty dawn of history, and back even beyond that, to disputes among warring spirits before the creation of the universe. Compromise was not an option in this cosmic context: Milton could not become a priest. But what were his options? Was there anything he could in fact become? What was he going to do?

II

BY THE TIME Milton left Cambridge in 1632, his parents had retired from the hubbub of London to the quiet village of Hammersmith, a few miles west of the city, although John Milton senior remained engaged in business affairs for several years afterward. Instead of taking holy orders, their twenty-three-year-old son moved back in with them and moved along with them three years later to the Berkshire village of Horton. During these years, as he later recalled, Milton "devoted myself entirely to the study of Greek and Latin writers" (4.i.613). This was not aimless reading. On the contrary, a letter from Diodati chastises Milton for his obsessive intellectual labors:

> But you, extraordinary man, why do you despise the gifts of nature? Why such inexcusable perseverance, bending over books and studies day and night? Live, laugh, enjoy your youth and the hours, and stop reading the serious, the light, and the indolent works of ancient wise men, wearing yourself out the while.[2]

In a later letter to his friend, Milton endorses this assessment: "[M]y temperament allows no delay, no rest, no anxiety—or at least thought—about scarcely anything to distract me, until I obtain my object and complete some great period, as it were, of my studies" (1:323). He worked hard because he believed that he was laboring in a divine vocation. Having decided against a clerical career, Milton had determined to serve God by other means. He looked for inspiration to the shadowy poet-priest-prophets who inhabit early mythology, before art and religion were separate spheres. He looked above all to Orpheus, who was able to move Hades by his song, who could make rocks and stones speak, and whose redemptive, death-defying power prefigured that of Christ himself. Orpheus appears in almost all of Milton's poetry as a source of inspiration but also, more daringly, as a model to which to aspire. To achieve that level of prophetic power, Milton felt it necessary to master the accumulated knowledge of humanity in its entirety before offering his own contribution. Before he could fulfill his prophetic and poetic destiny, he had to read everything.

He probably came as close to this impossible target as anyone ever has. He was born with considerable natural gifts, and he cultivated these by incessant study. No one could possibly have read more than Milton because, for the first thirty years of his life, reading was practically all he did. The leisure to live thus was purchased with the proceeds of usury, and it was not enjoyed without guilt. One of his first pamphlets admits that he has lived from "the sweat of other men." A letter to an unknown friend dated 1632 laments that he is "as yet obscure and unserviceable to mankind" and admits: "I am something suspicious of myself, and do take notice of a certain belatedness in me."[3] Since he was only twenty-three such sentiments testify more to his ambition than to his lethargy, and yet Milton would always be tormented by a nagging sense that he was wasting his talents. When he published his first book of poems in 1645 he dated some of his juvenilia a few years before they had actually been composed, as if to compensate for anxiety over his late development.

The poetry Milton produced in his twenties can be called minor only in comparison to his later work. If he had never put pen to paper after the age of thirty, Milton would still be recognized among the most technically brilliant, and certainly one of the most original, poets of his time. What catches our attention in the juvenilia is the fact that he is obviously and openly writing for posterity. The constant nods to his biographical circumstances, the repeated promises to produce a later, greater body of work, the insistent harping on the interlocking themes of sexual temptation and religious idolatry, which he treats in every conceivable register and examines from every possible perspective, and above all the developing interest in the Satanic, all testify to Milton's serene confidence that students like ourselves will be poring over his words for centuries to come, looking for clues in the early work to riddles posed in the later. He has even left us critical commentaries on his works in progress. Milton's correspondence often remarks on his literary endeavors, in what appears to have been a conscious effort to assist future biographers. The letter to his anonymous friend reveals the wary ambivalence with which he was now contemplating a career in the priesthood. He enclosed with it a sonnet that describes a distressing disproportion between his years and his achievements:

> How soon hath Time, the subtle thief of youth,
> Stol'n on his wing my three and twentieth year!
> My hasting days fly on with full career
> But my late spring no bud or blossom shew'th. ("On His Being
> Arrived to the Age of Twenty-three," 1–4)

The poet takes comfort, however, in the belief expressed in the final couplet: "All is, if I have grace to use it so, / As ever in my great Task-masters eye" (13–14). The meaning here depends on the central significance of the verb "to use." Milton intends "to employ" as a subsidiary sense, but the primary sense is "to practice usury." The construction "[a]s ever" means "like eternity," so Milton is saying that God will judge his life as if it were eternity. He will treat it as a whole, consider its accomplishments *en bloc*, and thus not condemn Milton for their temporal delay. But he will do this only "if I have grace to use it so," only if Milton is granted the grace to treat his life in the same way that he wants God to view it. And this means "using" his life, practicing usury with it, investing time in study while he is young so that it will bear the fruit of poetic accomplishments when he is old. Milton is thinking of the parable of the talents, in which servants are praised by their master for making money reproduce. Ten years later he would still be fretting that church reform might take place without any "contribution of those few talents, which God at that present had lent me" (1:804). The sonnet also alludes to the parable of the laborers in the vineyard, who received the same reward no matter what time they began their work. These parables are highly susceptible to interpretations that favor the rights of capital over those of labor, and this is the first of many passages in which Milton challenges his culture's conventional conception of usury as Satanic.

Milton was arriving at the belief that his vocation as a poet was itself a form of priesthood, superior to that available in the degenerate Anglican Church, and demanding a priestly, ascetic way of life. Elegy VI, a verse letter to Diodati dated 1629, illustrates the psychological pressure produced by such a self-conception. Charles also nurtured poetic ambitions, but Milton places his friend in the tradition of festive, hedonistic poets: "[Y]ou decant the store of your verses out of the wine-jar itself." As a heightened, intensified mode of language, poetry has often been compared to the heightened, intensified experience of intoxication; as Milton reminds his correspondent, "Song loves Bacchus and Bacchus loves songs." However he fastidiously separates himself from such company:

> But he whose theme is wars and heaven under Jupiter in his prime, and pious heroes and chieftans half-divine, and he who sings now of the sacred counsels of the god on high, and now of the infernal realms where the fierce dog howls, let him live sparingly . . . and let herbs furnish his innocent diet. Let the purest water stand beside him in a bowl of beech and let him drink sober draughts from this pure spring. Beyond this, his youth should be innocent of crime and chaste, his conduct irreproachable and his hands stainless. His character should be like yours, O Priest. (56–72)

At the age of twenty-one Milton already aspires to describe the affairs of immortal spirits in heaven and hell, and he dedicates himself to the chaste, sober lifestyle that he believes such aspirations demand. Although he will not go blind for almost twenty years, the young poet goes on to compare himself to such reputedly blind sages as Tiresias and Homer, respectively the greatest prophet and the greatest poet of the ancient world. Milton was already fascinated by the paradoxical concept of the blind seer, whose spiritual vision is keener for the loss of physical sight. As Milton's own sight deteriorated, his recollection that God had often anointed the blind as iconoclastic prophets by removing visual images from their perception would strengthen his confidence in his own grand vocation.

In Elegy VI Milton establishes another habit of a lifetime by comparing himself to "Orpheus in his old age, when he tamed the wild beasts among the lonely caves" (70). Orpheus's significance for Milton lies in the fact that he combined the two roles between which Milton was attempting to decide: priest and poet. The religion of Orphism is one of the earliest cults to hint at the possibility of individual redemption from death, and poetry is its vehicle of salvation. Orpheus descends to the underworld, where the beauty of his songs moves Pluto to allow Eurydice to return to earth, although the primitive status of the myth is suggested by the fact that her escape is only half successful. Orpheus may have been a historical figure, and the story that he was torn to pieces by Maenads, drunken female worshippers of Dionysus, presumably alludes to some historical conflict between two forms of religion. The opposition between the passionate, intoxicated transcendence available to Dionysian revelers and the measured, formal aesthetic of Orphic art would always fascinate Milton. In this elegy, almost forty years before the publication of *Paradise Lost*, Milton announces that the subject of his life's work will be the transactions and discussions of angels and demons and that its result will be a work of epic prophecy to rival, even to surpass, those of ancients. Such jaw-dropping ambition would be risible had Milton not fulfilled it.

Milton's letter was written at Christmastime or, as he puts it, during "the festivals which do honor to the heaven-forsaking god" (10). His phrasing here is oddly pagan, suggesting that Christ is merely one god among many, and this is an idea that Milton explores at length in the poem whose composition he announces in the letter. "On the Morning of Christs Nativity" is generally regarded as his earliest major work. It is a sweeping narrative description of cosmic history, interpreted from an idiosyncratic perspective that blends disparate pagan and Christian influences into an original but coherent unity. Milton portrays the nativity as an act of iconoclasm. It suspends the power of human rulers: "[K]ings sat still with awful eye, / As if they surely knew their sov'reign Lord was by" (59–60). Human authority is abolished by subjection to a greater power, and the pattern is repeated in a lengthy account of the banishment of the pagan gods. Milton signals his admiration for classical culture by the elegiac sorrow with which he describes the poignant departure of the nature deities. Monotheism forces us to abandon the childish belief that physical nature is animate, filled with spirits:

> From haunted spring and dale
> Edged with poplar pale,
> The parting Genius is with sighing sent,
> With flow'r-inwoven tresses torn
> The nymphs in twilight shade of tangled thickets mourn. (184–8)

These lines form an intriguing contrast with Elegy V, composed just one year earlier. That poem ends with a passionate appeal for the preservation of paganism: "And long may every grove possess its deities! And my prayer to you, O gods, is not to desert your forest home" (133). In the later work, however, Milton appears reconciled to the passing of polytheism, although hardly eager for it. The fall of the pagan gods is as necessary and inevitable as the end of spring, but also as regrettable. Two centuries later John Keats's "Ode to Psyche" echoed Milton's poem, lamenting the

passage of the era when "holy were the haunted forest boughs, / Holy the
air, the water, and the fire."[4] Keats announces that the pagan pantheon
has, in the modern world, been interiorized, expressed in psychological
terms, when he proclaims Psyche as the last of the classical gods. Like
Keats, Milton's ode also deals with the supersession of one system of
thought by another. He describes how the incarnation of Christ made the
Delphic oracle obsolete:

> The oracles are dumb,
> No voice or hideous hum
> Runs through the arched roof in words deceiving.
> Apollo from his shrine
> Can no more divine,
> With hollow shriek the steep of Delphos leaving.
> No nightly trance or breathed spell
> Inspires the pale-eyed priest from the prophetic cell. (173–80)

The birth of Christ cancels the prophetic power of Apollo. From
now on, true prophecy can only be inspired by the monotheistic God, to
whom Milton refers here as "mighty Pan." This was a common appel-
lation, arising from the fact that "pan" means "universal," but Milton
calls Christ by a pagan name in order to emphasize the supersessionist
nature of Christianity. Christianity does not simply abolish the pagan
gods, any more than Jesus abolishes the Jewish law. Rather, Christianity
assimilates paganism, like Judaism, into itself. By Keats's time the process of supersession had progressed to another stage, and Christianity
itself was being assimilated into modern disciplines like psychology and
philosophy. Thus Keats's ode bids farewell to the "faint Olympians" and
proposes the human mind as the source of its own inspiration. Addressing
Psyche, Keats declares:

I see, and sing, by my own eyes inspired.
So let me be thy choir, and make a moan
Upon the midnight hours;
Thy voice, thy lute, thy pipe, thy incense sweet,
From swinged censor teeming:
Thy shrine, they grove, thy oracle, thy heat
Of pale-mouth'd prophet dreaming. (43–49)

Milton anticipates the process Keats describes: the internalization of mythology. He had recently described this process in an academic exercise at Cambridge, which praises the Greeks as "the first to teach, by their divine inspiration, all the sciences which are known today, arraying them in the charming cloak of fable" (1:224). Mythology is a primitive expression of philosophical truth, so that the Greeks "have left to their successors the full development of that knowledge of the Arts which they so happily began" (ibid.). In the Nativity Ode, the pagan gods do not die, but they do depart from the material world. Although Milton allows himself a degree of nostalgia for the innocent nature deities, the pagan pantheon also possesses inimical, bestial gods whose humiliation is devoutly to be wished:

And sullen Moloch fled,
Hath left in shadows dread,
His burning idol all of blackest hue;
In vain with cymbals' ring
They call the grisly king,
In dismal dance about the furnace blue. (205–10)

Fled he may be, but Moloch is far from dead, and we will meet him again in *Paradise Lost*. The worship of idols cannot be abolished simply by destroying their temples, as the early Christians acknowledged when they translated the pagan gods into demons. The evil spirits can abandon their shrines and change their images, reappearing as abstract concepts or psychological experiences. The Nativity Ode inaugurates the detailed study of psychological idolatry which was to consume Milton's entire political and poetic career.

It was a timely subject. English people were already dividing into the camps of "Puritans" and "Cavaliers," and it was often possible to deduce a person's religious and political attitudes from his or her demeanor and attitude, from his or her dress and general deportment, from his or her character. In a letter dated 1638, Milton approved "the opinion of Plato that grave actions and mutations in the Republic are portended by changed custom and style in dressing" (1:329). A pair of companion poems, written around the time Milton left college, intervenes in this debate around the politics of personality, reflecting on the respective merits of the Cavalier and the Puritan lifestyles. Milton suggests that these ostensibly opposite approaches to life depend upon and define each other. "L'Allegro" describes "the mirthful man," while "Il Penseroso" depicts "the melancholy man." Mirth and melancholy are defined, first of all, by their opposites. "Hence loathed melancholy," exclaim the opening lines of "L'Allegro," while "Il Penseroso" begins "Hence vain deluding joys." Just as the Nativity Ode inaugurates the Christian era by the expulsion of the pagan gods, so the concepts of melancholy and mirth take shape through the exclusion of their contraries.

The poems explore the individual mind using the imagery of the classical pantheon, which Milton expertly manipulates for his purposes. He justifies this lifelong procedure in his first *Prolusion*: "Do not . . . hastily accuse me of arrogance, in shattering or altering the statements of all the ancient poets, without any authority to support me. For I am not taking upon myself to do that, but am only attempting to bring them to the test of reason, and thereby to examine whether they can bear the scrutiny of strict truth" (1:224). Milton's work uses a mythological vocabulary to make rational arguments. For example, "L'Allegro" gives "mirth" two different genealogies. She is first called the daughter of Venus and Bacchus, but Milton then offers an alternative, wiser or "sager" parentage, calling her the offspring of Zephyr and Aurora: the breeze and the dawn. Thus he denies that true mirth springs from sex and drink and instead traces its source to the wholesome enjoyment of nature. As in the early Elegies, virtue does not involve the rejection of sensual pleasure but rather a proper understanding of it, which actually increases it. The pleasurable activities in which the cheerful man indulges are certainly sensual, but they could be thought sinful only by the most rigid of Puritans: strolling around the countryside, drinking beer, going to the theater. Above all "L'Allegro" extols the pleasures of poetry itself, ending with a rapturous description of verse so powerful

> [t]hat Orpheus' self may heave his head
> From golden slumber on a bed
> Of heapt Elysian flow'rs, and hear
> Such strains as would have won the ear
> Of Pluto, to have quite set free
> His half-regain'd Eurydice.
> These delights if thou canst give,
> Mirth, with thee I mean to live. (145–52)

Poetry's aim is nothing less than redemption. The greatest poet ever, Orpheus himself, was only half-successful in pursuit of this aim, and Eurydice had to remain in the underworld. But Milton imagines a poetry that would persuade Pluto to set his captives completely free, and he believes he is the man to write it. Milton is arriving at the conclusion that the function of a priest is best fulfilled outside the church, that a poet may possess greater redemptive power than a priest. The poem ends on a conditional note, however. The cheerful man says that he will live with mirth "if" she is able to provide the delights he describes. He leaves open the possibility that mirth may prove inadequate to the task.

The pleasures described by "Il Penseroso" are determined by contrast with those of "L'Allegro." While the cheerful man enjoys his senses, the goddess Melancholy transcends them; her "saintly visage is too bright / To hit the sense of human sight" (13–14). Because she cannot be seen, she is "to our weaker view / O'erlaid with black staid Wisdom's hue" (15–16). Wisdom is melancholy's humanly perceptible aspect. Like mirth, melancholy is given a detailed genealogy. We are taken aback to find that she is the product of incest:

> Thee bright-haired Vesta long of yore
> To solitary Saturn bore;
> His daughter she (in Saturn's reign
> Such mixture was not held a stain).
> Oft in glimmering bow'rs and glades
> He met her, and in secret shades
> Of woody Ida's inmost grove,
> While yet there was no fear of Jove. (23–30)

The genealogy of mirth signals that her pleasures are innocent rather than sinful, but melancholy's genealogy transcends the categories of sin and innocence altogether. Her birth predates the triumph of Jove (Zeus) over his father Saturn (Kronos). She comes from a time before the Olympians, with Zeus as their king, expelled the Titans to Tartarus. Milton interpreted this ancient myth as a prefiguration of the war in heaven between the faithful angels and Satan's fallen legions, and so his genealogy informs us that melancholy is a figure beyond good and evil. Milton refers to the "unreproved pleasures" (40) of mirth, thus acquitting them of sin, but also admitting the possibility of their being reproved. In contrast, the pleasures of melancholy are not even brought to trial. Incest is a terrible sin in all human cultures, but before the victory of the Olympians imposed a moral order on the world there was no such thing as sin, no "fear of Jove." The pleasures of wisdom, of "melancholy," are not subject to the moral law, and therefore they are truly free.

Hence the superiority of melancholy to mirth. The mirthful and the melancholy men are both attractive, thoughtful, and sensitive characters, but Milton includes enough subtle hints to direct the reader clearly to his preference. He appeals to melancholy to "bid the soul of Orpheus sing / Such notes as, warbled to the string, / Drew iron tears down Pluto's cheek, / And made Hell grant what Love did seek" (105–8). Here, Orpheus's mission is described as wholly successful; Eurydice is not merely "half-regain'd" as in "L'Allegro." The poetry of melancholy, Milton suggests, actually does possess redemptive power. "Il Penseroso" is twenty-four lines longer than "L'Allegro," and in these final lines Milton seems to drop his persona and speak to us directly. At first he imagines a future for himself within the church: "And let my due feet never fail / To walk the studious cloister's pale" (155–6). The church's "antic pillars" and "storied windows" are described with enough loving detail to signal a slightly worrying sensuality, but this fascination with the beauty of holiness proves a passing phase. The final destination Milton anticipates is not a cathedral but a hermit's "mossy cell," where he dares to hope that "old experience may attain / To something like prophetic strain" (173–4). The falsely modest qualification should not conceal the audacity of Milton's pronouncement. Still in his early twenties, he is recording for posterity his ambition to become, or perhaps his sense that he already is, a prophet: a human mouthpiece for the word of God.

III

MAGNIFICENT AS THEY are, most of Milton's early works remained unpublished until 1645, and they represented small tangible recompense for the years that he was passing in his parents' house. The Latin poem "Ad Patrem" hints that the poet's father began to grow impatient with his unemployed son, now approaching his thirtieth birthday. Predictably, Milton's response directs his father to consider "Orpheus, who by his song . . . restrained rivers and gave ears to oaks, and by his singing stirred the hosts of the dead to tears" (52–54). He declares that "it has been my lot to have been born a poet" (61), appealing to the Calvinist notion of divine vocation, and he points out that his father himself pursues "sister arts and kindred interests" (63). The primary reference is to the senior Milton's musical composition, but it also hints at a kinship between art and finance, both of which were successfully practiced by father and son alike. But Milton also expresses gratitude that his father has allowed him to serve the Muses in his own way: "[Y]ou did not bid me go where the broad way stretches open, where it is easier to reap a harvest of lucre, and where the golden hope of piling up money shines bright and sure" (69–70), and he scornfully dismisses "whoever has an insane preference for the ancient treasures of Austria or the realms of Peru" (93–94). Such worldly enterprise is unflatteringly juxtaposed with Milton's own breathtaking intellectual ambition: "I who now have a place, albeit a low one, among the ranks of the learned, shall one day sit among those who are crowned with the victor's ivy and laurel. I shall not mingle unknown with the uncultivated throng, and my steps will shun the sight of profane eyes" (101–4).

In conclusion, Milton offers the poem itself as recompense for his parent's generosity: "[S]ince I cannot repay you as you deserve, or do anything to repay your gifts, let it suffice that I have recorded them" (111–4). "Ad Patrem" is itself the product of usury, the payment of a debt. Milton often describes his writings thus; in a 1630 letter to his school friend Alexander Gill he declares, "I think that each one of your letters cannot be repaid except by two of mine, or if it be reckoned more accurately, not even by a hundred of mine" (1:313). A wise father would be pleased by such a reward, for it will bring nothing less than immortality: "[P]erhaps these praises, and the name of the father celebrated in them, will be preserved as an example for future ages" (119–20). The prophecy has proved accurate, but it can have offered little immediate comfort to his anxious parent, and we must suspect that Milton is not primarily addressing his father here; indeed, his true audience does not yet exist. But the scrivener does seem to have used his influence to secure several commissions for the aspirant poet. Milton's first published verse is a sonnet among the poems prefacing the second folio of Shakespeare's plays, which appeared in 1632. Milton was completely unknown and was presumably asked to contribute only because his father was a trustee of Blackfriars theater, where Shakespeare's company was based, and had contributed a poem to the first folio in 1623. The younger Milton's earliest published lines express his lifelong iconoclasm: "What needs my Shakespear for his honored bones / The labour of an age in piled stones?" ("On Shakespeare," 1–2). As a poet, Shakespeare has built his own monument in the hearts of his readers, and this legacy obviates the need for any grandiose material tomb.

Milton's industrious father also secured his son a pair of commissions to write entertainments for aristocratic patrons. The conduit for these assignments was probably Henry Lawes, a well-known composer whom John Milton senior knew through his own musical activity and who wrote

the music that Milton's librettos accompanied. The first of these entertainments, known as "Arcades," was performed for the Countess of Derby in
1632. It is a conventional celebration of the lady's unparalleled virtue, notable for the manner in which Milton alludes to the music of the spheres:

> Such sweet compulsion doth in music lie,
> To lull the daughters of Necessity,
> And keep unsteady Nature to her law,
> And the low world in measur'd motion draw
> After the heavenly tune. (68–72)

Music constitutes the imposition of ideal form on physical nature and
thus the intersection between earth and heaven. This was the source of its
quasi-divine redemptive power: art, and music in particular, demonstrated
the existence of harmony in nature. They might even suggest the providential determination of history. In one of his university exercises, Milton
identified the music of the spheres as "a means of suggesting allegorically
the close interrelation of the orbs and their uniform revolution in accordance with the laws of destiny for ever" (1:235). Milton's rendition of this
conventional view in "Arcades" was well enough received that two years
later he was asked to write the words for a grander masque to celebrate the
appointment of the Earl of Bridgewater as Lord President of Wales. The
music for the occasion was again composed by Lawes, and it was presumably through this family connection that the obscure poet received such a
prestigious assignment. Milton would later reward Lawes with a sonnet
"On His Airs" that, like "Ad Patrem," promises to repay a debt to its recipient by assuring his immortality. With a certain lack of tact, it describes
Lawes's main accomplishment as his ability to provide appropriate accom-
paniment for Milton's own words: "To after age thou shall be writ the man
/ That with smooth air couldst humor best our tongue" (7–8).

The young Puritan could not have accepted this commission without reservations. Caroline England was the site of fierce and protracted cultural warfare, and all art was understood as intervention in the political and religious disputes that increasingly divided the nation. Theatrical entertainment was viewed with suspicion by many Puritans because it appealed primarily to the senses. It encouraged idolatry, by asking the spectators to assume that the actor actually was the character he represented. Milton had little sympathy with the dour anti-theatricalists; Elegy I and "L'Allegro" both celebrate the enjoyment to be derived from attending plays. But masques were a more dubious form of entertainment. They relied more heavily on visual spectacle, music, and dance. They were closely associated with Caroline court culture; Charles I and his Catholic wife, Henrietta Maria, often performed in them. Their ideological purport was to glorify the monarch and his household as the earthly manifestation of divine order, a message that seemed tinged with idolatry to its cultural opponents. In the same year that Milton's masque was first performed, the frantically zealous Puritan William Prynne had his ears cropped for calling Henrietta Maria a whore because of her participation in such lascivious spectacles.

So Milton must have been slightly taken aback at being asked to compose the libretto for a masque. He had been completely unemployed for two years, however, and his father was doubtless dropping heavy hints about the need to find gainful work. Henry Lawes was a family friend, and to rebuff his invitation would have been rude. Milton therefore accepted the commission, but the ideological pressure under which he labored is clearly visible in the result. His masque, which is known to posterity as *Comus*, challenges the most basic conventions and assumptions of the form. It is not so much a masque as the critical deconstruction of the masque genre. Masques generally celebrate and indulge the senses, but

Milton's masque explores the very darkest mode of sensuality, plumbing the moral depths to which unrestricted sexual desire can lead. Its theme is the sexual abuse of children. A young girl is abducted by a would-be rapist, and the masque's narrative recounts her efforts to avoid violation.

This choice of theme seems more than a little delicate, for just three years earlier the family for whom his masque was written had been embroiled in a real-life scandal involving child abuse. The new Lord President's wife's sister had been married to Mervin Touchet, the Earl of Castelhaven. In the most notorious sex scandal of the seventeenth century, Castelhaven had been tried, convicted and executed for a series of lurid sexual crimes. He had carried on affairs with his male servants, one of whom he had encouraged to rape his wife and daughter. He had forced his family to participate in orgies. The fact that the Earl was an adherent of the supposedly sensual Catholic religion confirmed his wickedness in the minds of upstanding English people, who followed his trial closely and debated its implications fiercely. Castelhaven's hapless family may even have been in the audience for the first performance of Milton's masque.

Comus shows what happens when appetite attempts to usurp the rule of reason in the mind. The eponymous protagonist is Milton's first detailed treatment of a figure who will preoccupy Milton's imagination for the rest of his life: the tempter. We have already met this figure in the Cupid of the early elegies, but here he takes on a much more complex and threatening guise. As usual in Milton, mythological genealogies hold the key to character, and Comus is announced as the son of Circe and Bacchus. He carries a rod and a cup, representing the twin temptations of sex and intoxication. Milton alludes to the episode in *The Odyssey* in which the hero is detained on his voyage home by the wiles of Circe: "Whose charmed Cup / Whoever tasted, lost his upright shape, / And downward fell into a groveling Swine" (51–53). The Fall takes place in the lives of individuals as well as in the history of the human race. It involves the abandonment of reason, which is the distinguishing characteristic of humanity and thus the reduction of human beings to the level of animals.

Comus's intended victim is named only as "The Lady," which may well be a conscious allusion to Milton's college nickname. She certainly exhibits the traits of character that Milton regarded as heroic. The masque displays the process by which she manufactures virtue out of temptation, which was Milton's lifelong psychological habit. We learn that Comus has come to live in "this ominous wood," where he tempts passers-by to drink from his magic cup. Most of them accept, and as a result "their native home forget, / To roll with pleasure in a sensual sty" (74–75). Milton is offering a Christian interpretation of *The Odyssey* in which Ithaca symbolizes heaven, the proper destination of life's journey, from which Circe aims to distract us. Homer's Circe is a witch, and Milton connects sensuality with magic on the grounds that both are irrational forces that work through visible or auditory symbols. He emphasizes the fact that Comus is a magician, who "[e]xcels his mother at that mighty Art" (63). Comus declares himself one of the "vow'd Priests" of the Thracian witch Cottyto, and a boon companion of Hecate, Queen of Witches.

This was topical material. Milton was writing at the height of the European "witch craze," in which tens, perhaps hundreds, of thousands of men and women were executed for having made a pact with Satan. Satan was believed to be energetically at work in the world, and witches were the human vehicles for his operations. The seduction of children by witchcraft was assumed to be a very real danger, and Milton's masque offers protection from this threat by illustrating the tactics employed by witches. His attitude has none of the confusion evinced by our own society on this subject. Most people in today's secular West will say that they do not "believe in" witchcraft, and they often decry the witch hunts of Milton's day as horrific and misogynist atrocities. But no one denies the existence of witches, and everyone knows that many people practice witchcraft. Perhaps, then, when people today say that they do not "believe in" witchcraft, they mean that they do not believe that witchcraft "works," that it is efficacious. But it was common for the prosecutors in seventeenth-century witch trials to admit that the accused was incapable of achieving his or her intended effects. The practical effects of witchcraft were not the point, and witchcraft was equally criminal whether its effects were evil, benign, or non-existent. The witch's crime was to *believe* that he or she could achieve objective effects through the manipulation of signs. Such a belief in itself constituted a pact with the devil.

The modern mind can accept the existence of witches, and it can accept that witches believe their magic to be efficacious. Post-Enlightenment insight into the psychosomatic has even enabled modern people to accept that, under certain circumstances, witchcraft "works." What the modern mind cannot accept is that the practice of magic involves a pact with the devil, for we see nothing morally wrong with the autonomous power of representation. But the people of Milton's time did. They believed that, although real effects did frequently follow the performance of magical rituals, those effects were not caused by the magic itself. They were caused, rather, by the devil, who performed them in order to delude both the witch and her victims into falsely believing that her magic was powerful. Satan's real aim was to propagate this belief. This logic is evident in Christopher Marlowe's *The Tragedy of Dr. Faustus*, the most famous example of the popular genre of "witch plays." When Mephistopheles first appears to Faustus, the magician demands: "Did not my conjuring speeches raise thee?" The devil's reply indicates the complex nature of magical causality:

That was the cause, but yet *per accidens*
For when we hear one rack the name of God,
Abjure the Scriptures and his Saviour Christ,
We fly in hope to get his glorious soul. (1.3.49–52)

Faustus's magic does have practical consequences, but it does not cause them directly. Rather, it allows the devil to cause them. To perform magic was to invite the devil into one's mind. Satan cannot enter the human mind uninvited, and to invite him in by performing magical rites constituted the crime of witchcraft. When a person believes in the efficacy of witchcraft, as evidenced by his or her practice of magic, that person has therefore made a "pact" with the devil.

Milton's masque was intended to teach its young audience and actors (the roles of the three children were played by Bridgewater's own offspring) how to resist the devil's offer of a pact. The tempter's most dangerous weapon is sexual desire, and the masque represents sexual temptation as a form of magic. As his earliest poems tell us, Milton had educated himself in sexual temptation through long, hard experience. The Lady is supposed to be assisted in her struggle by an "Attendant Spirit," who claims to protect "any favor'd of high Jove" (78). In Christian terms we might say that he is a guardian angel watching over God's elect. The fact that the Spirit disguises himself as a shepherd identifies him with the Christian priesthood, who were conventionally referred to as "shepherds" or "pastors." But Comus also dons a shepherd's costume, by "hurl[ing] / My dazzling Spells into the spongy air, / Of power to cheat the eye with blear illusion" (153–5). This "Magic dust" makes him "appear some harmless Villager." The Lady is thus faced with a choice between a good shepherd and an evil one.

Milton alludes to the choice facing every English person between the various churches competing for their allegiance. He takes pains to associate

Comus with Anglicanism. When the Lady rejects his advances, Comus
responds in the vocabulary that Anglicans were using against Puritans
in contemporary ecclesiastical debates: "This is mere moral babble, and
direct / Against the canon laws of our foundation" (807–8). The masque
has often been read as an allegory of the Anglicans' attempts to woo the
separatist Puritans into the established church. By 1634, when it was first
performed, the King's role in aggressively propagating Anglican doctrine
was well established, and Milton also associates Comus with monarchy:
when he first sees the Lady he declares "she shall be my Queen" (265),
he lives in a "palace," and he imprisons his prospective victim upon a
"throne." The Lady is easily deceived because, being unfamiliar with such
discourse, she fails to recognize Comus's aristocratic flattery:

> Shepherd, I take thy word,
> And trust thy honest offer'd courtesy,
> Which oft is sooner found in lowly sheds
> With smoky rafters, than in tap'stry halls
> And Courts of Princes, where it first was nam'd
> And yet is most pretended. (322–7)

These are bold lines to place in an entertainment celebrating an aris-
tocrat's acceptance of a royal appointment. The Lady separates courtesy
from the court, but in her virtuous innocence of courtly language she fails
to recognize Comus's address as insincere flattery. She is easily deceived
and follows him off to captivity in his palace. The scene then shifts to the
Lady's two brothers, who are searching for her in the wood. The younger
brother fears that she may fall into "the direful grasp / Of Savage hunger
or of Savage heat" (357–8). Milton indicates that the danger the Lady
faces is internal as well as external. Hunger and "heat" (which meant
sexual lust in the contemporary vernacular) are physical temptations that

constantly assail our psychological virtue, and the action of the masque can also be read as an allegorical psychomachia, a story whose real venue is the mind. The elder brother reminds the younger that their sister "has a hidden strength / Which you remember not" (415–6), and this puts his younger sibling to some confusion: "What hidden strength, / Unless the strength of Heav'n, if you mean that?" (417–8). This is a rather dismissive reference to divine assistance, and neither brother is prepared to abandon their sister to the protection of God alone. The elder refers rather to "a hidden strength / Which if Heav'n gave it, may yet be term'd her own: / 'Tis chastity, my brother, chastity" (418–20).

Milton is engaged in a philosophical commentary on Stoicism. "Chastity" is a feminized version of "virtue," which in the Stoics is the practical manifestation of rational morality. It may come from heaven, but it belongs to human beings—it is an inherent part of human nature, albeit one that has become occluded in most people. Milton does not understand chastity in negative terms, as the mere absence of sexual experience. He portrays it as an active, positive force that intervenes in the objective world and can even take material form: "I see ye visibly," as the Lady remarks to "thou unblemish't form of Chastity" (215–6). For the Stoics, virtue was the sole source of human liberty, because it is the only element of the self that cannot be affected by external circumstances. We cannot control what happens to us, and in this sense we are "slaves to fortune," but we can control our responses to events. The power to do so constitutes our "virtue," and only the virtuous are truly free.

Comus adapts Stoic virtue to the demands of Christianity, offering Milton's prescription for psychological liberty in a world of unremitting temptation. Liberty does not depend on external circumstances, and the brothers show a rather startling lack of interest in the Lady's physical safety. The younger brother draws an analogy between the sins of lust

and avarice, pointing out that both cause such powerful temptation that
their sister is almost certain to be sexually assaulted:

> You may as well spread out the unsunn'd heaps
> Of Miser's treasure by an outlaw's den,
> And tell me it is safe, as bid me hope
> Danger will wink on Opportunity,
> And let a single helpless maiden pass
> Uninjured in this wild surrounding waste. (398–403)

But the elder brother reveals a more subtle understanding of her situation. Protected by Chastity, the Lady may "set at nought / The frivolous
bolt of Cupid" (444–5). Chastity is the visible manifestation of reason, and
as Milton noted in his commonplace book, "[a] man's courage depends,
not upon his body, but upon his reason, which is man's strongest protection and defence" (1:373). In Stoic ethics, virtue rules over fortune, reason imposes form on chance, and the question of whether one is free or
enslaved is determined psychologically, not legally or literally:

> . . . [A]gainst the threats
> Of malice or of sorcery, or that power
> Which erring men call Chance, this I hold firm;
> Virtue may be assail'd but never hurt,
> Surpris'd by unjust force, but not enthrall'd. (586–90)

This sounds more like a philosophical consolation offered directly to
the masque's audience than the realistic practical advice of one character to another. Certainly the brothers prove ineffectual in their practical
attempts to rescue the Lady. From Milton's perspective, in fact, they are
incapable of rescuing her, because the threat she faces is psychological
rather than physical. Comus can use his magic to fix her on a throne,

making an idol of her, but as she reminds him: "Thou canst not touch the freedom of my mind / With all thy charms, although this corporal rind / Thou hast immanacl'd" (664–6). It is not the "corporal" but the "mind-forg'd manacles" that are the real danger. Comus attempts to forge them with a proto-capitalist economic argument, suggesting that the Lady ought to model her sexuality after the usurious pattern by which money is made to reproduce:

> Why should you be so cruel to yourself,
> And to those dainty limbs which nature lent
> For gentle usage and soft delicacy?
> But you invert the covenants of her trust,
> And harshly deal like an ill borrower
> With that which you received on other terms. (679–84)

Nature has made a loan of beauty to the Lady for the purpose of "usage" and expects that the Lady will let it out at interest by circulating her sexual favors: "Beauty is nature's coin, must not be hoarded, / But must be current" (739–40). Shakespeare had also put this argument into the mouth of a sexual tempter in his fourth sonnet, where the speaker informs a beautiful youth that "Nature's bequest gives nothing but doth lend, / And being frank she lends to those are free."[5] Nature expects the recipient of her loan to be "free" with it, and "lend" his beauty to his sexual partners. As the sons of usurers, Milton and Shakespeare were both acutely conscious of the erotic implications of financial affairs, and Milton alludes to the *Sonnets* when Comus compares sex to usury, thus revealing the lustful, concupiscent nature of his desire. His argument reprises the logical connection between usury and sodomy: Usury makes a naturally barren substance reproduce, while sodomy makes a naturally reproductive act barren. Comus has a fetishistic attitude to sex—he sees it as an end in itself, just as the worship of an idolater is addressed to the image and not to the idea it represents.

We may ask here how, given the obviously spurious nature of his arguments, Comus is able to successfully hold the Lady captive. The answer is that she is sexually tempted by him. The sorcerer's weapons are his "Charming Rod" and his "Glass." The glass is easily disposed of; the Lady effortlessly rejects Comus's "brew'd enchantments," and the brothers instantly snatch his cup when they invade his palace. Milton suggests that the temptation of intoxication is negligible compared to that of sex. Almost forty years later, the hero of *Samson Agonistes* recalls that he has always found it easy to resist the temptation of drink, "nor envied them the grape / Whose heads that turbulent liquor fills with fumes" (551–2). As he goes on to lament, however, Samson was incapable of similar resolve in the face of sexual attraction: "But what avail'd this temperance, not complete / Against another object more enticing?" (558–9). The Lady in *Comus* might say the same. The brothers' attempt to liberate their sister fails because they do not secure the magician's phallic "rod." As the Attendant Spirit angrily explains:

> What, have you let the false enchanter scape?
> O ye mistook, ye should have snatcht his wand
> And bound him fast; without his rod revers't,
> And backward mutters of dissevering power
> We cannot free the Lady that sits here. (814–8)

Sexual temptation is not as easy to resist as the temptation to intoxication. The Lady is eventually freed by Sabrina, a nymph associated with the river Severn, which flows through the grounds of Ludlow Castle, where the masque was first performed. In Geoffrey of Monmouth's *History of Britain*, which Milton knew well, Sabrina is the illegitimate daughter of King Locrine. His jealous wife defeats the King in battle, then drowns his lover and her daughter Sabrina in the river. As the product of an illegitimate union, Sabrina might seem an odd choice as a conduit for the power of chastity. But Milton's selection of Sabrina indicates his conception of what true chastity involves. He emphasizes Sabrina's own innocence, repeatedly referring to her as "guiltless" and "virgin." Sabrina dies because she is the product of sexual impropriety, but this is no fault of her own, as Milton takes great pains to stress. In fact Sabrina is made more chaste by being unjustly associated with unchastity. Her chastity is made perfect through contact with its opposite. The same is true of the Lady, who manufactures her virtue through the experience of resisting temptation. Any violation she might undergo would not destroy her innocence but increase it. For Milton, virtue and chastity were not physical but psychological conditions. By definition they could not be violated against their possessor's will, because they were themselves the assertion of that will.

Far from being an affront to chastity, temptation was the practical means by which chastity was produced, and Milton makes it quite clear that the Lady is tempted. Sabrina uses her own magic to quiet the Lady's lust: "[T]his marble venom'd seat / Smear'd with gums of glutinous heat / I touch with chaste palms moist and cold" (915–7). The fact that it takes a nature deity to liberate the Lady suggests that sexuality is a natural rather than a moral issue. Neither the Attendant Spirit nor the brothers nor even her own virtue is sufficient to free the Lady from temptation. The lines with which the Attendant Spirit closes the masque are revealingly imprecise about the ultimate source of her liberation:

> Mortals that would follow me,
> Love virtue, she alone is free,

She can teach ye how to climb
Higher than the Sphery chime;
Or if Virtue feeble were,
Heav'n itself would stoop to her. (1,018–23)

Milton's final position in *Comus* is unusual, even unique. He departs from Protestant Christianity by suggesting that we can be saved by our own virtue. But he also departs from Stoicism, by allowing the possibility of divine intervention if virtue proves "feeble." This ambiguity reveals his conviction that temptation, especially sexual temptation, is not something from which we ought to remove ourselves too hastily. The Lady is ultimately freed from her sticky seat, but only after successive attempts to liberate her have failed, and after it has been established that the experience of temptation is inevitable, even good. Milton is already exploring the way in which good arises out of evil, and already feeling his way toward the shocking consequences of this ethical position.

3

SAMSON SYBARITICUS

I

HISTORY DOES NOT record the Earl of Bridgewater's reaction to Milton's daring celebration of his investiture with an uncomfortably personal analysis of human sexuality. Nor does history record Milton's receiving any further commissions from the Earl of Bridgewater, or indeed from anyone else. After the masque's performance in 1634 Milton sank deeper into studious obscurity. In fact, his lack of productivity during his energetic twenties was truly heroic. I do not mean to be comic here. Milton was living according to the strategy he had outlined in the sonnet "How Soon Hath Time." He was investing the years of his youth in activity that would pay dividends later. He was practicing usury with his very life.

He was also gambling with it. Milton spent the 1630s in frenetic study, on the assumption that he would be granted the time and health to compose the epic works for which his Herculean but anonymous youthful labors were supposed to be preparing him. As he put it at the age of twenty-eight, in a letter to Diodati:

Listen, Diodati, but in secret, lest I blush; and let me talk to you
grandiloquently for a while. You ask what I am thinking of? So
help me God, an immortality of fame. What am I doing? Growing
my wings and practicing flight. (1:327)

This was taking a heroic risk. For if, as happened very often in the
seventeenth century, Milton was to die young, before his intellectual
investments had matured, his life would be utterly wasted. He would
have squandered his talents and would have to face the fate that the Bible
assigns the querulous servant in the parable, which Milton fearfully called
"the terrible seizing of him that hid the talent" (1:320). He could not even
claim the libertine's consolation of having fully savored the pleasures of
the flesh, for he had sacrificed them too, keeping himself chaste and sober
as the sacred roles of poet, priest and prophet demanded. As the years
of his youth passed without bearing visible fruit, as the reproaches of
his father grew louder, as the continued lack of audience began to sow
the seeds of self-doubt, Milton's anxiety grew. It seems to have reached
a climax in 1637, the year in which his mother died. Milton left no lines
grieving for her, but he did compose a lengthy meditation on the nature of
death itself. That August he received news that a Cambridge contemporary named Edward King had drowned, shipwrecked on his way to take
up an ecclesiastical appointment in Ireland. King was just twenty-five,
three years younger than Milton, and like Milton he had been an aspirant
poetaster. Although they had not been especially close, Milton was deeply
affected by King's death, because it brought home to him the frightening
fact of his own mortality. When the deceased's family asked Milton to
contribute to a memorial volume of verses commemorating their son, he
gladly accepted.

Such literary tributes to the recently departed were commonplace in the seventeenth century. They did not require any particular poetic ability from the contributors, for the sincere expression of emotion was more important than technical virtuosity. But just as the subject matter of *Comus* seems odd given its original audience, so the scope and ambition of "Lycidas" must have surprised the people at whose behest it was composed. The other poems in the volume are heartfelt, even moving, but mostly unskilled and inarticulate. Milton's contribution was almost inconceivably inappropriate to this context. "Lycidas" is an intricate, obscure, profound meditation on human mortality—it has even been called the greatest short poem in the English language—but as a contribution to a memorial volume it is practically an insult. The very title is tactless; Lycidas is a sailor mentioned in Lucan's *Pharsalia,* an epic poem much revered by English radicals because of its republican politics. If the bereaved knew the reference, they cannot have been comforted by Lucan's gruesome description of Lycidas's horrible death: "rent in twain he hung; nor slowly flowed / As from a wound the blood; but all his veins / Were torn asunder."[1] But Milton was not thinking of the bereaved; the poem does not even mention Edward King. Rather, Milton exploits the opportunity to display his astounding technical abilities and baffle his readers with his convoluted philosophical speculations. More obviously than ever before, Milton is writing for posterity. He never cared about his immediate audience; he aimed only to impress his "fit audience, though few" of like-minded individuals, who were mostly as yet unborn. The opening lines of "Lycidas" make sense only to an audience that is aware of Milton's entire biography. They would certainly have made no sense to Edward King's grieving family. Milton opens with a lengthy complaint that he is being forced to write poetry before he is ready:

Yet once more, O ye Laurels, and once more
Ye Myrtles brown, with Ivy never sear,
I come to pluck your Berries harsh and crude,
And with forc'd fingers rude,
Shatter your leaves before the mellowing year.
Bitter constraint, and sad occasion dear,
Compels me to disturb your season due. (1–7)

The lament is ironic, but only future students of Milton will get the joke. The weary "[y]et once more" contradicts the fact that Milton had written almost nothing over the three years preceding this poem. The notion that the poem is composed before its "season due" will be coherent only to one who knows the poet to be in the midst of an arduous course of preparation for his greatest work. The next line does mention that "Lycidas is dead," but the poet's reflections on that subject immediately take a direction that can only be described as selfish:

So may some gentle Muse
With lucky words favour my destin'd Urn,
And as he passes turn,
And bid fair peace be to my sable shrowd. (19–22)

It soon becomes clear that Lycidas is basically a surrogate for Milton himself. The poem addresses his greatest fear: that he will defraud God of the interest on his talent, by dying before he has written any great poetry. Milton notes that he and King were friends at university or, as he puts it in the terms of the pastoral convention: "[W]e were nurst upon the self-same hill, / Fed the same flock, by fountain, shade, and rill" (23–24). The generic conceit of pastoral poetry is that the characters are shepherds, and Milton had good biographical reasons for composing "Lycidas" in pastoral form. Shepherds were conventional symbols of both priests and poets. Milton had recently reached the conclusion that, in present-day England, poets were more effective shepherds than priests. Edward King, a minor poet who had become a priest, had made the opposite decision, and the pastoral medium provides the perfect vehicle to consider the relative merits of these choices.

That medium might also have allowed Milton to reminiscence about his student days with King. He mentions that, after a long day's sheepherding, he and Lycidas would adjourn to hear "th'oaten flute," where "rough Satyrs danc'd, and Fauns with clov'n heel" (34). This is not the kind of company we would expect a Puritan undergraduate to be keeping. But the poem eschews any further revelations and instead laments the impotence of various deities in the face of death. Even "the Muse herself that Orpheus bore" had been unable to save her son from dismemberment at the hands of "the rout that made the hideous roar" (61). Orpheus's mother, Calliope, was the Muse of epic poetry, to which Milton had dedicated his life, and her poignant helplessness at the death of her son surely reflects the recent demise of Milton's own mother. The thought of Orpheus's death brings Milton to the brink of despair. He regrets the lost sexual opportunities of his chaste youth:

> Alas! What boots it with uncessant care
> To tend the homely slighted Shepherd's trade,
> And strictly meditate the thankless Muse?
> Were it not better done as others use
> To sport with Amaryllis in the shade,
> Or with the tangles of Neaera's hair? (64–69)

Approaching thirty, Milton feels a pang of jealousy as he considers how others "use" their lives. He is using his time as an investment for the

future, but others are wallowing in the immediate, sensual pleasures of
the moment. The poem now shifts into a rapid pattern of proposition and
response, as Milton reasons his way to a justification of his vocation. It
is not wasteful to neglect carnal delights, he decides, in pursuit of the far
greater satisfaction of fame: "Fame is the spur that the clear spirit doth
raise / (That last infirmity of Noble mind) / To scorn delights and live
laborious days" (70–72). But Milton knew that fame was a long way off.
He was still only preparing himself for its pursuit. What if, like Edward
King, he should die before achieving it?

> But the fair Guerdon when we hope to find,
> And think to burst out into sudden blaze,
> Come the blind Fury with th'abhorred shears,
> And slits the thin-spun life. (73–76)

At this dramatic moment the first of the poem's characters makes
his appearance: "'But not the praise,' / Phoebus repli'd, and touch'd my
trembling ears" (76–77). Phoebus (Apollo), the classical god of poetry,
touches Virgil's ears in the sixth *Ecologue*, so Milton is once again claiming parity with the greatest epic poets of all time, now with the added
implication that he is divinely inspired. Phoebus instructs the poet not to
concern himself with an earthly audience:

> Fame is no plant that grows on mortal soil,
> Nor in the glistering foil
> Set off to th' world, nor in broad rumour lies,
> But lives and spreds aloft by those pure eyes,
> And perfet witnes of all judging Jove;
> As he pronounces lastly on each deed,
> Of so much fame in Heav'n expect thy meed. (78–84)

Milton's investment of his youth in the service of God through poetry would bear fruit in heaven if not on earth. Milton's "fit audience" is not to be found among human beings at all. A procession of divine, allegorical, and mythical figures now passes through the poem, offering various reflections on Lycidas's demise. The prefatory note that Milton appended when he published "Lycidas" in 1645 describes it as a "monody," a song for one voice. This would appear to be manifestly contradicted by the poem itself, in which six or seven different voices address us. But Milton's insistence that "Lycidas" is a "monody" reveals a key to his poetic procedure: he uses figures like Phoebus, Camus, Hippotades, and the poem's other characters to express various aspects of his own mental processes. Even *Paradise Lost,* which features over twenty different voices, is in this sense a "monody."

The 1645 preface also claims that "Lycidas" "foretells the ruin of our corrupted clergy then in their height." That is a rather generous reading and reveals a slight over-eagerness to claim prophetic powers. But the poem does contain a stinging criticism of the Church of England, spoken by "[t]he Pilot of the Galilean lake," St. Peter. Milton's portrayal of Peter indicates that, as late as 1637, he was still basically sympathetic to the Church of England as an institution. The saint has "Mitred locks," suggesting that he is a bishop, just as the Anglicans claimed. But Peter is scathing in his attack on the personal characters of the men currently entering the priesthood, who "for their bellies' sake / Creep and intrude and climb into the fold" (114–5). Such avaricious hirelings will "shove away the worthy bidden guest" (118) and discourage those who have a genuine calling, like Milton himself, from joining the church. They thus leave the way open for Roman Catholicism, "the grim wolf," to devour the flock. Milton ends this denunciation with an unmistakably apocalyptic but studiedly imprecise prophecy: "But that two-handed engine at the door / Stands ready to smite once, and smite no more" (130–1). Critics have identified this mysterious power as variously the "double-edged sword" of Revelation, the Bible with its two testaments, and the two houses of Parliament. But Milton's mechanism of vengeance is deliberately vague, and the image is more lugubriously threatening than would have been possible had the instrument of the church's future downfall been explicitly named.

Two separate, even contradictory consolations are offered for the death of Lycidas. One is the conventional Christian notion that he is now "mounted high / Through the dear might of him that walked the waves" and ensconced in "the blest Kingdoms meek of joy and love" (177). A few lines later, however, Lycidas receives a pagan, earthly apotheosis: "Henceforth thou art the Genius of the shore" (183). Lycidas has become a local deity, a spirit or "genius" of a particular place, although this process is quite incompatible with the heavenly reward he was offered earlier. Milton's poem debates the relative merits of the classical and Christian responses to death and is finally unable to decide between them. In fact this immature hesitancy is ultimately revealed as the poem's true subject. At the very end, we are abruptly informed that the entire poem up to this point has been in reported speech. We have been listening to a character within the poem:

> Thus sang the uncouth Swain to th'oaks and rills,
> While the still morn went out with sandals gray;
> He touch't the tender stops of various quills,
> With eager thought warbling his Doric lay:
> And now the sun had strech't out all the hills,
> And now was dropt into the Western bay;
> At last he rose, and twitch't his mantle blue:
> Tomorrow to fresh woods, and pastures new. (186–93)

Again, these lines make sense only to a future, or perhaps a heavenly, audience. Milton ends "Lycidas" as he began it, by locating the poem within the larger framework of his overall poetic career. It is, he informs us, a piece of juvenilia, the work of an "uncouth Swain," but it is to be the last such piece. From now on, Milton vows, his life and work will enter a new phase. These "pastures new" may be taken either metaphorically or literally. Milton would now start writing a very different kind of literature from the sonnets and odes of his youth. But he was also about to literally visit new pastures. He was on his way to Italy.

II

AT THE BELATED age of thirty Milton prized himself out of his studious retirement to embark on the final stage of a seventeenth-century gentleman's education: the "grand tour" of the sites of classical antiquity. He raised funds for the journey by his customary usurious means, loaning out £150 at 8 percent interest, which enabled him to hire a manservant to accompany him. He secured letters of introduction to various continental intellectuals from Sir Henry Wotton, Provost of Eton, former ambassador to Venice, and a great admirer of Milton's masque. Perhaps divining his young friend's outspoken tendencies, Wotton passed on a motto he had been given about how a Protestant Englishman should behave in the homeland of Catholicism: "*I pensieri stretti, ed il viso sciolto* [thoughts close, countenance open] will go safely over the whole world."[2] Milton would follow only half of this advice.

Milton's friend Cyriack Skinner recorded that he had "no admiration"[3] for the French, and there is plenty of evidence to support him. In his tract *Of Education* (1644) Milton would sneer at "the Monsieurs of Paris" for their tendency "to take our hopefull Youth into their slight and prodigal custodies and send them over back again transform'd into Mimicks, Apes, and Kicshoes" (2:393). This latter epithet derives from the French *quelque chose,* and the Oxford English Dictionary lists this as the first usage meaning "a fantastical, frivolous person." In a letter of 1667 Milton praised his friend Richard Jones for "despising the luxuries of Paris,"[4] and Milton's nephew Edward Phillips remembers the Council of State, which Milton later served, "scorning to conduct their affairs in the wheedling, lisping jargon of the cringing French" (1,033). Unsurprisingly, France did not detain Milton long, although he found time to meet Hugo Grotius, the famous Protestant theologian, in Paris. He traveled south to Nice, sailed from there to Genoa, and proceeded through Pisa to Florence. Italy was the native country of both classical civilization and the Renaissance, and Milton blossomed in its fertile soil. In Florence, especially, he found his spiritual home. He was introduced to many of its most famous inhabitants, including the seventy-five-year-old Galileo, then under house arrest by the Inquisition and also suffering from blindness. Milton mentions Galileo in *Paradise Lost,* and he clearly came to perceive a kinship between the astronomer's circumstances and his own.

Above all, Milton was delighted at the favorable responses that his poems won in Florence's literary salons. His letters of introduction gained him admission to the meetings of the private academies, modeled on the school of Plato, which characterized the city's intellectual life. They were gathering places for free-spirited young men, where discussion of art, politics, and sex could take place away from prying clerical eyes. Milton attended several of these groups, especially the Svogliati (the Will-less) and the Apatisti (the Passionless). He had brought along copies of his own poems and was delighted to find that the Florentine exotics admired his writings fervently. After his return to England he recalled that:

in the private academies of Italy, whither I was favoured to resort, perceiving that some trifles which I had in memory, composed at under twenty or thereabout, (for the manner is, that every one must give some proof of his wit and reading there,) met with acceptance above what was looked for; and other things, which I had shifted in scarcity of books and conveniences to patch up amongst them, were received with written encomiums, which the Italian is not forward to bestow on men of this side the Alps. (4.i.416)

In August 1638, while Milton was in Florence, his beloved Charles Diodati died. We do not know the cause, nor do we know when the sad news reached Milton, but it may be significant that during his Florentine sojourn he formed a passionate attachment to another spiritually sympathetic younger man, a nineteen-year-old former pupil of Galileo's named Carlo Dati. A homoerotic ambience pervaded the spiritual successors of Plato's academy, and the Italians showed none of the Calvinist reticence on sexual matters that Milton was used to in England. Another Florentine acquaintance, Antonio Malatesti, presented him with a copy of his risqué sonnet sequence, *La Tina, Equivoci Rusticali*. Milton found the academies full of well-balanced individuals, who were libertine without being sensualist, and spiritual without being ascetic. He must have noted the contrast with England, where people's personalities seemed to be drifting to opposite and mutually exclusive extremes.

From Florence he traveled to Rome, which had a deserved reputation as a perilous place for Protestants. Milton seems to have positively courted danger, accepting an invitation to dinner from the community of exiled English Jesuits. The details of their conversation are lost to history, but they can be inferred from the fact that Milton later reported hearing of "plots laid against me by the English Jesuits, should I return

to Rome, because of the freedom with which I had spoken about religion" (4.i.619). Before leaving England he had resolved that "I would
not indeed begin a conversation about religion, but if questioned about
my faith would hide nothing, whatever the consequences" (ibid.). He was
as good as his word, and he evidently expressed himself with the same
robust conviction that was to characterize his career as a pamphleteer.
According to the Dutch poet Nicolaas Heinsius, who traveled in Italy
later: "The Englishman [Milton] was hated by the Italians . . . on account
of his over-strict morals, because he both disputed freely about religion,
and on any occasion whatever prated very bitterly against the Roman
Pontiff."[5]

He also made Roman friends, however, including Lucas Holstein,
the librarian of the Vatican, who introduced him to the Pope's nephew,
Cardinal Barberini. Milton's correspondence shows how flattered he was
by this prelate's attentions (1:334) and despite his theological anti-Cathol-
icism, he never displayed the slightest personal antipathy to Catholics. His
own brother Christopher became a Catholic convert, but it does not seem
to have affected their relationship in the least. It was also in Rome that
Milton heard the famous Leonora Baroni sing, which inspired three short
poems in her praise. From Rome he continued south to Naples, which was
then ruled by England's political arch-enemy, Spain. His companion on
the last leg of the journey was "a certain Eremite friar," who introduced
him to the Marquis of Manso, a former patron of the great epic poet
Tasso. The nobleman's hospitality was somewhat thwarted, however, by
Milton's continued insistence on speaking his mind on matters of faith.
He later recalled that Manso had "wished to show me many more attentions, [but] he could not do so in that city, since I was unwilling to be
circumspect in regard to religion" (4.i.618). Manso presented the young
Englishman with an encomium that hints at some sensitive interchanges

on theological matters: "If your mind, for grace, features and manners were equaled by your religion, / Then, by Hercules, you would be no 'Angle' but a very angel." Milton rewarded him with a poem, "Manso," which transpires to be more of a tribute to Milton's ambition than to the aged Italian's achievements. Just as Milton had broken off his mourning for Edward King in "Lycidas" with the speculation that "[s]o may some lucky Muse favor my destin'd urn," so his preservation of Manso's fame leads him to speculate on how his own reputation might be guarded by his future admirers. The poem ends with a rapturous vision of Milton relishing his posthumous glory:

> Then, if faith has any meaning, if rewards are assured for the righteous, I myself, having been transported to the celestial realms of the heavenly gods, where labour, a pure mind, and ardent virtue lead, shall see these events (so far as the Fates allow) from some part of that secret world, and with a wholly serene mind and my smiling face suffused with rosy light, I shall joyfully clap my hands on heavenly Olympus. (94–100)

Milton's original plan had been to continue to Sicily and then Greece, but at some point in late 1638 he received tidings of civic unrest and political crisis in his native country. This struck him as the vocation he had been waiting for. As he later recalled, "I thought it base that I should travel abroad at my ease for the cultivation of my mind, while my fellow-citizens at home were fighting for their liberty" (4.i.619). He was having the time of his life, however, and he took his time returning. War between England and Scotland broke out in March 1639, but Milton found leisure to revisit Rome, in spite of the Jesuits' threats and, as he bragged, "for almost two more months, in the very stronghold of the Pope, if anyone attacked the orthodox religion, I openly, as before, defended it" (ibid.). He made another lengthy stay in Florence, then spent a month in Venice, where he encountered the music of Monteverdi, famed for having fashioned the story of Orpheus into one of the earliest operas. He next sojourned in Geneva, where he visited Charles Diodati's uncle Giovanni, the renowned theologian, with whom he held daily discussions, doubtless concerning the dramatic changes in his personal and political circumstances since the death of Charles and the outbreak of war. He did not arrive back in London until the late summer of 1639.

Milton found lodgings near St. Paul's, in the neighborhood where he had grown up, later moving to his own house in nearby Aldersgate Street. He set himself up as the master of a small private academy, initially boasting only two students—his sister's sons, aged eight and nine—then also admitting a few sons of friends. He began to settle into an agreeable routine of work interposed with leisure; his nephew Edward Phillips recalls how "once in three weeks or a month" he would "drop into the society of some young sparks of his acquaintance, the chief whereof were Mr. Alphry and Mr. Miller, two gentlemen of Gray's Inn, the beaux of those times (but nothing near so bad as those nowadays). With these gentlemen he would so far make bold with his body as now and then to keep a gaudy-day" (1,030). It is hard, at this distance, to gauge just what Phillips meant by "beaux," but the word doubtless suggests a fun-loving disposition, and such company belies any suggestion that Milton was overly puritanical in his personal life. In these pleasant circumstances he embarked on a detailed study of English history, as the notes in his surviving commonplace book show. Among them is a summary of Bede's story about "an Englishman who was suddenly made a poet by divine Providence" (1:381). There can be no doubt about the direction his thoughts were leading.

He was now at the stage of making notes for the great epic poem that he at last felt himself qualified to write. His jottings include drafts of epic poems on British heroes like Arthur and Alfred, and fragmentary musings on biblical subjects like *The Golden Calf, Gideon Idoloclastes,* and *Abram in Egypt.* There is an intriguing sketch called *Cupid's Funeral Pile,* or *Sodom Burning,* in which the inhabitants of Sodom were to be described "each evening every one, with mistresse, or Ganymed, gitterning along the streets." Ganymede, the beautiful boy who served as Jove's cup bearer, signified a homosexual lover. Milton's notes expand on the biblical story of two angels who visit Sodom disguised as beautiful young men. In his version, they try to teach the citizens about "love and how it differs from lust" but, failing to "win" the Sodomites to appreciation of this distinction, invoke "the thunders, lightnings, and fires" to "hear the call and command of God to come and destroy a godless nation." Milton's Sodom appears to be a symbol of excessive sensuality in general, rather than of homosexuality in particular. He seems to have intended a prophetic jeremiad to accompany the revolutionary purge of London's social and political corruption that was taking place outside his window as he wrote.

But the most portentous section of his notes from this period is the three germinal fragments entitled *Paradise Lost,* and another brief treatment under the heading *Adam Unparadis'd.* Milton's nephew reports being shown ten lines from the latter that found their way unaltered into the published version of *Paradise Lost,* as part of Satan's opening soliloquy in book four. Milton's epic was evidently in the process of composition at least twenty-five years before its publication. *Paradise Lost* is effectively his life's work. But its progress, like that of all of Milton's private literary ambitions, was soon swamped and engulfed in England's national political crisis.

III

THE EARLY YEARS of Charles I's reign had been dominated by increasingly acrimonious quarrels between the King and Parliament. The King's demands for increased taxes, which he needed to finance his extravagant court, had been met by Parliament's recalcitrant requests for political and religious reform, and after the disastrous "addled" session of 1629, Charles had refused to summon Parliament at all. He instituted a repressive system of government known as "Thorough," forcibly raised taxes of dubious legality, guided national policy by his personal whim, and aspired to the mode of absolutism that was coming to characterize the French political system. This kind of personal rule struck most English people as Popish, and Milton's Italian idyll was interrupted by the news that Charles's system was becoming impractical. The final catalyst for the English civil war was the King's rash attempt to impose the English Book of Common Prayer on the fiercely Presbyterian nation of Scotland. It would take an army to enforce this decision, but the English army was weak and impoverished, described by its commander as composed of men "fit for Bedlam and Bridewell,"[6] and it unsurprisingly proved inadequate to the task of intimidating the Scots.

To raise the funds necessary to strengthen the army, Charles was finally forced to call a Parliament in April 1640. The demands for redress of grievances that the Commons immediately placed before him seemed intolerable to Charles, and he angrily prorogued what has become known as the "short Parliament" after only three weeks. Mobs swarmed through the streets in protest; on May 11, Archbishop Laud noted in his diary that "[a]t midnight my house at Lambeth was beset by 500 of these rascal routers."[7] On the fifteenth two London prisons were stormed and the prisoners released. The King responded to the Scots' defiance by launching a disastrous invasion, in which the English army was trounced and which ended with the Scots in control of the north of England. The need to pay the ransom they demanded compelled the King to summon Parliament again in November. This time the members were determined to bring about fundamental and irreversible reforms to the English state, reforms so radical that historians recognize them as the English Revolution.

Events now moved very rapidly. The Long Parliament met on November 3, 1640. The King's most prominent advisor, the hated Earl of Strafford, was charged with treason on the eleventh. The iconoclastic spirit of the times appears to have invaded even the subconscious of Archbishop Laud: A week before Parliament assembled he wrote in his diary of a visit to his "upper study":

> In that study hung my picture, taken from the life; and, coming in, I found it fallen down upon the face, and lying on the floor, the string being broken by which it was hanged upon the wall. I am almost every day threatened with my ruin in Parliament; God grant this be no omen![8]

His prayer was not granted; denounced as "the Sty of all Pestilential Filth that hath infested the State and Government of this Commonwealth,"[9] Laud was voted a traitor on December 18 and imprisoned. Parliament freed the noisy zealot William Prynne and the future Leveller John Lilburne, along with other Puritans who had been imprisoned by Laud. The parliamentary leader John Pym listed grievances and specified the ways in which the rights of Parliament had been violated over the previous eleven years. In February 1641 Parliament passed the Triennial Act, mandating that it should meet every three years, and in May it declared itself dissoluble by no exterior force. On May 12 the Earl of Strafford, to whom Charles had recently pledged assurance "upon the word of a King, you shall not suffer in life, honour or fortune," was executed. The King's word was no longer law, it was not even good. Parliament, and not the King, was now England's highest political authority.

As he explained in one of his earliest tracts, Milton's decision to involve himself in these events entailed considerable self-sacrifice. He had spent his entire life preparing himself for the role of epic poet, to which he believed he had been called by God. He recalls "an inward prompting which now grew daily upon me, that by labour and intense study, (which I take to be my portion in this life,) joined with the strong propensity of nature, I might perhaps leave something so written to aftertimes, as they should not willingly let it die" (1:810). He dares to hope that "what the greatest and choicest wits of Athens, Rome or modern Italy, and those Hebrews of old did for their country, I in my proportion, with this over and above, of being a Christian, might do for mine" (1:812). Milton is laying down a pledge, taking out a loan of credibility, which he intends to redeem with the greatest epic poem ever written. The reference to the "Hebrews of old" even hints that he aspires to surpass the Bible itself. But given his conviction that the individual soul and the political nation were organically connected, Milton now felt himself unable to accomplish his aesthetic aim until England had "enfranchised herself from this impertinent yoke of prelaty, under whose inquisitorious and tyrannical duncery, no free and splendid wit can flourish" (1:820).

Accustomed as he was to playing the role of debt collector, Milton was aware that the interest on his talent would accumulate during this delay, and he begs indulgence from his creditors: "Neither do I think it shame to covenant with any knowing reader, that for some few years yet I may go on trust with him toward the payment of what I am now indebted" (ibid.). A lengthy digression wrestles with the implications of his turn to politics, as Milton addresses himself, once again, to a select audience that dwells mostly in posterity. As in "Lycidas" he complains that he is forced to put pen to paper prematurely and that the results will likely be hurried, controversial, and in any case written in prose, a medium to which he is not naturally suited:

> I would be heard only, if it might be, by the elegant and learned reader, to whom principally for a while I shall beg leave I may address myself. To him it will be no new thing, though I tell him that if I hunted after praise, by the ostentation of wit and learning, I should not write thus out of mine own season when I have neither yet completed to my mind the full circle of my private studies, although I complain not of any insufficiency to the matter in hand; or were I ready to my wishes, it were a folly to commit any thing elaborately composed to the careless and interrupted listening of these tumultuous times. Next, if I were wise only to my own ends, I would certainly take such a subject as of itself might catch applause, whereas this hath all the disadvantages on the contrary, and such a subject as the publishing whereof might be delayed at pleasure, and time enough to pencil it over with all the curious touches of art, even to the perfection of a faultless picture; whenas in this argument the not deferring is of great moment to the good speeding, that if solidity have leisure to do her office, art cannot have much. Lastly, I should not choose this manner of writing, wherein knowing myself inferior to myself, led by the genial power of nature to another task, I have the use, as I may account, but of my left hand. (1:807–8)

Milton envisioned his transition to political prose as a necessary but temporary distraction from his real vocation. He knew that the longer he delayed repaying the loan of his talent, the heavier the burden would grow, but he also knew there were other accounts that must be settled

first. The military battles of the civil war were preceded by equally ferocious literary exchanges. The Long Parliament abolished the Court of
Star Chamber in 1641, thus removing the royal censorship and unleashing a startlingly voracious public appetite for controversy. A tidal wave
of pamphlets streamed from the presses. Pamphleteering was an uncon-
trolled, readily accessible and inexpensive means to a potentially wide
audience, strongly reminiscent of the Internet in our own time. There
must have been enormous pent-up intellectual energy among the people
of London, hundreds of whom now rushed to publish their opinions and
proposals on every important issue of the day. The most important such
issue, perhaps surprisingly for a modern reader, was church government,
and London was awash with pamphlets, news books, broadsheets, published sermons, and mass petitions taking every conceivable position on
the subject.

Milton immediately perceived that the question of how the church
should be governed would determine the outcome of every other debate.
His first five pamphlets were ferocious attacks on the Anglican institution of "episcopacy": rule by bishops. At this early stage in his career
Milton preferred the Presbyterian system of ecclesiastical organization, although his position already contained an implicit objection to
all state churches and even to organized religion as such. The church
was an unrivaled source of ideological power, everyone legally had to
attend its services, and whoever controlled its government would rule
the souls of the English people. The model of authority provided by
the church would be replicated in the state, the family, and even within
the mind. The habits of thought formed by idolatrous church liturgy
would produce willing slaves to political tyrants. In *The Reason of
Church Government*, Milton describes "prelaty ascending by a gradual
monarchy from bishop to archbishop, from thence to primate, and . . .

from primate to patriarch, and so to pope." The attack on episcopacy contained a covert criticism of patriarchal authority in general, and the removal of the bishops would entail a fundamental reorganization of the English state and psyche: "no bishop, no king," as the contemporary slogan had it. Milton understood all this with crystal clarity. He later recalled how the need to dethrone the bishops

> awakened all my attention and my zeal. I saw that a way was opening for the establishment of real liberty; that the foundation was laying for the deliverance of man from the yoke of slavery and superstition; that the principles of religion, which were the first objects of our care, would exert a salutary influence on the manners and constitution of the republic. (4.i.622)

Milton's studies in theology and church history had equipped him perfectly for this battle, and he carefully leveled his aim at the bishops' miters. Of course, one did not become a bishop in seventeenth-century England by being meek or stupid. The prelates, well aware of what was at stake, defended their position with aggression and intelligence, throwing a powerful early punch in the form of Bishop Joseph Hall's *Episcopacie by Divine Right* (1640), which Hall followed up with a *Humble Remonstrance* to Parliament in January 1641. A traditional Calvinist (and a noted opponent of usury), whose rebarbative prose had won him the title "the English Seneca,"[10] Hall pointed out the democratic conclusion to which the abolition of episcopacy was likely to lead: "John a Nokes and John a Stiles the Elders! Smug the Smith, a Deacon."[11] He was quite right—the disruption of ecclesiastical hierarchy would indeed inspire many working men and women to exercise a vocation to preach. Hall's mistake lay in assuming that his Presbyterian opponents would perceive the same dangers as he in such democratic developments and that they would therefore draw back from the precipice. Instead they boisterously engaged him, and prominent among the authors crowding into the melee was the pseudonymous "Smectymnuus." This personage was actually an acronym constructed from the initials of five Presbyterian pastors, among them Milton's former tutor and close friend Thomas Young.

Milton's anti-prelatical tracts are interventions in the wider pamphlet war between the Smectymnuans and various Anglican bishops, Hall in particular. His first published piece of prose, *Of Reformation,* appeared in spring 1641, and ecclesiastical controversy occupied his attention for the next year. He acknowledged that, in one sense, writing political pro-paganda was a distraction from his prophetic vocation. In another sense, however, politics was prophecy in practice. Our last three centuries have been full of political revolutions, so it is hard for us to imagine just how shocking the English revolution seemed to contemporaries. It was a virtu-ally unprecedented series of events. Whenever earlier monarchs had been overthrown, they had simply been replaced by new kings. The Dutch had thrown off the yoke of Spanish oppression and established a Protestant republic, but theirs was primarily a revolt against foreign occupation. Never since ancient times had a nation deposed its ruler over issues of political principle. Never before had a monarch been convicted of crimes against his own people, still less executed for them. The sheer novelty of the revolution led many of those who made it to believe they were tools in the hands of the Almighty, who was preparing the ground for his return by the physical elimination of Antichrist. It was easy for Milton to con-clude that he had been divinely appointed as God's iconoclast. He began casting around for idols to smash.

Milton embarked on his pamphleteering career with his customary eye on posterity. Although *Of Reformation* appeared anonymously, he made sure that his authorship was known, even taking the trouble to present a copy to the Bodleian library. He was fully aware of the significance of the events in which he was about to participate, and he wanted his participation recorded. *Of Reformation* thrusts the profound and various implications of church government upon the reader, shaping the concept of "reformation" into a theoretical justification of revolution, both political and psychological. A finely honed philosophy springs fully fledged from the opening pages; it is immediately obvious that we are encountering a highly idiosyncratic, even eccentric, but remarkably fierce intelligence. It is like watching a dam burst. The pent-up energy produced by decades of anonymous, largely silent reading and thinking is released with overwhelming exuberance: Milton invents an entirely new polemical style, sometimes even coining new words in his excitement, as in his dismissal of "the finicall goosery of your neat Sermon-actor" (1:935).

Milton's case against prelacy streams and expands over the course of five tracts, but it culminates in the following position: the Church has been seduced, perverted, and rendered "more antichristian than antichrist himself," by the power of commodity fetishism. The bishops have established an ecclesiastical market economy, and this has brought about a magical and idolatrous attitude to religion, which turns people's souls into things. Who, Milton asks, can defend the ecclesiastical justice system

> where fees and clamours keep shop and drive a trade, where bribery and corruption solicits, paltering the free and moneyless power of discipline with a carnal satisfaction by the purse? Contrition, humiliation, confession, the very sighs of a repentant spirit, are there sold by the penny. That undeflowered and unblemishable

> simplicity of the gospel, not she herself, for that could never be,
> but a false-whited, a lawny resemblance of her, like that air-born
> Helena in the fables, made by the sorcery of prelates, instead of
> calling her disciples from the receipt of custom, is now turned pub-
> lican herself; and gives up her body to a mercenary whoredom
> under those fornicated arches, which she calls God's house, and in
> the sight of those her altars, which she hath set up to be adored,
> makes merchandise of the bodies and souls of men. (1:849)

The commodification of spiritual matters produces idolatry as the
whorish apparition of "air-born Helena," familiar to Milton's audience
as the archetypal idol in the Faust story, materializes out of the financial
"sorcery of prelates." Milton was writing at the time when commodity fetishism was just beginning to manifest itself outside the church, in
the vast and sudden expansion of the secular market, which abolished
restraints on usury and stimulated money into artificial life. As prominent
participants in, and beneficiaries of, the growing market economy, Milton
and his family were better aware than most of the market's psychological effects. We live in an era when commodity fetishism has colonized
every corner of the world and every recess of the mind: it is so familiar
as to be barely perceptible. But Milton saw it with the clarity of novelty,
he explored its impact on every aspect of thought and experience, and
that is one of the many reasons why it is salutary to read him today. He
describes the bishops as ecclesiastical capitalists who "feast and riot upon
the labours of hireling Curats" (1:952), and he warns his readers that the
market mentality will not rest until it has commodified every aspect of
life. The market economy may have developed and grown to maturity in
the womb of the Church, but now it is ready to migrate into the social
and political spheres:

that they may want nothing to make them true merchants of
Babylon, as they have done to your souls, they will sell your bodies, your wives, your children, your liberties, your parliaments, all
these things; and if there be aught else dearer than these, they
will sell at an outcry in their pulpits to the arbitrary and illegal
dispose of any one that may hereafter be called a king, whose
mind shall serve him to listen to their bargain. (1:851)

Protestantism had been founded as a result of Luther's protest against
the sale of "indulgences," which he considered an idolatrous commodification of penitential labor. The sale of the sacraments was also held to
have a violently deleterious effect on the soul. A sacrament was a genuinely efficacious sign, while a commodity is given a fetishistic, artificial
efficacy by human custom. To commodify the sacraments was to reduce
divine efficacy to the level of magic. The technical term for commodification in ecclesiastical discourse was "simony," and Milton's anti-prelatical
tracts identify "simony" as the root historical cause of church's degrada-
tion. The sin is named after Simon Magus, the sorcerer who attempted
to buy St. Peter's miraculous healing power. As a professional magician,
Simon automatically assumed that this power was a thing, a commodity
that could be bought and sold, just as the modern priests "buy and sell
. . . and prostitute every inducement of grace, every holy thing to sale"
(1:558). Milton often alludes to the popular Faust myth, which expresses
in fictional terms exactly what "the Babilonish Marchants of Soules"
(1:592) were daily practicing in reality: the sale of the soul. He rails that
the bishops "extract heaps of gold, and silver out of the drossie Bullion of
the people's sins" (1:719). He scorns those who seduce the church to "lie
prostitute to sordid fees" and imagine they can derive "the divine gift of
learning from the den of Plutus, or the cave of Mammon." Furthermore,

since "Antichrist is Mammon's son," the commodification of the church will lead directly to the imposition of fetishistic religion: "If the splendour of Gold and silver begin to lord it once again in the Church of England, wee shall see Antichrist shortly wallow here, though his chief Kennell be at Rome" (1:590).

The commodity fetishism produced by a market economy is, in an ecclesiastical context, expressed as liturgical idolatry. The idolatrous liturgy and traditional hierarchy of the church drag people's attention from the spirit to the flesh. The bishops interpose themselves between the individual believer and God, blocking the soul's access to divinity. The icons with which they fill their churches represent God in material form. This causes the congregation to focus on the images to the exclusion of what they represent, and this produces an absurdly literalistic interpretation of scripture. Just as people in church concentrate on the beautiful ornaments and so are distracted from their spiritual referents, so readers of the Bible focus on the "letter," the surface significance of the text, what the words *appear* to mean. They are thus distracted from the "spirit" of the words, their underlying, symbolic, essential meaning. Milton would have found the literalistic religious fundamentalists of our own day to be no better than atheists. He deplores the degeneration in interpretative skills by which "men came to scan the Scriptures, by the Letter," and he argues that such an approach to religion amounts to slavery. He drives home the identity between episcopacy and slavery with a wild, biting wit: The bishops are "Egyptian task-masters of Ceremonies," who have

> Magnifi'd the external signs more then the quickning power of
> the Spirit, and yet looking on them through their own guiltinesse
> with a Servile feare, and finding as little comfort, or rather ter-
> ror from them againe, they knew not how to hide their Slavish

approach to Gods behests by them not understood, not worthily receav'd, but by cloaking their Servile crouching to all Religious Presentments, sometimes lawfull, sometimes Idolatrous, under the name of humility, and terming the Py-bald frippery, and ostentation of Ceremony's, decency. (1:522)

These words sound King Charles's death knell, by translating objections to Anglican liturgy into denunciations of political oppression. If episcopacy is idolatry, it is also slavery. If it is slavery, it is tyranny. If the King enforces episcopacy, the King is a tyrant. Tyrants must be deposed. This revolutionary reasoning is not yet explicit; indeed, Milton claims to be defending the King against his evil, ecclesiastical advisors. But revolution simmers just beneath the surface of the text, bubbling into sight infrequently but unmistakably. Milton argues that episcopal church government is a school of slavery, where people are habituated to the mental tendencies that issue in social and political enslavement:

[P]relaty, whom the tyrant custom begot, a natural tyrant in religion, and in state the agent and minister of tyranny, seems to have had this fatal gift in her nativity, like another Midas, that whatsoever she should touch, or come near either in ecclesial or political government, it should turn, not to gold, though she for her part could wish it, but to the dross and scum of slavery, breeding and settling both in the bodies and the souls of all such as do not in time, with the sovereign treacle of sound doctrine, provide to fortify their hearts against her hierarchy. The service of God who is truth, her liturgy confesses to be perfect freedom; but her works and her opinions declare, that the service of prelaty is perfect slavery, and by consequence perfect falsehood. (1:853)

In Milton's tracts we see the epochal historical process by which religious reform evolved into political revolution taking place within the mind of a single man: "looke what the grounds, and causes are of single happiness to one man, the same shall ye find them to a whole state" (1:572). The personal is the political: the cleansing of the mind from idols will require and produce the abolition of the political powers that enforce idolatrous religion. By the summer of 1642 Milton was referring to true religion and political liberty as "two things [which] God hath inseparably knit together, and hath disclos'd to us that they who seek to corrupt our religion are the same that would inthrall our civill liberty" (1:923–4).

By repudiating the very earliest history of institutional and theological Christianity, *Of Reformation* comes close to suggesting that all organized religion is necessarily apostasy. A state church certainly is; Constantine's adoption of Christianity as the state religion of the Roman Empire was the beginning of apostasy, and purity in the church was found only in "the most virgin times between Christ and Constantine" (1:551). The writings of the first church fathers were already full of "the foul errors, the ridiculous wresting of Scripture, the Heresies" (ibid.) that characterize apostasy. Constantine himself is ridiculed for his magical attitude to relics; Milton mocks his alleged discovery of the True Cross, "some of the nailes whereof he put into his Helmet, to beare off blows in battell" (1:556), and his fetishizing of "[p]art of the Crosse, in which he thought such Vertue to reside, as would prove a kind of Palladium to save the Citie where ever it remain'd" (ibid.). This magical "Vertue" which Constantine attributed to the material body of the cross is in reality the power of Satan, who tempts us to put our faith in magical signs, symbols, and icons. It is the diametrical antithesis of the interior, psychological "virtue" evinced by the Lady in *Comus,* which consists precisely in the ability to resist the appeal of such images. Milton is arguing that Antichrist has taken control of the church by forcibly marrying it to the state and that this marriage has produced copious offspring in the form of psychological idols. Now he demands a divorce.

Apostasy began under Constantine and advanced rapidly after his death: "at this time Antichrist began first to put forth his horne, and that saying was common that former times had their wooden Chalices and golden Priests; but they golden Chalices and Woodden Priests" (1:557). The English Reformation failed to dissolve the Antichristian marriage of church and state, and as a result Antichrist remained powerful, working now through the episcopal hierarchy and Laudian liturgy. Milton loathes the visual and auditory beauty of Anglican ceremony, which he dismisses as "the gaudy allurements of a Whore" (ibid.). With scatological wit he imagines the bishops literally wiping their behinds with the divine image: "the dark overcasting of superstitious copes and flaminical vestures, wearing on their backs, and I abhor to think, perhaps in some worse place, the inexpressible image of God the Father." Such antipathy to ornamentation might seem surprising in an artist, but of course Milton is not unappreciative of sensual beauty as such. His objection is to the deployment of beauty as an aid to religious worship. He saw that people would soon come to worship the beauty itself, rather than what it stood for.

He also understood how sensuality can be enlisted in the service of political oppression. In 1633 King Charles had struck a blow against the Puritans by issuing the *Book of Sports*, which explicitly legalized many of the destructive and lascivious popular pastimes that Puritan local authorities were quite sensibly attempting to regulate. Milton presents the royal intervention as a deliberate administration of opium to the people: "To make men governable in this manner their precepts mainly tend to break a nationall spirit, and courage by count'nancing upon riot, luxury, and ignorance . . ." (1:572). The bishops have

hamstrung the valour of the Subject by seeking to effeminate us all
at home. Well knows every wise Nation that their Liberty consists
in manly and honest labours, in sobriety and rigorous honor to the
Marriage Bed, which in both Sexes should be bred up from chast
hopes to loyall Enjoyments; and when the people slacken, and fall
to loosenes, and riot, then doe they as much as if they laid downe
their necks for some wily Tyrant to get up and ride. (1:589)

This is revolutionary Puritanism in its classic form. Sensual indulgence comes from and leads to political tyranny. King Charles was fully
aware of how useful sensuality could be as a way of distracting the people
from politics, and he went out of his way to encourage what Milton calls
"gaming, jigging, wassailing, and mixt dancing" (ibid.). In *The Reason of
Church Government,* Milton advocates by contrast a Spartan "managing
of our public sports and festival pastimes; that they might be, not such
as were authorized a while since, the provocations of drunkenness and
lust, but such as may inure and harden our bodies by martial exercises
to all warlike skill and performance." Milton forms part of the tradition of revolutionary asceticism stretching back to the Catos and forward
through Robespierre, Lenin, and Che Guevara, even to the ayatollahs and
jihadis of our own day.

But his most violent abuse is always reserved for the merchants and
usurers of the ecclesiastical economy. He denounces those who claim to
save souls through "the truccage of perishing Coine, and the butcherly
execution of Tormentors, Rooks, and Rakeshames sold to lucre" (1:591).
He condemns "the fogging proctorage of money" and "that banking den
of thieves that dare thus baffle, and buy and sell" spiritual commodities; he
scorns priests who live by "the ignoble Hucksterage of piddling Tithes."
The Reason of Church Government alleges that the prelates manipulate

the market, deliberately withholding access to scripture, in order to make their own goods seem more alluring to consumers:

> the great merchants of this world, fearing that this course would soon discover and disgrace the false glitter of their deceitful wares, wherewith they abuse the people, like poor Indians with beads and glasses, practise by all means how they may suppress the vending of such rarities, and at such a cheapness as would undo them, and turn their trash upon their hands. (1:802)

Milton was venturing into potentially dangerous territory here. As a professional usurer himself, who had always lived, as he put it, "of the sweat of other men," he was obviously vulnerable to the charge of hypocrisy. Perhaps his intemperate rage against the financial corruption of his enemies is also a self-criticism, his extreme vehemence an indication of guilty neurosis. *Of Reformation*'s tone is violent throughout, but it ends with a burst of jaw-droppingly incandescent fury that causes serious concern about its author's emotional well-being. Not content with anticipating the bishops' political defeat, Milton pursues the prelates beyond the grave, slavering with anticipation at the prospect that:

> after a shamefull end in this Life (which God grant them) [they] shall be throwne down eternally into the darkest and deepest Gulfe of Hell, where under the despightfull controule, the trample and spurne of all the other Damned, that in the anguish of their Torture shall have no other ease than to exercise a Raving and Bestial Tyranny over them as their Slaves and Negros, they shall remaine in that plight for ever, the basest, the lowermost, the most dejected, most underfoot and downe-trodden Vassals of Perdition. (1:616–7)

The tradition of perverted sadism in Christian depictions of Hell stretches back to Tertullian's second-century gloating: "How shall I admire, how laugh, how rejoice, how exult, when I behold so many proud monarchs, and fancied gods, groaning in the lower abyss of darkness."[14] Nietzsche attributed it to the *resentiment* of slaves against their masters, which, since it could not be expressed in this life, was projected into eternity. In Milton, however, such base impulses have a thematic coherence that goes some way toward excusing them. He is concerned with communicating the fact that idolatry is slavery, he is aware that idolatry seems attractive to many people, and so he desires to convey slavery's true horror to the complacent among his audience. He had absorbed from his reading of Dante the notion that punishments in Hell will be ironically adapted to the nature of the sins they chastise. Because the bishops are slave-masters on earth, they will be slaves in Hell. But despite all this, Milton's decision to end his first published prose in such bloodcurdling fashion is hardly redolent of a soul at ease with itself.

IV

WE CAN ASSUME that this fact was communicated to Milton by friend and foe alike. While hardly less vehement in tone, the tracts that followed *Of Reformation* do at least attempt to rationalize their ferocity. At every stage of his life, the virulence of Milton's abuse is shocking, even by the standards of his time. He was aware of this, proud of it even, and he often draws the reader's attention to what he calls "a sanctifi'd bitternesse against the enemies of truth" (1:901). He offers various excuses for his intemperance, suggesting that it is not self-interested but rather generated by his outrage at seeing the cause of righteousness defamed: "I conceav'd myself to be now not as mine own person, but as a member incorporate into that truth whereof I was perswaded . . ."[15] He points out that "Christ himselfe . . . scruples not to mention the Dunghill and the Jakes" (1:895). He sometimes provides a parental advisory before some especially brutal passage: "In the following Section I must foretell ye, Readers, the doings will be rough and dangerous, the bating of a Satir."[14] The preface to *Of Reformation* unconvincingly claims that the abuse Milton is about to heap upon his sixty-eight-year-old opponent is an appropriate response to Bishop Hall's own vitriol: "I suppose and more then suppose, it will be nothing disagreeing from Christian Meeknesse to handle such a one in a rougher accent, and to send home his haughtinesse well bespurted with his owne holy-water" (1:662). But Milton's claim to be "without all private and personal spleene," to feel "a sad and unwilling anger" that forces him to express "grim laughter," is instantly undermined by the joyous, abandoned relish with which he leaps into controversy. He obviously enjoyed abusing his enemies, and we do not need to excuse his sadism. But the derision does serve a purpose. In addition to ecclesiastical and political reform, Milton is proposing a cultural revolution in personal conduct, which will dispense with the hypocritical niceties of courtly discourse. The English revolution affected every area of experience, involving aesthetic issues of dress and style as well as political and ecclesiastical matters. Milton drew a causal connection between personal morality and stylistic facility: "[H]ow he should be truly eloquent who is not withal a good man, I see not" (1:874). His tracts against the bishops ostentatiously ignore courtly convention, expounding instead a quite new form of political discourse that combines the range of a scholar with the tone of the alehouse.

Just as Milton was convinced of the fusion between the individual soul and the political state, so he claimed that the salvational power of the church depended upon the character of its clergy. He noted that "many

worthy preachers," when "left to their own disciplining at home," prove
"deficient" in regulating their body in such a way as "to render it more
pliant to the soul, and useful to the commonwealth." He rather recklessly
asserted that

> those Priests whose vices have been notorious, are all Prelaticall,
> which argues both the impiety of that opinion, and the wicked re-
> misnesse of that government. We hear not of any which are call'd
> Nonconformists that have been accus'd for scandalous living; but
> are known to be pious, or at least sober men. Which is a great
> good argument, that they are in the truth and Prelats in the error.
> (1:945)

Because he believed that political and religious opinions arose out of
personal morality, Milton felt entirely justified in noting that many Anglican
priests "spend their youth in loitering, bezelling, and harlotting, their studies in unprofitable questions, and barbarous sophistry, their middle age
in ambition, and idleness, their old age in avarice, dotage, and disease"
(1:677). It cannot have surprised him when the prelates turned such accusations back upon him. Although his first tracts were ostensibly anonymous,
Milton allowed his authorship to become known, and it was not long before
Bishop Hall was denouncing him as "a scurrilous mime, a personated and
(as himself thinks) a grim, lowering, bitter fool" who, after a scandalous
career at Cambridge, had been "at length vomited out thence into a suburb
sink about London,"[15] where he allegedly spent his time hanging around
playhouses and brothels. This provoked Milton into a defensive description
of his real daily activities, which, although self-interested, probably does
bear a reasonably close resemblance to the truth. As throughout his youth,
he spent most of his time studying, but now he claims also to be readying
his body for the service of the revolutionary cause:

Those morning haunts are where they should be, at home, not sleeping, or concoting the surfeits of an irregular feast, but up, and stirring, in winter often ere the sound of any bell awake men to labour, or to devotion; in Summer as oft with the Bird that first rouses, or not much tardier, to reade good Authors, or cause them to be read, till the attention bee weary, or memory have his full fraught. Then with usefull and generous labours preserving the bodies health, and hardinesse; to render lightsome, cleare, and not lumpish obedience to the minde, to the cause of religion, and our Countries liberty, when it shall require firme hearts in sound bodies to stand and cover their stations, rather than to see the ruine of our Protestation, and the inforcement of a slavish life. (1:885–6)

As Milton clearly appreciated, the disputes between Parliament and the King could now only be settled by "inforcement." By this stage the political tide had turned against the bishops. A bill for the "root and branch" abolition of episcopacy was introduced into the Commons in May 1641, and in August, thirteen bishops, including the Smectymnuans' arch-enemy Joseph Hall, were impeached for collusion with Laud's repression and sent to the Tower. On September 1, Parliament launched an official campaign of iconoclasm, and images, altar rails, statues, paintings, and relics were ripped out of the churches. Autumn brought the dreadful news of revolt in Ireland; the natives had risen against the English and Scots colonists and, according to exaggerated but by no means groundless reports, were butchering them in horrific numbers and with terrible cruelty. By November it was said that every Protestant family in Ulster had been slaughtered or evicted. English and Scots people believed the most salacious reports of atrocities: "eighteen Scotch infants hanged on clothiers' tenter-hooks, and one fat young Scotchman murdered and candles made of his grease."[16]

Obviously an army must be sent to save the defenseless colonists, but Parliament could not trust the King with command of such a power. In an act of open and obvious rebellion, Parliament began mustering its own forces, and people began to understand that the battles currently being fought with pen and paper would soon come to involve other weapons.

The tracts the prelates produced in self-defense now took an increasingly desperate tone. Both sides were starting to realize that they were literally fighting for their lives. Bishop Hall continued to attack Milton even from his prison cell; it is poignant to consider the disgust he would feel on learning that he was known to posterity primarily as the object of his target's satire. Just before Hall's imprisonment, Milton published his *Animadversions upon the Remonstrant's Defence,* another personal attack on the aged prelate. Milton's tract is written in a remarkably modern, even postmodern form. He reproduces Hall's previous work in its entirety, interspersing his own scornful responses between the bishop's words. The result resembles nothing so much as an Internet "flame-war," and the tract's demotic, colloquial tone gives a unique flavor of seventeenth-century tavern talk:

> *Remonstrant:* No seduc't persons reclaim'd?
>
> *Answerer:* More reclaimed persons seduc'd.
>
> *Remonstrant:* No hospitality kept?
>
> *Answerer:* Bacchanalia's good store in every Bishop's family, and good gleeking.
>
> *Remonstrant:* No great offenders punish'd?
>
> *Answerer:* The trophies of your high Commision are renown'd.
>
> *Remonstrant:* No good offices done for the publique?
>
> *Answerer:* Yes, the good office of reducing monarchie to tyrannie, of breaking pacifications, and calumniating the people to the King.

Remonstrant: No care of the peace of the Church?

Answerer: No, nor of the land, witnesse the two armies in the
North that now lies plunder'd, and over-run by a liturgie.

Remonstrant: No diligence in preaching?

Answerer: Scarce any preaching at all.

Remonstrant: No holinesse in living?

Answerer: No.

Remonstrant: Truly brethren I can say no more; but that the fault
is in your eyes.

Answerer: If you can say no more than this, you were a proper
Remonstrant to stand up for the whole tribe.

Remonstrant: Wipe them and looke better.

Answerer: Wipe your fat corpulencies out of our light. (1:731–2)

To Hall's baseless boast that "[n]o one Clergie in the whole Christian
world yeelds so many eminent schollers, learned preachers, grave, holy and
accomplish'd Divines as this Church of England doth at this day," Milton
simply answers, "Ha, ha, ha" (1:726). He blends the most abstruse and
arcane intellectual arguments with a bluntly popular accent that evokes
the democratic, liberated ambience of revolutionary London. The tract's
anti-ceremonial fury extends even to the domestic rituals of set meals:

Call hither your Cook. The order of Breakfast, Dinner, and Supper,
answere me, is it set or no? Set. Is a man therefore bound in the
morning to potcht eggs, and vinegar, or at noon to Brawn, or
Beefe, or at night to fresh Sammon, and French Kick-hoes? May
he not make his meales in order, though he be not bound to this,
or that viand? (1:681–2)

The fact that we consume three meals a day does not compel us always to eat the same food. Milton offers this "Kitchin physick" as part of his argument against set forms of prayer, which is in turn a protest against ritual and custom in every sphere of life. Precedent and established practice are no arguments for continuing to do things as they have been done in the past. In fact, Milton suggests, all traditional mores must be swept aside in the continual, incessant motion of reformation. Custom is a "tyrant" in need of overthrowing. Milton has arrived at the belief that human practices and institutions, especially religious ones, should ceaselessly change and adapt to historical circumstances. To those who argue that episcopacy is a venerable institution and its challengers upstart newcomers he responds, "This was the plea of Judaisme, and Idolatry against Christ and his Apostles, of Papacie against Reformation . . ." All arguments from "Succession, Custome and Visibility" (1:703) are inherently invalid. The logical, though not yet explicit, conclusion of Milton's argument is the complete abolition of organized religion. By early 1642, he was already convinced that "the functions of church-government ought to be free and open to any Christian man, though never so laic, if his capacity, his faith, and prudent demeanour, commend him" (1:844).

Events were compelling Milton's mind toward these increasingly radical positions. In January 1642, King Charles determined on a decisive display of his personal authority. With 500 armed men he rode down Whitehall to the House of Commons to arrest the five most prominent leaders of the rebellious faction. But they had disappeared into the city of London, whose inhabitants were delighted to shelter them. The King asked the Speaker of the House where they were, and was told: "I have neither eyes to see nor tongue to speak in this place, but as the House is pleased to direct me, whose servant I am here."[17] This was undisguised defiance of the Royal will and could mean only one thing. Charles abandoned his hostile capital and moved his court to Windsor, then to far-away York. Both sides spent the winter in fruitless negotiation and the spring in preparation for battle, as Milton sweated over his raging denunciations of the prelacy. Finally, on the twenty-second of August 1642, Charles unfurled the Royal standard at Nottingham. The English civil war had entered its military phase.

4

REVOLUTION AND ROMANCE

I

MILTON WAS THIRTY-THREE when hostilities commenced, healthy in body and, by his own account, a skilled swordsman. He believed passionately in the causes for which the revolutionaries were fighting. He was certainly no pacifist, and he later even expressed relish at the thought that his rhetoric might have killed his polemical adversaries. Why did he not join the Parliamentary army? The notion was apparently contemplated in 1645; his nephew recalled, "I am much mistaken if there were not about this time a design in agitation of making him Adjutant-General in Sir William Waller's army" (1,032). This largely administrative role would not have involved much fighting, and the "design" was in any case never realized. But Milton did not remain above the physical fray because of any scruples about wreaking havoc and destruction among his enemies. On the contrary, he concentrated on waging a war of words because he believed that he could do more damage with the pen than with the sword.

As was usual with Milton, this biographical dilemma became deeply integrated into his work. One of the themes to which he ceaselessly returns is the nature of heroism. His thought shows a constant but developing effort to redefine the traditional, Homeric conception of the hero as a man of physical strength and martial valor. His notes on possible subjects for the great epic poem he was planning to write show that he considered treating the military exploits of British monarchs like Arthur and Alfred, and his skill in depicting such subjects is evident in *Paradise Lost*'s gripping account of warfare in heaven. As Milton takes care to remind the reader, however, the military conflict in *Paradise Lost* is futile to the point of absurdity, because its outcome is predetermined by Providence. The heroic exploits of the protagonists are ironized; their true significance is concealed from them. Although Michael, Gabriel, and the other warrior angels experience themselves as behaving heroically, the reader is aware that they are merely going through the motions, acting out a drama whose script is already finished. The poem's battle can be won only by the intervention of the Son of God, whose merit lies not in traditional heroic prowess but in his capacity for self-sacrifice.

Milton assumed that the English civil war was being guided by Providence in the same manner. No matter how brave their battlefield conduct might be, the soldiers were merely tools in the hands of the Almighty, and true heroism began with acknowledging that fact.[1] Milton frequently recalled how primitive Christianity shocked the uncomprehending pagan world by making heroic virtues of worldly weakness, humility, and the willing acceptance of defeat. In early works like the *Elegies* and *Comus*, he explores the possibility of a negative heroism that consists in resistance to temptation: the cultivation of inner virtue through exposure to, followed by renunciation of, the concupiscent pleasures of the flesh. In the polemical career on which he was now embarking, Milton would apply his idiosyncratic understanding of heroism to the task of selecting the most appropriate political leaders for the nation. He insisted, for example, that Oliver Cromwell had earned the right to rule England, not because of his military victories but because of his personal virtue. Handy with a sword as he might be, Milton knew that his own special gift lay in verbal rather than physical skirmishing. His literary talent was the investment on which God had trusted him to recoup the interest. But he was resolved that his work in the service of the revolution would manifest on paper a virtue at least as heroic as the bravery his revolutionary colleagues were displaying on the battlefield. He often uses martial metaphors to describe his literary conflicts, describing his rhetorical strategy against Bishop Hall as using "some kinde of military advantages to await him at his forragings, at his watrings . . ." (1:872) Milton saw his pamphleteering as war conducted by other means. While Fairfax, Cromwell, and the other generals won the military war for Parliament, Milton would be winning the war of ideas.

The prophetic temper of the age, and the startlingly novel nature of its events, encouraged seventeenth-century English people to scrutinize their individual lives for signs of the divine Providence that was revealing itself so unmistakably on the wider political stage. It seemed that God was rejuvenating the English nation, even re-creating it, and many people felt themselves personally reborn as well, their souls swept along on the tide of history. They did not imagine, as we tend to, that their minds were hermetically sealed off and impervious to political events; they were fully conscious that the sphere of personal experience is inseparable from the political realm. But even more than most of his contemporaries, Milton could not help but acknowledge the peculiar parallels between his biography and wider historical developments. Even had he not been accustomed by habit and inclination to draw such connections, the striking convergence of crises in his emotional life and the political life of the nation would have forcibly concentrated his attention upon them.

There was little money to be made by ecclesiastical polemic, and Milton's tracts were in any case too convoluted and abstruse to rank among the best-sellers. Fortunately for the history of English literature, he continued to reap the benefit of his father's ingenious exploitation of the new, capitalist route to financial independence. In the early 1640s Milton was still supporting himself as he always had: by small-scale usury. This was not the kind of moneylending that financed corporate enterprises or global trading projects; rather, Milton or his father would typically lend small sums at high interest for personal use by individuals who were already in financial difficulties. This meant that much of their time was necessarily devoted to the arduous and unpleasant business of debt collection. The breakdown of the English state in 1641–2 pushed many improvident debtors over the edge of bankruptcy, and petty usurers like Milton had to move quickly to protect their investments.

The Milton family's roots lay in Oxfordshire, where the poet's father had been born and raised and where there are still several villages bearing the family name. John Milton senior appears to have retained strong business ties in the region, many of whose inhabitants owed him money. In February and May 1642 the Cope family of Hanwell, Oxfordshire, defaulted on their quarterly interest payments, and the Powells of nearby Forest Hill were also having trouble making the eight percent rate of payment on their large debt. Fifteen years earlier Milton's father had loaned Richard Powell £300 and had received as security a "statute staple," or bond, for £500. The senior Milton bestowed this debt and its revenue on his son, so that it became the younger Milton's responsibility to collect it. Richard Powell's finances were in a terrible condition; he spent the first part of 1642 desperately casting about for credit among his neighbors, and it became obvious that he would have difficulty making June's payment on the loan from Milton.

Clearly a business trip to Oxfordshire was called for, and Milton set off in early June. He seems to have kept the reasons for his journey secret from his closest family. Edward Phillips remembers "nobody about him certainly knowing the reason, or that it was any more than a journey of recreation."[2] This secrecy is perhaps the strangest element of this strange story. Why would Milton neglect to tell anyone that he was traveling to Oxfordshire in order to collect an overdue debt? It is true that the age held usurers in small esteem, but Milton's family was well aware of his profession and happy to live off its proceeds. Milton's peculiar reticence about the reasons for his journey suggests that it had an ulterior motive. It suggests that his marriage, which biographers have sometimes portrayed as a sudden, unexpected blossoming of love between two young innocents, was in some sense, and to some degree, a prearranged business transaction.

Whatever may have been the details of the arrangement, the fact is that Milton returned from Forest Hill married to Richard Powell's eldest daughter, seventeen-year-old Mary. The marriage took place less than a month after the couple's first meeting. Perhaps our postmodern attitude to such matters is more cynical than the post-Romantic ideas of Victorian and Edwardian biographers, but it is surely difficult to believe that this was a spontaneous match. It is easy to believe that it was primarily a business arrangement, and although the precise nature of its benefits are difficult to discern, we can assume that Milton would have been more inclined to show financial mercy to relations than to strangers. We should recall in this context that creditors had the power to imprison defaulting debtors, which would doubtless have been a powerful inducement for Richard Powell's daughter to forgo any objections she may have had to marrying a stranger almost twice her age.

Mary Powell was one of eleven children. Her family was Cavalier in both the political and the social sense; they were monarchists, and they seem to have been a jolly, raucous crew. If the patriarch's attitude to money is any guide, the Powells' approach to life was happy-go-lucky, even devil-may-care, and thus in diametrical opposition to the austere, disciplined rationalism that guided Milton's daily routine. There must have been a jarring clash of cultures when several of the Powells accompanied Mary back to her new husband's house in London, where the celebrations continued for many days after the wedding. When the festive crew departed, leaving the naïve teenager trapped with the greatest mind in England, she must have felt lonely for the first time in her life. John Aubrey recounts that, having been "brought up and lived where there was a great deal of company and merriment," Mary now "found it very solitary, no company came to her; oftentimes heard his nephews beaten and cry."[3] We should not make too much of Milton's violent pedagogy, which was the age's universal practice, but according to Aubrey she found the studious, intellectual ambience of her new home "irksome." After she had "led a philosophical life," as Edward Phillips euphemistically put it, for around a month, Mary and her family combined to entreat Milton that she should be allowed to return to Forest Hill until the end of September.

That was two months away, and the newlyweds had been together less than half that long. Such an unusual request must have been preceded, and may have been precipitated, by a considerable number of strained conversations between husband and wife. On the evidence of Milton's ferociously argumentative style in his published work, it is difficult to avoid concluding that between the departure of her relatives and Mary Milton's own decamping, the Miltons' married life must have been a perpetual torment of frustrated recrimination. It is not even wholly clear that the separation took place at Mary's request; in 1651 her mother referred to Milton's "having turned away his wife heretofore for a long space upon some other occasion."[4] On the other hand, it appears from the fact that Milton never pursued an annulment that the marriage was successfully consummated. We know nothing of either party's previous sexual experience. Although there are good grounds for believing that Milton had enjoyed some sort of adolescent romance with Charles Diodati, it is impossible to say whether this ever took a physical form. Keenly aware of posterity's likely interest in his proclivities, however, Milton appears to have left us some hints. For example, we know how important he considered the second-century BC Book of Tobit, which is apocryphal in Protestantism and canonical in Catholicism. Milton alludes to it throughout his life, most extensively in *Paradise Lost,* large portions of which are narrated by the angel Raphael, who also features in Tobit as the teacher and guide of Tobit's son, Tobias. In *Paradise Lost* Milton introduces him as "the sociable spirit that deign'd / To travel with Tobias, and secured / His marriage with the sev'n times wedded maid" (5:221–3).

One does not need a prophetic gift to find Tobit's prefiguration of Milton's biography uncanny, even today. In an age trained in the techniques of biblical typology, whereby the events described in scripture were scrutinized for the minutest resemblances to contemporary history, they must have seemed revelatory. Like John Milton senior, Tobit is the faithful son of an idolatrous father. Exiled in Nineveh, he continues to serve Jehovah while his family worships Baal. He displays his piety by arranging for the burial of Jewish dead left to rot in the open by Persian law. In old age he has two problems: he is blind, and he is owed money. He sends his son Tobias to collect the money, and God sends Raphael, disguised as a human being, to accompany him. The angel leads Tobias to Sarah, a beautiful young woman who has been married seven times. On each occasion her husband was murdered on their wedding night, before the marriage could be consummated, by Ashmodai, a demon associated with sexual concupiscence in general and with homosexual lust in particular. The verse explaining that "Ashmodai loved Sarah" implies that the demon's desire for a female was anomalous: he loved Sarah in particular, rather than women in general. Raphael helps Tobias drive the demon away, and he successfully consummates his marriage to Sarah. Raphael collects the money for him, and the party returns to Tobit's house, where the angel helps Tobias heal his father's blindness. Raphael then reveals his true identity before departing, having instructed Tobias to "write all things which are done in a book."[5]

Parallel myths occur in many ancient Middle Eastern and European cultures, and they are known as "grateful dead" legends. They generally involve a youth who generously pays the debts of a dead man and receives an unexpected reward, often in the form of a wife. They frequently intersect with "poison maiden" stories, in which sexual contact with a wife is fatal to the husband.[6] This folktale seems to express, and attempt to resolve, anxieties about the connections between usury and sexuality. Paul Haupt reports a typical version:

In an Armenian legend, a well-to-do man, riding through a forest, finds some men treating a dead body rather unceremoniously. They tell him that the dead man owed them money. He pays the debts and buries the body. In his native town there is a rich man with an only daughter. She had been married five times, but her husbands had always died the first night after the marriage. An unknown servant advises him to marry the widow. In the wedding night a snake comes out of the mouth of the bride and threatens to kill him. The unknown servant, who has been on guard, kills the snake and saves the groom. The unknown servant turns out to be the dead man whom he had buried in the forest.[7]

The vindictive usurers and the dangerous, phallic snake are twin obstacles, and disarming the former proves to be the means by which the youth escapes the latter. This story thus connects usury with homosexuality and presents both of them as stumbling blocks to a fertile marital union. The parallels between the Book of Tobit and Milton's life are not quite exact. Sarah was his mother's name rather than his wife's, it was he rather than his father who went blind, and we know of no previous lovers enjoyed by Mary Powell. But the similarities are nevertheless striking and must have seemed even more so to a mind accustomed to scan scripture for personal relevance on a daily basis. The Book of Tobit implies the need to purge the demon of homosexuality as a prelude to successful marriage. We cannot say whether Milton perceived in this detail the close reference to his own life that is so obvious elsewhere in the story. But he undoubtedly felt the force of Tobit's warning to his son: "[T]ake a wife of the seed of thy fathers, and take not a strange woman to wife, which is not of thy father's tribe" (Tobit 4:12). Milton returns to the difficulties caused by taking an alien bride on many occasions, notably in *Samson Agonistes,* where the hero is betrayed by his Philistine spouse, Delilah. The Puritan revolutionaries conceived of themselves as the new Israel, the modern embodiment of God's chosen people. Within that typological context, to marry the daughter of Royalists was to take a bride from among the heathen. The analogy must have weighed heavily on Milton's mind as the peal of his wedding bells blended with the rapport of the civil war's opening barrages.

It is surely obvious that Milton acquired his bride through usury. We can presume that Milton and Mary Powell would never have married had not Richard Powell owed Milton a lot of money. We can also assume that this fact exerted some influence on their intimate relations. The people of the seventeenth century did not separate economic matters from ethics, or from sexuality. Moreover, they conceived of usury as a specifically sexual sin: a "sodomy in nature," because it made money breed. If Mary Powell essentially *was* the interest on her father's loan, how would that have affected the couple's sex life? Usury certainly played on Milton's mind as he meditated on his marriage. Apart from his lengthy and unpublished Latin theological treatise, *De Doctrina Christiana,* every single mention of "usury" in Milton's prose is found in the divorce tracts. Referring to the Jews in *The Doctrine and Discipline of Divorce,* Milton remarks that "[t]heir hearts were set upon usury, and are to this day, no Nation more; yet that which was the endammaging only of their estates, was narrowly forbid" (2:289). He alludes here to the law whereby Hebrews were allowed to practice usury in their dealings with Gentiles but not with fellow Israelites, because usury was a hostile act calculated to "damage the estate" of the borrower. Milton's argument assumes that this is an accurate conception of usury, which makes one wonder how he regarded his relations with his wife's family. As Royalists, the Powells were aliens, Gentiles to the Puritan Israelites; did Milton apply the biblical distinction between strangers and brothers to his business dealings with his in-laws, or to his emotional interactions with his wife?

The law of Moses allowed divorce, but many argued that this was not an example for Christians to follow, but rather God's method of miring the Jews deeper in sin. Milton points out that this is to make the law a predatory usurer, exploiting the debtor's lack of discipline to entice him deeper into debt, and the technical language Milton uses in such passages may reveal some familiarity with the sharp practices he describes. He finds it blasphemous to imagine Moses conspiring "to let the dettor Israelite the seed of *Abraham* run on upon a banckrout score, flatter'd with insufficient and insnaring discharges, that so he might be halhal'd to a more cruel forfeit for all the indulgent arrears which those judicial acquitments had ingaged him in" (2:401). If Milton's wife was indeed a "forfeit" on her "banckrout" father's debt, such passages acquire a defensive tone, as Milton dismisses the idea that the law might act as such a "shamelesse broker of our impurities."[8] It was the law of England, not the law of Moses, that was in need of reform. England's government, as Milton notes, "permits usury" but bans the much less harmful practice of divorce. This strikes him as paradoxical:

> As for what they instance of Usury, let them first prove Usury to be wholly unlawful, as the Law allows it; which learned Men as numerous on the other side will deny them. Or if it be altogether unlawful, why is it tolerated more than Divorce? He who said, *Divorce not,* said also, *Lend, hoping for nothing again, Luk.* 6. 35. But then they put it, that Trade could not stand, and so to serve the commodity of insatiable trading, Usury shall be permitted; but Divorce, the only means oftimes to right the innocent and outragiously wrong'd, shall be utterly forbid. This is egregious doctrine, and for which one day Charity will much thank them. (2:425)

He asks "why wee should strain thus at the matter of divorce, which may stand so much with charity to permit, and make no scruple to allow usury esteem'd to be so much against charity." But this reveals a telling contradiction in Milton's argument. Elsewhere he deploys usury as an example of a practice that is *mistakenly* construed as uncharitable by overly scrupulous, moralistic literalists. He explicitly exonerates usury of uncharity: "[U]sury, so much as is permitted by the Magistrate and demanded with common equity, is neither against the word of God, nor the rule of charity." But since the popular estimation of usury as uncharitable is in Milton's view mistaken, usury's legality cannot logically be used to argue that divorce ought also to be permitted because it is more

charitable than usury. Milton's thinking on the subject of usury is unchar-
acteristically confused, and the reader gets the distinct impression that it
made him uncomfortable.

The same can be said of his musings on the subject of sexuality. Even
if John and Mary Milton were both virgins when they married, the fact
that their courtship presumably consisted of negotiations over usury, the
sodomy in nature, must have ensured that their union came fraught with
considerable sexual baggage. The complete lack of evidence describing
the couple's personal relations over these weeks means that gauging the
weight of that baggage is a task for the novelist rather than the biographer.[9] We do, however, know Milton's opinions on sex in general. These
are often rather surprising. Discussing divorce in the *Commonplace
Book,* he remarks that "[t]he reason why it ought to be permitted is that,
as physicians and almost all others acknowledge, [copulation] without
love is cold, unpleasant, unfruitful, harmful, bestial, abominable . . ."
(1:414). The idea that sex without love is disgusting was most certainly
not endorsed by "almost all" Milton's contemporaries; indeed it was
loudly and explicitly denied by the Cavaliers, who frequently made the
opposite argument, that sex is most enjoyable when anonymous and promiscuous. Cavalier poets like John Suckling and Richard Lovelace saw
their hedonistic lifestyle as the correlative to their Anglican religion and
Royalist politics. In "The Grasshopper," Lovelace offers "Greek" revelry
as a defiant response to the regicide:

> Dropping *December* shall come weeping in,
> Bewayle th' usurping of his Raigne;
> But when in show'rs of old Greeke we beginne
> Shall crie, he hath his Crowne againe![10]

Milton is making a political as well as an erotic point when he locates the source of sexual pleasure in the spirit rather than the flesh, for such asceticism was at odds with the Cavalier celebration of carnal delight. Even the anti-prelatical tracts often digress into discussions of sexuality, as Milton associates indulgence in carnal pleasure for its own sake with the relish for sensory beauty expressed in Anglican liturgy. He recalls how, in the course of his youthful reading:

> I learnt of chastity and love, I meane that which is truly so, whose charming cup is only vertue which she bears in her hand to those who are worthy. The rest are cheated with a thick intoxicating potion which a certaine Sorceresse the abuser of loves name carries about. (1:891)

Sexual lust, liturgical idolatry, and magic coalesce into the potion wielded by Circe, who embodies the temptations of the flesh in the *Odyssey* and later becomes the mother of Milton's Comus. Milton conceives of life as a continuous act of resistance to such temptation, out of which is manufactured the kind of virtue that can truly be called heroic. This battle is waged both internally and externally; the struggle against the bishops is another form of the spiritual warfare against Circe and Comus. The chastity that Milton felt indispensable to authentic heroism was manifested on the personal level by the subordination of the flesh to the spirit. At the political level it took the form of resistance to Anglican Church government and, later, monarchical government of the state. These were different fronts in the same war, and thus the painful crisis in Milton's romantic life propelled his economic, political, philosophical, and religious thought yet further ahead of his age.

II

IT SEEMS THAT Milton and his wife may have had different expectations as to how their separation would be resolved. The original arrangement had been that Mary would return to London at the end of September. When she failed to do so, Milton wrote her several letters, which went unanswered. He eventually dispatched a messenger who, as Edward Phillips recalls, was "dismissed with some sort of contempt."[11] This, in Phillips's recollection, left Milton "incensed" against his wife. The convergence between personal and political affairs now impressed itself yet more forcefully upon him. From November 1642, King Charles's court was resident at Oxford, and the Powells must have regretted marrying their daughter into what was now quite literally the enemy camp. Mary's brothers were working as actively for the King's cause as her husband was for Parliament's. If, as was widely expected, Charles should secure a quick and easy victory over his rebellious foes and exact due vengeance upon them, the name of Milton would not be a fortuitous addition to any family.

In any case, battle lines rapidly formed between London and Oxford. October 1642 saw the first major engagement of the civil war: the battle of Edgehill, which ended inconclusively but left five thousand dead. The King now marched on London, and an exhilarating panic gripped the city. Barricades were thrown up in the streets, the people took up arms, fanatics proclaimed the coming of the Apocalypse, and the sense of impending judgment suddenly transformed many respectable men and women into democrats, socialists, communists, anarchists, polygamists, and feminists. Scores of surviving radical tracts and pamphlets testify to the fact that every kind of social and political experimentation suddenly seemed possible. Such a hectic atmosphere is typical of beleagured, revolutionary cities, and being in London in 1642 must have been much like being in Munster in 1535, Paris in 1871, or Barcelona in 1938. Unlike those cities, however, revolutionary London was strong enough to survive the assault of reaction.

Like everyone else, Milton braced himself for attack. He composed a sonnet for the occasion and, according to an anonymous note appended to the manuscript, posted it on his front door. The poem appeals to any "Captain, or Colonel or Knight at Arms" who discovers it to protect the house's inhabitant. Milton promises any such merciful soldier the same reward he had promised to his father and the Marquis of Manso. He will make them immortal by his verse: "He can requite thee, for he knows the charms / That call Fame on such gentle acts as these, / And he can spread thy Name o're Lands and Seas" (5–7). This serene assurance of posthumous fame must have been a source of immense resilience in these dangerous days. On November 13 Charles's army reached Turnham Green, on the western outskirts of the city. There they were confronted by twenty-four thousand armed civilians of the "trained bands," a people's militia that had existed before the war but whose ranks had grown exponentially since its outbreak. The decision of the trained bands to support Parliament reveals where the sympathies of most ordinary Londoners lay. Although much better armed and organized, the King's army was less than half the size of the citizens' forces, and after a lengthy standoff, Charles retreated. The Londoners celebrated their momentous victory with a mass picnic.

When the winter of 1642 descended with both armies still in the field, it became clear that the conflict was to be lengthy. From January 1643 all traffic between Oxford and London was forbidden. Milton must have concluded that he and his wife were now permanently estranged. It is unclear whether John Aubrey had any first-hand knowledge of Milton's feelings when he reflected: "[W]hat man (especially contemplative) would like to have a young wife environed [and stormed] by the sons of Mars, and those of the enemy party."[12] But we can certainly assume that, whether or not they involved sexual jealousy, Milton's contemplations were far from happy. He was in a highly delicate predicament. Marriages could be annulled on grounds of impotence or frigidity, and divorces might be granted in cases of adultery. But these were not the problems with the Miltons' marriage. Mary had not run away from John because of any sexual incapacity but because their characters were irreconcilably divergent, and neither civil nor canon law accepted psychological incompatibility as grounds for divorce. Unless he was prepared to live in adultery (and also to find a woman similarly prepared), the laws of England condemned Milton to perpetual solitude.

Fortuitously, or as Milton saw it providentially, the laws of England were in the process of being rewritten. Parliament was rapidly dismantling the institutional mechanism of Charles's personal rule and disposing of the personnel who had manned it. From the summer of 1643 the Westminster Assembly of Divines was in session, hammering out a church settlement that deposed episcopacy and seemed likely to institute Presbyterianism as the state religion. Milton immediately saw the possibilities these developments held for his personal situation. If the tyrannical English church and state were to be reformed, the oppressive legal restrictions on divorce might also be struck down. The synchronies between his own desire for divorce and the English people's reformation of their public sphere struck Milton as a revelation, and he felt compelled to spread his newly acquired insight as widely as possible throughout the land. He interpreted the pain of his personal situation as God's goad, driving him to reveal new truths to a nation that, initially at least, he seems to have hoped might provide a receptive audience. In that hope he was to prove very sorely mistaken.

Milton spent the year following his wife's desertion immersed in a prolonged study of divorce, both in theory and in historical practice. Just as *Of Reformation* subjected the concept of "reformation" to such minute scrutiny as to reveal its implications for every sphere of life, so Milton's divorce tracts make the matter of divorce into a fundamental political and religious principle. And divorce was in the air: the English people were separating from their church and their state. Milton had described events in these terms as early as *The Reason of Church Government*:

> If we have indeed given a bill of divorce to Popery and superstition, why do we not say as to a divors't wife; those things which are yours take them all with you, and they shall seepe after you? Why were not we thus wise at our parting from Rome? Ah like a crafty adultresse she forgot not all her smooth looks and inticing words at her parting; yet keep these letters, these tokens, and these few ornaments; I am not all so greedy of what is mine, let them preserve with you the memory of what I am? No, but of what I was, once faire and lovely in your eyes. Thus did those tender hearted reformers dotingly suffer themselves to be overcome with harlots language. And she like a witch, but with a contrary policy did not take something of theirs that she might still have power to bewitch them, but for the same intent left something of her own behind her. (1:942)

Witches typically needed to steal from their victim a lock of hair, a fingernail clipping, or some other small body part in order to cast effective spells over them. Milton describes the witchcraft of Catholicism as operating in similar fashion, except that Rome has left physical parts of herself—her ornaments, icons, and vestments—within the Anglican liturgy, to enable her to retain control over the minds of the congregation. Even before his own marriage, Milton is meditating on the benefits of divorce. He considers the purification of the English church as finalizing its divorce from Rome, and he would soon be describing the revolution as an act of divorce presented by the people to the King.

Despite the personal pain it brought him, Milton's fervent desire to divorce Mary drove him into a perspective on reformation and revolution that was far in advance of his compatriots. But approaching the issue from a personal angle also brought his motives into question and laid him open to all kinds of damaging accusations. Divorce at will was a sufficiently novel and shocking subject to be saleable; the first edition of Milton's *Doctrine and Discipline of Divorce* was published in the summer of 1643, sold out its 1,200 copies within six months, and was reissued in a much-expanded second edition in January 1644. For the first time in his life, Milton had the public's ear. He appended a direct address to Parliament, acknowledging the Houses as the sovereign power in the realm and urging them to seize the opportunity to effect permanent social change: "[Y]e have now in your hands a great and populous Nation to Reform" (2:226). He endeavored to forge a connection between his case for divorce and reformation in general. He knew that his proposals would seem outrageous to many, so he began by attributing this response to the power of habit and superstition to foster systematic illusion:

> If it were seriously askt, and it would be no untimely question, Renowned Parlament, select Assembly, who of all Teachers and Maisters that have ever taught, hath drawn the most Disciples after him, both in Religion, and in manners, it might bee not untruly answer'd, Custome. . . . Custome being but a meer face, as Eccho is a meere voice, rests not in her unaccomplishment, untill by secret inclination, she accorporat her selfe with error, who being a blind and Serpentine body without a head, willingly accepts what she wants, and supplies what her incompleatnesse went seeking. Hence

it is, that Error supports Custome, Custome count'nances Error. And these two betweene them would persecute and chase away all truth and solid wisdome out of humane life, were it not that God, rather than man, once in many ages, calls together the prudent and Religious counsels of Men, deputed to repress the encroachments, and to work off the inveterate blots and obscurities wrought upon our minds by the subtle insinuating of Error and Custom. (2:223–4)

Milton is offering what in modern terminology we might call a theory of false consciousness. He is trying to explain how people can come to believe what is not only untrue but also in manifest contradiction to their own interests. His answer is that "custom," which was often referred to as a "second nature," has the power to turn evident falsehood into apparent truth. Custom could easily become an idol, and the people whom Milton elsewhere calls "the prostrate worshippers of custom" (2:439) would grow as impervious to reason as the acolytes of Moloch or Baal. This was potentially an extremely radical position. It could quickly expand into an assumption that customary practice was *always* bad, that all habitual, socially sanctioned institutions and values ought to be abandoned, or at least reassessed. In the heady days of the 1640s, many people did in fact arrive at just that position. The idea that it was the right, even the duty, of elect Christians systematically to violate every kind of custom spread widely, particularly among the lower classes. Strange "antinomian" sects like the Ranters and the Quakers emerged suddenly, as if from nowhere, though it is probable that their ideas had been current in subterranean form for generations. The revolution allowed them to reveal themselves.

The antinomians believed that, because Christ died to forgive our sins, it was now impossible for the saved to commit sin, no matter what they did: "to the pure all things are pure." The whole moral law, and all conventional morality, was thus undermined. The Ranters in particular made ostentatious displays of their freedom from the law with public drunkenness, swearing, and sexual promiscuity. Some Quakers interrupted church services with bizarre speeches and walked the streets naked. Milton never countenanced such behavior, but he was often accused of doing so, and it is not hard to see why. His divorce tracts argue that sexuality should be regulated by the conscience, not by the law. In his opinion, the kind of unbridled lust exhibited by the extremist sects was produced, rather than restrained, by legal prohibitions:

> [S]eeing that sort of men who follow *Anabaptism, Familism, Antinomianism,* and other fanatic dreams (if we understand them not amisse) be such most commonly as are by nature addicted to Religion; of life also not debausht, and that their opinions having full swinge, do end in satisfaction of the flesh, it may be come with reason into the thoughts of a wise man, whether all this proceed not partly, if not chiefly, from the restraint of some lawfull liberty, which ought to be giv'n men, and is deny'd them. (2:437)

This is a momentous psychological insight. Milton understands that the law is a form of temptation. Forbidding sin is the surest way to encourage it. If Parliament liberalizes the divorce laws, Milton claims, "they shall reclaime from obscure and giddy sects, many regain from dissolute and brutish licence."[13] The idea that the law creates sin informs Paul's epistles and is strongly stressed in the seminal texts of Protestantism, especially Martin Luther's biblical commentaries. Milton was among the first Englishmen to advocate its practical application in reforming the laws of the land.

The time was right for such innovation. The rapid changes that the revolution was bringing about had convinced Milton that truth was by nature historical. God's revelation was not finished or static; it continued in and through the movement of history. *The Doctrine and Discipline* attacks conservatives who behave "as if the womb of teeming Truth were to be clos'd up" (2:224). The announcement of new truths was the work of prophecy, and Milton now publicly claims the prophet's mantle that he had always privately regarded as his birthright. He declares himself called "to be the sole advocate of a discount'nanct truth: a high enterprise Lords and Commons; a high enterprise and a hard, and such as every seventh Son of a seventh Son does not venture on. . . ." The following year, addressing Parliament in another pamphlet, he bluntly claims that "I could allege many instances, wherein there would appear cause to esteem of me no other than a passive instrument under some power and counsel higher and better than can be human" (2:433). Throughout *The Doctrine and Discipline* he tries to persuade Parliament that his fight is also theirs, claiming that a man's right to divorce rests on the same principle as a people's right to change their government:

> He who marries intends as little to conspire his own ruine, as he
> that swears Allegiance: and as a whole people is in proportion to
> an ill Government, so is one man to an ill mariage. If they against
> any authority, Covnant, or Statute, may by the sovereign edict of
> charity, save not only their lives but honest liberties from unworthy
> bondage, as well may he against any private Covnant, which hee
> never enter'd to his mischief, redeem himself from unsupportable
> disturbances to honest peace, and just contentment. (2:229)

The health of the state is dependent on the happiness of the household: "no effect of tyranny can sit more heavy on the Common-wealth, then this houshold unhappines on the family. And farewell all hope of true Reformation in the state, while such an evil as this lies undiscern'd or unregarded in the house" (ibid.). The outcome of "our Christian warfare" will be determined by Parliament's ability to abolish not only religious idolatry and political tyranny but also "imaginary and scarecrow sins at home." Milton was well aware that the case for divorce on the sole grounds of psychological incompatibility would sound to many like an argument for "divorce at pleasure," but that was due to a fault in the audience rather than in his argument:

> What though the brood of Belial, the draffe of men, to whom no liberty is pleasing, but unbridl'd and vagabond lust without pale or partition, will laugh broad perhaps, to see so great a strength of Scripture mustering up in favour, as they suppose, of their debaucheries; they will know better, when they shall hence learne, that honest liberty is the greatest foe to dishonest licence. (2:225)

The kind of licentious behavior practiced by "the brood of Belial" was not the opposite of the law but its accomplice. The hypocrite who imposes legalistic restrictions on sexual freedom does not eliminate but encourages promiscuity: "'tis he that commits all the whordom and adultery, which himselfe adjudges." The very concept of license presupposes the existence of law, from which temporary exemption is granted to the licensee. But true liberty, like true libertines, acknowledges no law but conscience. Milton believed that the revolutionary changes England was undergoing would implement true liberty by freeing people to follow their conscience in matters of religion and morality. The abolition of laws regulating sexuality would not bring about an explosion of licentious behavior. To the contrary, Milton predicted that "places of prostitution wil be lesse haunted, the neighbours bed less attempted, the yoke of prudent and manly discipline will be generally submitted to, sober and well order'd living will soon spring up in the Common-wealth" (2:230). He assumed that once freed from the oppressive injunctions of the law, people would no longer lust after what the law forbade but would voluntarily renounce sin. It is the prohibition of sin that makes it tempting. Milton would later make this idea the central element of his greatest epic poem.

There are no explicitly autobiographical references in Milton's divorce tracts; presumably he did not wish to give his opponents the ammunition to dismiss his argument as self-interested. But we can at least guess at the nature of Milton's own experience of marriage by the inventively virulent phrases he uses to describe unhappy unions: "a familiar and co-inhabiting mischiefe," "a remediless thraldom," "a drooping and disconsolate houshold captivity" "a living soule bound to a dead corps," "deadly enemies in a cage together." Yet more disturbing are the epithets he applies to the unfit spouse: "an image of earth and fleam," "one that must be hated with a most operative hatred," "a helpless, unaffectionate and sullen mass," a "causeless tormenter and executioner." Generations of critics have detected misogyny here, as well as in Milton's dismissal of the "[p]alpably uxorious" argument that divorce was instituted for the protection of women against tyrannical husbands. Milton angrily claims that this ignores the harm suffered by men trapped in unhappy marriages: "What an injury is it after wedlock not to be belov'd, what to be slighted, what to be contended with in point of house-rule who shall be the head, not for any parity of wisdom, for that were something reasonable, but out of a female pride" (2:324). Amid the bluster, however, Milton is making a remarkably progressive point. He does not say, in fact he explicitly denies, that the husband must always rule over the wife. Where there is "parity of wisdom" it is "reasonable" that authority should be shared.

Milton's position is that the most rational partner in the marriage should be dominant. Empirically that partner would usually be the man, but this could be attributed to the lack of educational and professional

opportunities available to women. Milton differs from the vast majority of his male contemporaries in allowing the possibility that it might,
in theory, be "reasonable" for a woman to rule over a man. In another
of his divorce tracts, *Tetrachordon*, he repeats the conventional formula
subjecting women to men, before making a surprising qualification:

> Not but that particular exceptions may have place, if she exceed
> her husband in prudence and dexterity, and he contentedly yeeld;
> for then a superior and more naturall law comes in, that the wiser
> should govern the lesse wise, whether male or female. (2:589)

Reason, not gender, ought to determine where marital authority lies.
By the same logic, rationality rather than birthright should dictate the
distribution of political power, and reason rather than passion or appetite
ought to motivate the actions of a human being. The reversal of these natural relations of authority results in what Milton calls "slavery." We must
assume that this was the logic he applied to his relations with his wife. It
is doubtful whether he managed to give much serious consideration to the
emotional fears and anxieties of his teenage bride, but this is no indication of what we call "sexism," and certainly not of misogyny. Although
the divorce tracts avoid overtly autobiographical arguments, they contain
several passages that would be recognized as self-referential by readers
who are already aware of Milton's life story. Large parts of *The Doctrine
and Discipline* are addressed to the "fit audience" that Milton anticipated
in posterity. A year later, in the preface to *The Judgment of Martin Bucer*,
Milton repeats his determination to record "those thoughts, which may
render me best serviceable, either to this age, or, if it so happen, to posterity" (2:440). In *The Doctrine and Discipline* he envisions his posthumous
readership as cognizant of his personal history and so able to recognize
the autobiographical tenor of his examples:

The soberest and best govern'd men are least practiz'd in these affairs; and who knows not that the bashful muteness of a virgin may oft-times hide all the unliveliness and natural sloth which is really unfit for conversation; nor is there that freedom of access granted or presum'd, as may suffice to a perfect discerning till too late: and where any indisposition is suspected, what more usual than the persuasion of friends, that acquaintance, as it increases, will amend all. And lastly, it is not strange though many who have spent their youth chastely, are in some things not so quick-sighted, while they haste too eagerly to light the nuptial torch; nor is it therefore that for a modest error a man should forfeit so great a happines, and no charitable means to release him. . . . the sober man honouring the appearance of modesty, and hoping well of every sociall vertue under that veile, may easily chance to meet, if not with a body impenetrable, yet often with a mind to all other due conversation inaccessible, and to all the more estimable and superior purposes of matrimony uselesse and almost liveles: and what a solace, what a fit help such a consort would be through the whole life of a man, is lesse pain to conjecture then to have experience. (2:249–50)

If we are justified in discerning a commentary on Milton's own marriage here, we can distill from this passage the following scenario: Richard Powell's debts have mounted to the point where drastic action is required. He has no collateral, but he has a lot of daughters. He offers his eldest as a bride to his main creditor, in the hope that such a family connection will dispose him to financial mercy. Inexperienced with women but eager to marry, and in no pressing need of Powell's money, Milton is interested. On being introduced to Mary, however, he finds her dull and uncommunicative. The seventeen-year-old country girl does

not provide conversation acceptable to one of the most learned men
in Europe. Perceiving the usurer's displeasure, Powell assures him that
although Mary is quiet and shy with strangers, her bashful modesty con-
ceals hidden depths. Milton's ignorance of women allows this strategy
to prevail, the marriage takes place, and the deceit is revealed. Mary's
dull exterior concealed a yet duller interior. Sexual intercourse of some
kind occurs, and her body is penetrated, but this fails to induce spiritual harmony between the couple. They quarrel and separate. And there,
according to the extant law of the land, the matter must rest until death
legally parts them.

These circumstances brought Milton's private life under the direct
influence of the debates regarding the roles of church and state that were
raging in revolutionary London. The divorce tracts brilliantly demonstrate the logical connection between the Anglicans' approach to liturgy
and their view of marriage. Their attitude to these, as to every other issue,
is tainted by idolatry: "[T]o enjoyn the indissoluble keeping of a mariage
found unfit against the good of man both soul and body . . . is to make
an Idol of marriage . . . as if it were to be worshipt like some *Indian*
deity" (2:276). Since idols exist only in the mind of the idolater, this line
of reasoning allows Milton to claim that a marriage that fails to fulfill its
primary purpose of affectionate companionship does not even exist. As
he puts it in *Tetrachordon*: "[T]he prime ends of Marriage, are the whole
strength and validity therof, without which Matrimony is like an Idol,
nothing in the world" (2:629).

Just as their addiction to beautiful ornamentation and their preference for set forms of prayer reveal the carnal orientation of their souls, so
the Anglicans are incapable of conceiving any other purpose to marriage
than physical reproduction. They ignore the central importance of spiritual intercourse. Because they conceive reproduction as marriage's main

purpose, they are quite happy to permit divorce on grounds of sexual inadequacy. But because they do not recognize psychological companionship as the highest end of marriage, the Anglicans cannot understand that its absence also justifies divorce. If a couple "have tasted in any sort the nuptiall bed," and have been "found suitably weapon'd to the least possibility of sensuall enjoyment," they will "be made, spight of antipathy to fadge together" (2:244) without any possibility of relief, no matter how miserable their emotional relations may become.

In short, the existing law fetishizes sex. It assumes sex to be the main purpose of marriage. As Milton puts it: "[H]e who affirms adultery to be the highest breach, affirms the bed to be the highest end of marriage, which is in truth a gross and borish opinion" (2:269). This reverses the natural ethical hierarchy within the human soul, by subordinating the mind to the body, thus instituting an interior, psychological slavery and making the mind "a servant of its own vassal." As ever, Milton is concerned with communicating the political implications of this mistake. As he puts it in *Tetrachordon*: "What is this, besides tyranny, but to turn nature upside down, to make both religion, and the mind of man wait upon the slavish errands of the body" (2:598). Milton is determined to liberate himself from all forms of slavery, and he regards the bondage of an unhappy marriage as "the ignoblest, and the lowest slavery that a human shape can be put to" (2:626). He politicizes his theory of sexuality, describing loveless sex as "an unmanly task of bondage." To have sex with an unfit partner is "to grind in the mill of an undelighted and servile copulation" (2:258). What is servile is also bestial, and Milton describes sexual intercourse in the absence of spiritual union as "a sublunary and bestial burning," "the sting of a brute desire," an "animal and beastish meeting," "a brutish congresse," "the prescrib'd satisfaction of an irrational heat," "the promiscuous draining of a carnal rage," "a prone and savage necessity," and "the quintessence of an excrement." Sex without love is emotional slavery, which Parliament ought to abolish along with political and religious slavery.

It is perhaps a novel idea to us, or at any rate one that we choose not to express much, but Milton is convinced that loveless sex is a hostile, aggressive act, "a benevolence that hates" and that transforms the marriage bed into "the compulsive stie of an ingratefull and malignant lust, stirr'd up only from a carnall acrimony . . . an old haunt of lust and malice mixt together." He candidly explores the paradox whereby sexual attraction can coexist with, or even exacerbate, spiritual antipathy:

> When love finds it self utterly unmatcht, and justly vanishes, nay rather cannot but vanish, the fleshly act indeed may continue, but not holy, not pure, not beseeming the sacred bond of Marriage; being at best but an animal excretion, but more truly worse and more ignoble than that mute kindliness among the herds and flocks: in that proceeding as it ought from intellective principles, it participates of nothing rational, but that which the field and the fold equals. For in human actions the soul is the agent, the body in a manner passive. If then the body do out of sensitive force, what the soul complies not with, how can Man, and not rather something beneath Man, be thought the doer? (2:609)

Sex without spiritual love is beneath the dignity of a human being. It is true, Milton admits, that St. Paul prescribes marriage as a remedy for "burning . . . but what might this burning mean? Certainly not the mere motion of carnal lust, not the mere goad of a sensitive desire; God does not principally take care for such cattle."[14] Properly understood, claims Milton, the "rational burning that marriage is to remedy" is the need for "a fit soul" with whom to engage in "meet and happy conversation."

How then have the Anglicans grown so deluded as to encourage, even to compel, their salacious view of marriage as sanctified whoredom?

The answer lies in their literalistic method of biblical interpretation, which Milton, following Paul, describes as another form of carnality. Milton anticipates that his argument in *The Doctrine and Discipline* will meet with "two severall oppositions: the one from those who having sworn themselves to long custom and the letter of the Text, will not out of the road: the other from those whose grosse and vulgar apprehensions conceit but low of matrimoniall purposes, and in the work of male and female think they have all" (2:240). But as the tract progresses it becomes clear that these oppositions are not "severall," or distinct, but actually identical. Literalism and carnality are errors of the same kind—they are both manifestations of a slavish mentality: "obstinate literality" constitutes "alphabetical servility" and reflects the "letter-bound servility of the Canon Doctors" (2:338).

This allows Milton to circumvent the rather formidable objection to his argument that Christ explicitly forbids divorce, by denying that his words were to be taken literally. Jesus allowed divorce only in cases of "fornication," which the Anglicans understand to mean sexual adultery. But Milton deploys his linguistic skills to argue that the Hebrew and Greek words for "fornication" primarily imply spiritual infidelity. When Jesus said "Whosoever shall put away his wife, except it be for fornication, and shall marry another, committeth adultery,"[15] he was addressing the Pharisees and consciously working to confuse them, in order to tie them up in the knots of their own literalism: "[T]heir Answer will be such as is fittest for them; not so much a teaching, as an intangling" (2:642). In order to comprehend Christ's teaching, we must be able to read metaphorically. The ability to look beneath the surface meanings of words, like the ability to look beneath the surface appearances of things, is a necessary component of religious faith. That is why Jesus addresses his followers through the medium of parables. Interpreted literally, parables are insignificant or absurd; their true meaning becomes apparent only when they are read figuratively.

As Milton notes, figural interpretation is fundamental to Protestant doctrine. Christ's words forbidding divorce "are as much against plain equity, and the mercy of religion, as those words of *Take, eat, this is my body*, elementally understood, are against nature and sense" (2:325). The Catholic doctrine of transubstantiation takes Jesus's words at the Last Supper literally, rather than metaphorically, and Protestants believe that this induces an idolatrous view of the sacrament. But now the Anglicans, who claim to be Protestants, are repeating the same error with regard to divorce, "persisting deafly in the abrupt and papistical way of a literal apprehension" (2:437). Milton reminds "the extreme literalist" of the painful folly of Origen who, taking a biblical verse in an insanely literalistic fashion, actually castrated himself:

> And if none of these considerations with all their wait and gravity, can avail to the dispossessing him of his pretious literalism, let some one or other entreat him but to read on in the same 19. of *Math.* till he come to that place that sayes, *Some make themselves Eunuchs for the kingdom of heaves sake.* And if then he please to make use of *Origens knife,* he may doe well to be his own carver. (2:334)

Having established the servile nature of literalism, Milton can easily dispose of Christ's prohibition of divorce "except it be for fornication." Only a carnal slave would take "fornication" literally, as referring to extramarital sexual intercourse. On the contrary, as Milton explains in *Tetrachordon,* "the word fornication in mariage hath a larger sense then that commonly suppos'd." It included sexual perversion: Milton cites Justin Martyr's story of a wife granted a divorce because her husband "against the law of nature and of right sought out voluptuous waies" and "endeavour'd som unnaturall abuse." But the term need not be sexual at all. According to Milton it "signifies also any notable disobedience, or intractable carriage of the Wife to the Husband," as well as "the love of earthly things, or worldly pleasures," "the least suspicion of unwitting Idolatry," "disobedience to any the least of God's Commandment," a "distrust only in God, and withdrawing from that nearness of zeal and confidence which ought to be," "a constant alienation and disaffection of mind," "the continual practice of disobedience and crossness from the duties of love and peace," and in fact any situation "when to be a tolerable Wife is either naturally not in their power, or obstinately not in their will" (2:673). "Fornication," for which even Jesus permits divorce, can in fact mean just about anything.

By the end of *The Doctrine and Discipline,* divorce has been elevated to a metaphysical principle, nothing less than the basis of creation itself. Milton rhapsodizes about it as a kind of miracle, an instantaneous solution to problems "wherof no amends can be made, no cure, no ceasing but by divorce, which like a divine touch in one moment heals all." Divorce is the Alpha and the Omega, "the first and last of all [God's] visible works; when by his divorcing command the world first rose out of Chaos, nor can be renew'd again out of confusion but by the separating of unmeet consorts" (2:273). Divorce is the ordering principle of creation, for identity depends upon differentiation. Milton conceived of creation as God's stamping particular forms upon the chaos of primal matter. In order to be knowable by the human mind, phenomena must first be divorced from the undifferentiated mass of surrounding material. The process of reformation also demands the divorce of "unmeet consorts," a phrase that includes not only ill-matched spouses but also the religious elect and the reprobate and, by implication, the King and the people of England. In a progression typical of Milton's thought, the difficulties he experienced in communicating with a seventeen-year-old country girl have expanded into a profound and innovative theory of ontology, as well as a convincing rationalization of political revolution. Mary Powell would have been astonished to learn of the indirect influence she was to wield on future generations.

III

THE THRILLING CONVERGENCE of erotic and political crises in his life seems to have misled Milton into expecting that his ideas on divorce would be received with due, respectful consideration. By dedicating *The Doctrine and Discipline* to Parliament he revealed an aspiration to reform the laws of the land so as to allow him to break the bonds of wedlock, and he evidently regarded this as a realistic goal. This was a serious miscalculation; the vocal but marginal radical fringe aside, English people were not prepared to receive proposals for what they called "divorce at pleasure" as anything but disgracefully libidinous. Milton was three centuries ahead of his time, and his opponents flew to attack him in print. His critics included his old adversary Bishop Hall, who remembered in 1649:

> I have heard too much of, and once saw, a licentious pamphlet, thrown abroad in these lawless times in the defence and encouragement of Divorces (not to be sued out; that solemnity needed not, but) to be arbitrarily given by the disliking husband to the displeasing and unquiet wife. . . . Woe is me! To what a pass is the world come that a Christian, pretending to Information, should dare to tender so loose a project to the public?[16]

The indefatigable William Prynne railed against "the late dangerous increase of many Anabaptistical, Antinomian, Heresiacall, Atheisticall opinions, as of the soules mortalitie, divorce at pleasure &c."[17] On August 12, 1643, Herbert Palmer preached a sermon before the Houses of Parliament in which he announced that "a wicked book is abroad and uncensored, though deserving to be burnt, whose author hath been so impudent as to set his name to it and dedicate it to yourselves." The book in question was *The Doctrine and Discipline*, and Milton had good reason to be concerned about the fate of his only published work to have achieved any degree of success. Just the previous week the Commons had ordered the public burning of *The Bloody Tenent* by Roger Williams, for the crime of advocating complete toleration in religion. A good friend of Milton's, Williams had arrived back in London that summer, fresh from his practical experiments with toleration in Rhode Island. The fact that the revolution was now attracting such wild men was deeply disturbing to the more conservative Parliamentarians, who were beginning to wonder what kind of forces they had unleashed.

On August 26 the Company of Stationers presented a petition to Parliament protesting the printing of *The Doctrine and Discipline*, among other unlicensed publications. Parliament referred the matter to its Committee for Printing, which was "diligently to inquire out the authors, printers, and publishers of the pamphlets against the immortality of the soul and concerning divorce."[18] On December 28 two wardens of the Stationers' Company appeared before the House of Lords and "complained of the frequent printing of scandalous books by divers, as Hezekiah Woodward and John Milton."[19] But there is no record of any further action against Milton, and indeed his career began notably to flourish from this point on. It seems likely that he already had powerful friends among the radical leaders of the revolution. Men like Henry Vane and Oliver Cromwell, who were sympathetic to at least some of Milton's ideas, and who were later to give him important employment, were beginning to wrest control of events away from the dismayed Presbyterians.

It was starting to look as if the upheaval in process might turn out to be far more fundamental than its original architects had intended. It had become clear that the Earl of Essex, the commander of the parliamentary forces, had no real desire to defeat the King on the battlefield. Like most of the Presbyterian aristocrats, he aimed to force Charles to negotiate a compromise settlement. Angered by his timidity, a "win-the-war" party emerged on the Parliamentary side, and in July 1644 the decisive Parliamentary victory at the battle of Marston Moor was credited to the troops of Oliver Cromwell's Eastern Association. These men were not Presbyterian but Independent in religious sympathy. They did not want to impose a new form of state church on the English people but rather to allow each congregation to determine its own mode of worship. In December 1644 the Self-denying Ordinance removed the leading Parliamentary commanders from their posts, but Cromwell cunningly circumvented its strictures. The Independents' hand was further strengthened after his defeat of the King at the battle of Naseby in June 1645. Charles's personal correspondence was captured, studied, and later published by Cromwell's men. It revealed that while the King had been negotiating with the Parliamentarians, he had simultaneously been trying to secure military support against them from various continental Catholic powers. It was clearly dangerous to trust him.

As they felt the initiative slipping away, the Presbyterians responded with bitter invective against their enemies. It must have been disturbing for one so proud of his virtue and chastity as Milton to find himself denounced as a licentious libertine. Knowing as he did that his motives for wanting a divorce were irreproachably pure, he watched in horror

as his name become a byword for libidinous sexuality. In 1645 Ephraim
Pagitt's *Heresiography* identified a sinister sect known as the "Divorcers"
who "would be quit of their wives for slight occasions, and to main-
taine this opinion, one hath published a Tractate of divorce, in which the
bonds of marriage are let loose to inordinate lust."[20] In the next year the
Presbyterian Thomas Edwards published *Gangraena*, a prurient account
of the vile heretical views he found flourishing amid London's ideological chaos. These included the antinomian opinions that "if a man by the
Spirit knew himself to be in the state of grace, though he did commit mur-
der or drunkenness, God did see no sin in him," that "even in the Articles
of Faith and principles of Religion, there's nothing certainly to be believed
and built on; only that all men ought to have liberty of conscience and
liberty of prophesying," that "all the earth is the Saints and there ought
to be a community of goods," and that "'tis lawfull for women to preach,
and why should they not, having gifts as well as men?"[21] He also reported
people baptizing cats, and soldiers urinating in the font. The second edition of this catalogue of horrors recounted a conversation between two
gentlemen of the Inns of Court and a Mrs. Attaway, who

> spake to them of Master Milton's *Doctrine of Divorce*, and asked
> them what they thought of it, saying it was a point to be consid-
> ered of, and that she for her part would look more into it, for
> she had an unsanctified husband that did not walk in the way of
> Sion, nor speak the language of Canaan. And how accordingly
> she hath practiced it, in running away with another woman's hus-
> band, is now sufficiently known.[22]

It was bad enough that the name of Milton was invoked by the
reprobates to justify their excesses. That was doubtless infuriating to
a man who prided himself on always having cultivated "that vertue

which abhorres the society of Bordello's" (1:891), but it was perhaps predictable, and Milton later expressed regret at not having published *The Doctrine and Discipline* in Latin, where its subversive implications would have been hidden from the "unlearned." More insulting, however, was the misrepresentation of his views by intelligent men who should have known better. In November 1645 Robert Baillie, one of the Scottish Presbyterian leaders, wrote of "Mr. Milton, who in a large treatise hath pleaded for a full liberty for any man to put away his wife whenever he pleaseth, without any fault in her at all, but for any dislike or dyspathy of humour . . ."[23] Daniel Featley appealed for the suppression of "a Tractate of Divorce," which advocated "putting away wives for many other causes besides that which our Saviour only approveth."[24] The Royalist poet Christopher Wasse coined the phrase "the froward Miltonist"[25] and we can imagine the ribald guffaws ringing throughout the taverns of London as the Cavaliers made sport of this hypocritically horny Puritan.

Milton responded to such critics with a pair of sonnets: "On the Detraction Which Followed upon My Writing Certain Treatises." He denounces his mockers as "hogs" unfit to receive his pearls of wisdom and as "owls and cuckoos, asses, apes and dogs" who attempt to drown out his sage counsel with their "barbarous noise" (143). The fact that many readers were apparently intimidated by the very title of *Tetrachordon* causes Milton to sneer that his age hates "learning worse than toad or asp." He knew he was ahead of his time, as he admitted in that tract: "I fear to be more elaborat in such perspicuity as this; lest I should seem not to teach, but to upbraid the dulnes of an age" (2:692). But one poem includes a penetrating diagnosis of the reasons behind the public's incomprehension. Milton's critics are the kind of people

That bawl for freedom in their senseless mood,
And still revolt when truth would set them free.
Licence they mean when they cry liberty;
For who loves that, must first be wise and good.[26]

The conservative Presbyterians share with the radical antinomians, their ostensible opposites, an inability to distinguish between licence and liberty. Only a "wise and good" person can make this distinction, because it involves obedience to the law of conscience. It does not involve obedience to the laws of church or state, which the conservatives advocated, but neither does it involve the abandonment of law altogether, which the antinomians practiced. Both groups assumed that in claiming the right to divorce Milton was claiming exemption from, or proclaiming disregard of, the law. But Milton thought of himself as strictly obeying the interior law of conscience, which was the only law he recognized. He understood that legalism and licentiousness, the conservatives and the antinomians, were secretly, unconsciously, in alliance, and he was determined to defeat both of them together.

In early 1645 Milton published two prose responses to his critics, in accordance with his policy of dividing his audience into worthy and unworthy recipients of his wisdom. *Tetrachordon* is a learned, meticulous exposition of all the biblical texts referring to divorce, while *Colasterion* ("place of punishment" in Greek) is a joyous, abandoned thrashing of his wretched adversary. The former tract is prefaced with fulsome praise of Parliament for having resisted the clamour to suppress *The Doctrine and Discipline,* and as usual Milton reminds the recipients of his gratitude that it will make them famous in posterity, offering "such thanks perhaps . . . as shall more then whisper to the next ages" (2:579). *Colasterion* repeats the offer of posthumous fame for his opponent, but in rather different terms. Milton challenges his anonymous adversary to reveal his identity: "[I]f in this penury of Soul hee can bee possible to have the lustiness to think of fame, let him but send mee how hee calls himself, and I may chance not fail to endorse him on the backside of posterity, not a *golden*, but a brazen Asse" (2:757).

The object of Milton's scorn wisely declined the invitation. But the work that provoked the poet's wrath is in fact a perfectly sensible series of objections to *The Doctrine and Discipline*'s wildly impractical proposals. *An Answer to a Book Entitled The Doctrine and Discipline of Divorce* was published anonymously in November 1644, but it contained a preface by the government's licenser Joseph Caryl, who approved it as a precaution against the likely effect of Milton's ideas on "unstaid mindes and men given to change." Milton himself had worried that *The Doctrine and Discipline* might be taken up by libertines and antinomians to justify their loose morality, and such concerns were by no means unwarranted. *An Answer* asks the reader to imagine what would happen if Milton's proposals were put into effect: "[H]ow many thousands of lustfull and libidinous men would be parting from their wives every week and marrying others."[27] Again, this is a problem that Milton had recognized, though he blithely dismissed it as insignificant. Indeed, *An Answer* scores several palpable hits against Milton's case. *The Doctrine and Discipline* advocates divorce on grounds of psychological disagreement, but as the answerer notes, "there is between all married people some contrariety or disagreement of mindes" (5), and Milton has suggested no criterion to judge when such differences are sufficient to justify divorce. The tone of the *Answer* is respectful throughout, and sometimes even flattering. The author sympathizes with the difficulties Milton has experienced in finding a fit partner but tactfully points out that his is an exceptional case:

If every man were of your breeding and capacity there were some colour for this plea, for we believe you count no woman to due conversation accessible as to you, except she can speak Hebrew, Greek, Latin, and French, and dispute against the canon law as well as you, or at least be able to hold discourse with you. But other gentlemen of good quality are content with meaner and fewer endowments, as you know well enough. (12)

In fact the author seems well intentioned, earnest, and genuinely curious to know the details of Milton's difficult argument. *The Doctrine and Discipline* had asserted the possibility of an absolute, irreconcilable psychological difference between marriage partners. But as the answerer notes, "[T]here is no such disposition in nature as is unchangeable," so he politely asks Milton to clarify his meaning: "[W]e desire the next time you write, to tell us the meaning of this fit conversing soul. We have heard that angels converse with one another as they are spirits; but for husbands and wives . . . we know no conversing with one another but what is by words and actions."[28]

These mild and reasonable objections cast Milton into a paroxysm of rage. The intemperance of his response tells us much about his psychological condition during the critical years of the mid-1640s and also about the general climate of the times. Milton was convinced that only a miserable slave could fail to see that "fit companionship" was more important in a marriage than physical sex. It was therefore immediately obvious to him, as he claims, "that this Author could for certain bee no other then som mechanic" (2:725), a manual laborer. To his delight, he soon discovered that the truth was even better: His opponent's true profession was "no other, if any can hold laughter, and I am sure none will guess him lower, then an actual Serving-man" (2:726). This fortuitous circumstance spurs

Milton into a veritable orgy of snobbery. The answerer had dared to mention the fate likely to be suffered by the children of women divorced by their husbands while pregnant. In response Milton sneers that this "must needs bee good news for Chamber-maids, to hear a Serving-man grown so provident for great bellies" (2:734). The answerer had honestly, and understandably, admitted that he did not grasp what Milton meant by "the gentlest ends of marriage." In response Milton scoffs:

> I beleev him heartily: for how should hee, a Servingman both by nature and by function, an Idiot by breeding, and a Sollicitor by presumption, ever come to know, or feel within himself what the meaning is of gentle. . . . Yet altogether without art sure hee is not; for who could have devis'd to give us more breifly a better description of his own Servility? (2:741)

A natural slave, who in this case happens appropriately also to be a literal servant, will obviously be incapable of conceiving any other form of conversation than physical intercourse. Milton dismisses his objections with the haughty claim that "[a]ll persons of gentle breeding (I say gentle, though this Barrow grunt at the word) I know will apprehend, and bee satisfy'd in what I spake, how unpleasing and discontenting the society of body must needs bee between those whose mindes cannot bee sociable" (2:747). But in fact Milton is highly unusual in his opinion that loveless sex is actively unpleasant. Many people might agree that sex is more pleasant when the partners love each other, but few would concede that sex as a means to purely physical satisfaction is inherently a hostile and degrading act. Not only does Milton believe this, however, it seems so obvious to him that he assumes anyone who feels otherwise is a disgustingly salacious pervert: "But what should a man say more to a snout in this pickle, what language can be low and degenerat anough?" (ibid.)

It might seem that Milton is simply a Puritan killjoy, opposed to and afraid of sexual pleasure. But nothing could be further from the truth; in fact Milton is arguing for a sexualization of all intercourse between husband and wife, both physical and psychological. Convinced that sex takes place primarily in the mind, Milton attacks those who would restrict its sphere of influence to the body. The vehemence with which he upbraids his answerer arises from his fear that sexuality is being artificially and unnaturally restricted, relegated to the lowest element of human activity, rather than spreading through the entire person, soul as well as body. The author of *An Answer* claims that if marriage had been intended primarily for spiritual conversation,

> then would it have been every wayes as much, yea more content and solace to Adam; and so consequently to every man, to have had another man made to him of his rib instead of Eve: this is apparent by experience, which shews that man ordinarily exceeds woman in naturall gifts of minde, and in delectablenesse of converse; upon which we suppose it may be plainly concluded, that the solace and meetnesse of a helper to Adam which was spoken of, was not that which you seem to speak of as contrary to discord only, but is a solace and a meetnesse made up chiefly as of different sexes, consisting of male and female. (12)

But Milton had not been referring to the kind of spiritual companionship that a man can derive from the company of other men. He conceives of a companionable conversation that, although not carnal, is nevertheless sexual and specifically heterosexual. With men, he argues, a man may experience the "society of grave freindship," but with a woman he can expect a different form of spiritual intercourse, "another amiable and attractive society of conjugal love, besides the deed of procreation, which of itself soon cloies, and is despis'd, unless it be cherisht and re-incited with a pleasing conversation" (2:740). The specific delights that a man can derive only from a woman's company are not limited to bodily pleasure. Sexual intercourse is spiritual as well as sensual, and anyone who fails to understand that has a bestial conception of sex. Thus Milton incessantly pours scorn upon his opponent with animalistic imagery: "I mean not to dispute Philosophy with this Pork, who never read any. . . . Came this doctrin out of som School or some stie?" (2:739)

We do not need to endorse Milton's railing abuse to note that it possesses a rigorous thematic coherence, nor to admit that it clarifies the political implications behind his theory of sexuality. To allow divorce only for impotence or adultery reveals a carnal, and therefore bestial, view of sex: to be a beast is to lack the definitive human capacity of reason; reason is true liberty; insofar as human beings are irrational they are enslaved; servility produces idolatry; idolatry supports monarchy. A perfectly logical chain of cause and effect connects Milton's demands for divorce with his ecclesiastical and political opinions, and it is doubtful whether he could have arrived at his radical views in those spheres had he not been impelled in their direction by the crisis in his romantic life. That is certainly how he chose to view the matter, and it confirmed his conviction that he had been divinely anointed as a prophet to the nation. And now, at long last, his prophecy was being heard.

5

WAR ON TWO FRONTS

I

Unlike its French and Russian successors, the English revolution did not devour its children. But it did disown them. The moderate, Presbyterian aristocrats who were only trying to make the King see reason proved unwilling to or incapable of decisively beating him in battle, and as the war dragged into its third and fourth years they found themselves displaced by sturdier souls. Foremost among these was Oliver Cromwell, who molded the New Model Army into the most disciplined and effective fighting force in Europe, one which would hold the keys to political power in England for the next decade. It was in many ways the first modern army, using uniforms and drills to discipline its soldiers' individual bodies into the organized service of a collective cause. Its soldiers were ideologues, convinced that they served divine Providence, which they identified with religious Independency, constitutional republicanism, political democracy and economic egalitarianism. The New Model gained a major advantage from Cromwell's insistence that ability rather than birth should secure advancement. As he put it: "I had rather have a plain, russet-coated Captain, that knows what he fights for, and loves what he knows, than what you call a Gentleman and is nothing else."[1] Nor was Cromwell averse to exploiting the zealotry of the extreme radicals among his troops. Challenged about the prevalence of unorthodox opinions in the army, he declared: "Ay, but the man is an Anabaptist. . . . Admit he be, shall that render him incapable to serve the public?"[2] The range of acceptable political and religious opinion was sharply radicalizing, and this movement would not easily be reversed.

By the end of the war in 1646 Cromwell was the most powerful man in England. Political and religious opinion in the country as a whole, but especially in the army, had swung massively toward what we would call "the Left" since 1642, and the Independency that Cromwell advocated in religion soon replaced Presbyterianism as the predominant faith of the revolutionaries. The New Model Army was more truly representative of the English nation than of Parliament, which was elected on a strictly limited, property-based franchise, and the experience of fighting together in a basically ideological war had molded them into a classical revolutionary force. Cromwell had seized the political initiative while Parliament dithered, and the army he commanded had now replaced Parliament as the dominant power in the country. Deep, radical social change, including universal male suffrage and an egalitarian redistribution of property, was, though most people outside the army did not fully realize it, suddenly and for the first time in England becoming a practical possibility.

Remarkable as it seems, Milton's miserable marriage had played a significant role in these developments. The incomprehension and hilarity that had greeted his arguments for divorce had infuriated him. Not only did the public's ignorant response condemn him to involuntary and perpetual celibacy, the calls made by prominent Presbyterians to suppress his pamphlets threatened to deprive him of the sole modicum of fame he had yet achieved.

Over the years 1643–4, Milton brooded on the personal affronts he was suffering, hammering them out onto paper as matters of public principle. In the postscript to *The Judgment of Martin Bucer* he warned that even the as-yet-modest gains of the revolution were already under threat:

> I refer me to wisest men, whether truth be suffered to be truth, or liberty to be liberty, now among us, and be not again in danger of new fetters and captivity after all our hopes and labours lost: and whether learning be not (which our enemies too prophetically feared) in the way to be trodden down again by ignorance. Whereof while time is, out of the faith owing to God and my country, I bid this kingdom beware; and doubt not but God who hath dignified this parliament already to so many glorious degrees, will also give them (which is a singular blessing) to inform themselves rightly in the midst of an unprincipled age, and to prevent this working mystery of ignorance and ecclesiastical thraldom, which under new shapes and disguises begins afresh to grow upon us. (2:479)

These "new shapes and disguises" were worn by the Presbyterians who, as Milton now perceived, were simply trying to seize power in the English church and state for themselves, not to institute any genuinely liberating reforms. They were even willing to restore most of his powers to the defeated King, whom they now held prisoner in Scotland, if he would recognize their religion as the state church of England. For Milton, as for Cromwell and the soldiers of the New Model, this would be a despicable betrayal, merely replacing one tyranny with another. The fact that Presbyterians like Herbert and Prynne had led the cry to ban his books enabled Milton to understand the true nature of their aims long before most of his compatriots. They might be prepared to remove the physical icons from the churches, but only in order to redirect the people's idolatrous impulses inward, toward the ideological fetishes and images that supported their own interests. In one of his most brilliant political sonnets, "On the New Forcers of Conscience under the Long Parliament," Milton accuses the Presbyterians of having seized the lucrative assets of the Anglican church "[f]rom them whose sin ye envi'd, not abhor'd" (4). He castigates their proposed institution of their own faith as the new state church as an attempt "[t]o force our Consciences that Christ set free" (6), and he allows himself spiteful digs at the men who had personally attacked him in print, like Thomas Edwards and Robert Baillie, to whom he refers as "shallow Edwards and Scotch what d' ye call" (12).

By 1644, when this poem was written, Milton's mind was marching rapidly, in step with a small but powerful and determined section of the nation, away from Presbyterianism and toward Independency. Like many of the soldiers who were now grasping the initiative from the politicians, Milton had come to oppose any state church whatsoever. Ecclesiastical and political affairs must undergo a divorce, the state must separate from the church, and individual congregations, indeed individual people, must be free to determine their own modes of religious observance. The Presbyterians' attempt to deny the English people these freedoms made them as bad as, or even the same as, the Anglicans against whom they were allegedly fighting: "*New Presbyter* is but *Old Priest* writ Large" (14), as Milton memorably put it. Two or three years previously such opinions had been confined to what was regarded as the lunatic fringe of separatist sects like the Brownists and Anabaptists. But as early as 1642, Milton had welcomed the spread of such groups as a sign of vibrant, healthy debate among Christians:

> If sects and schisms be turbulent in the unsettled estate of a church,
> while it lies under the amending hand, it best beseems our Christian

courage to think they are but as the throes and pangs that go before the birth of reformation, and that the work itself is now in doing. For if we look but on the nature of elemental and mixed things, we know they cannot suffer any change of one kind or quality into another, without the struggle of contrarieties. (1:795)

Milton was fully confident that the revolutionary events unfolding before his eyes were manifestations of the divine will. God was revealing his nature in and through human history. The "struggle of contrarieties," the dialectical conflict between opposed social and ideological forces, was necessary for progress, and it was in and through progress that God made Himself manifest. Conflict between religious opinions was not to be repressed but, rather, welcomed as the motor of history. The Anglicans' efforts to suppress the separatists recalled the Pope's attempts to repress Protestants and provided "the very womb for a new sub-antichrist to breed in." The bishops claimed that episcopal authority was all that stood between the church and theological anarchy, warning that "if they be put down, a deluge of innumerable sects will follow; we shall be all Brownists, Familists, Anabaptists" (1:786). But Milton had much sympathy with such sectaries who, like himself, had been "church-outed by the prelates":

Noise it till ye be hoarse, that a rabble of sects will come in; it will be answered ye, no rabble, sir priest, but an unanimous multitude of good protestants will then join to the church, which now, because of you, stand separated. This will be the dreadful consequence of your removal. (1:787–8)

Milton is thinking his way toward another momentous breakthrough in the history of ideas. He is coming to believe in religious toleration. And

because he had been brought to that belief by the Presbyterians' attempts
to suppress his divorce tracts, he was further led to conclude that freedom
of speech is a prerequisite of a healthy society. This notion is so basic an
assumption of modern liberal democracy that it seems almost banal today,
but that is not how it seemed in Milton's time. In the 1640s the idea that
anyone should be allowed publicly to express his opinion about anything
appeared to most people a reckless and destructive argument guaranteed,
and in all probability designed, to bring about complete social, political
and economic chaos. It seemed plain common sense to ban and suppress
ideas that were clearly dangerous to society. The concept that a society
might actually benefit from allowing the expression of all thought, however evil or crazy, was not part of commonly acceptable discourse. Milton
has a good claim to have invented it. In 1642 he applauded the emergence
of outlandish opinions, on the grounds that truth can be identified only
through the rejection of error:

> If God come to try our constancy, we ought not to shrink or stand
> the less firmly for that, but pass on with more steadfast resolution
> to establish the truth, though it were through a lane of sects and
> heresies on each side. Other things men do to the glory of God;
> but sects and errors, it seems, God suffers to be for the glory of
> good men, that the world may know and reverence their true for-
> titude and undaunted constancy in the truth. Let us not therefore
> make these things an incumbrance, or an excuse of our delay in
> reforming, which God sends us as an incitement to proceed with
> more honour and alacrity: for if there were no opposition, where
> were the trial of an unfeigned goodness and magnanimity? Virtue
> that wavers is not virtue, but vice revolted from itself, and after a
> while returning. (1:794–5)

Vice is necessary for the creation of virtue, truth would be unknowable without falsehood, good could not exist without evil. Therefore, the public expression of a variety of contradictory opinions benefits society as a whole. Milton has achieved a profound philosophical insight that would not be matched until Hegel elaborated his dialectical view of history in the early nineteenth century. He understands that identity is relational, that everything is defined by its relation to what it is not. Human thought works through mutually definitive binary oppositions, such as those between good and evil, male and female, God and Satan. Each pole of such oppositions is necessary for the existence of the other. By the time of *Paradise Lost*, Milton had fully worked out the profound ramifications of this epistemology for human, angelic and even divine life, but the essential elements of his mature philosophical system were already present by 1644, in the most famous of all Milton's prose tracts, *Areopagitica*.

II

SINCE THE LONG Parliament's abolition of the Court of Star Chamber in July 1641, there had been no legally effective censorship in England. This resulted in a torrent of unorthodox opinion appearing in print for the first time, including Milton's initial prose pamphlets. By June 1643 the Presbyterians who controlled Parliament were determined to stamp out this dangerous and contagious epidemic of popular opinion, and they passed a Licensing Order, requiring all publications to be licenced at Stationers' Hall before they could be printed. Since Milton's *Doctrine and Discipline of Divorce* had been mentioned in Parliament as one of the most outrageous books requiring repression, it is not surprising that he took this as a personal affront. By now, however, Milton was accustomed to turning personal affronts into public issues.

The Court of the Areopagus had been the Athenian Parliament, which the philosopher Isocrates had famously addressed in his capacity as a private citizen. Isocrates described it as "a body which was composed exclusively of men who were of noble birth and had exemplified in their lives exceptional virtue and sobriety,"[3] but the restriction to the aristocracy was later dropped, and Milton intended the Areopagus to represent legislative authority in the hands of the most personally virtuous citizens. Milton always espoused this classical republican view that personal moral rectitude was the best qualification for political power. The main thrust of Isocrates's argument was that "virtue is not advanced by written laws but by the habits of every-day life" and that "written statutes" are unimportant beside the "justice in [men's] souls" (7:40). Milton's tract notes that Isocrates's argument converges with the doctrines of Christianity elaborated three centuries later. He points out that the Gospel frees God's people from legal bondage, writing the law in the heart rather than in tablets of stone.

This was reasonably conventional Protestant theology, but in 1644 Milton's argument had obvious and dangerous antinomian implications. It could easily be misread by anarchistic hotheads as endorsing the abolition of law altogether. As his opponents had loudly proclaimed, Milton also lacked any official platform for his views, but he signaled his right to address Parliament by the title of the tract he submitted to them. Like ancient Athens, Milton suggested, England could become a participatory, direct democracy, in which virtue and reason, rather than wealth or breeding, would be the qualifications for participating in public life. Milton was drawing on the tradition of ancient republicanism, expressed both in Athens and Rome, in which the exploits of republican heroes like Pericles, Cato and Brutus provided the model for heroic conduct during the civil war. Recently revived by Machiavelli and other Italian civic humanists, classical republicanism was, along with radical Protestantism, the ideological inspiration of the English revolution, and the two strains of thought blend harmoniously throughout Milton's tract.

Areopagitica begins by establishing the credentials that give Milton the right to be heard by the nation's governing body. Primary among these is his "life wholly dedicated to studious labours," added to certain "natural endowments," which, Milton confidently asserts, compels Parliament to obey "the voice of reason from what quarter soever it be heard speaking; and renders ye as willing to repeal any Act of your own setting forth, as any set forth by your predecessors" (2:490). Milton anticipates here the Trotskyite theory of "permanent revolution," which he calls "the reforming of Reformation itself." By its very nature, reformation can never be finished. It is a continual, incessant process of re-examination, alteration and improvement, and its purpose is to replace the traditional conception of government and social order as static, fixed and divinely ordained. The course of history is ordained by God, who reveals his will through the process of reformation. Human beings should not experience God as an immutable set of ideas, rules or practices, for that would be idolatry. Rather, human beings should experience God as a thrilling, shocking, ceaselessly new and novel series of spectacular events and discoveries:

> Truth is compared in Scripture to a streaming fountain; if her waters flow not in a perpetual progression, they sicken into a muddy pool of conformity and tradition. A man may be a heretic in the truth; and if he believe things only because his pastor says so, or the Assembly so determines, without knowing other reason, though his belief be true, yet the very truth he holds becomes his heresy. (2:543)

We see here how rapidly Milton's thought was developing during
these months. In 1643 he began *The Doctrine and Discipline* by describing "custom" as the greatest ally of error. Now, little more than a year
later, he draws the concomitant conclusion, that change is a necessary
component of truth: "[t]he light which we have gained was given us, not
to be ever staring on, but by it to discover onward things more remote
from our knowledge" (2:550). If any body of doctrine, or even any man's
personal opinion, fails to take account of changing historical circumstances, this is sufficient proof of its falsity:

> [H]e who thinks we are to pitch our tent here, and have attained
> the utmost prospect of reformation that the mortal glass wherein
> we contemplate can show us, till we come to beatific vision, that
> man by this very opinion declares that he is yet far short of truth.
> (2:549)

Clearly such an ever-changing, endlessly mutating, sinuous and ser-
pentine concept of truth is incompatible with dogmatic religion. It is
irreconcilable with any organized faith that sets down a catechism of
indelible credo. It is difficult to reconcile with Christianity itself, and
it can only be reconciled with those kinds of Christianity that eschew
any and all hierarchical forms of church discipline, whether episcopal
or Presbyterian. Little more than ten years after vowing to uphold royal
supremacy over the Church of England, as he had done before receiving
his MA, Milton now refuses to recognize any other authority than his
own conscience in matters of faith. This is no indication of hypocrisy,
however, but a sign of how rapidly and radically the minds of English
people were being cast into new molds by the events through which they
were living. This psychological insurrection brings Milton to a position
that is almost indistinguishable from outright antinomianism. He quotes

the antinomians' favorite line of scripture from St. Paul: "To the pure, all things are pure; not only meats and drinks, but all kind of knowledge whether of good or evil; the knowledge cannot defile, nor consequently the books, if the will and conscience be not defiled" (2:512).

A modern reader could be forgiven for concluding that Milton is arguing that everybody should be able to read absolutely anything at all. But his true position is subtly but vitally different. In the divorce tracts he had made it very clear that he was not advocating "divorce at pleasure" for "hard-hearted and licentious men," but only the right of a "good and peaceable man" to liberate himself from an objectively "remediless thraldom." This was what had confused people like the author of *An Answer*, and it is easy enough to see why. Milton believed that God had created laws to control the reprobate only. The law was not supposed to bind the elect, who were at liberty to act according to their rational conscience, and Milton extended this belief to the civil and canon laws of England, as well as to the Mosaic law. Like the antinomians, he believed that all is pure to the pure.

Milton differed from the antinomians, however, in limiting the "pure" to a vanishingly small number of highly educated, morally immaculate, politically, philosophically and theologically advanced individuals closely resembling himself. Whereas the more radical antinomian sects believed in universal salvation, and so included everybody under the category of "the pure," Milton limited admission to this exalted group to a handful of like-minded lofty souls. He therefore denies "introducing license, while I oppose licensing" (2:493), and supports the post-publication suppression of books whose effects prove deleterious to the commonwealth. He is well aware of the practical impact books can have on public affairs: "I know they are as lively, and as vigorously productive, as those fabulous dragon's teeth; and being sown up and down, may chance to spring up armed men" (2:492). He has no intention of allowing the revolution to be defeated by permitting the spread of Royalist or Catholic propaganda. He is not, despite the best efforts of many of his posthumous admirers to present him as such, an advocate of free speech: "I mean not tolerated popery, and open superstition, which, as it extirpates all religions and civil supremacies, so itself should be extirpate" (2:565).

Stanley Fish, the most prominent Milton critic of the twentieth century, set the pattern for modern interpretations of this sentence when he argued that Milton is exempting from toleration only those who are themselves intolerant. The problem there, however, is that by our standards virtually everyone in seventeenth-century England was religiously intolerant. It is true that in this passage Milton exempts only "popery and open superstition" from toleration, but he considered any religious observance that used icons, incense, vestments or set forms of prayer to be openly superstitious. Milton and his fellow Puritans did not consider the use of such devices to be a matter of conscience. Such devices were attempts to *do* things, to bring about objective alterations in the condition of the material world. They were, in the parlance of the day, magic. Thus Oliver Cromwell saw no contradiction when, speaking in Ireland in 1649, he declared that "I meddle not with any man's conscience. But if by liberty of conscience you mean a liberty to exercise the Mass, I judge it best to use plain dealing, and to let you know, where the Parliament of England have power, that will not be allowed of."[4] The Mass was not something that took place in the conscience; it was an attempt to transform one objective substance into another by means of ritual incantation. It was magic, and since magic bypassed the conscience altogether, magical rites lay beyond the freedom that Milton was willing that the conscience should enjoy.

In one of *Areopagitica*'s later passages, furthermore, Milton seems to advocate a repressive pre-emptive strike against the Presbyterians.

Because they "are already with one foot in the stirrup so active at suppressing, it would be no unequal distribution in the first place to suppress the suppressors themselves." So when Milton mentions that he is willing to tolerate "neighbouring differences, or rather indifferences" in religion, we should not take him as advocating any significant degree of latitude by modern standards. But if *Areopagitica* is not quite so epochal a breakthrough in the history of free-speech theory as it has sometimes been considered, it is yet more philosophically radical than most readers have realized. In making his case that good men can be made better by reading bad books, Milton is led to the astounding revelation that goodness is actually composed of evil. This is true logically: since Milton believes that identity is relational, that things are defined by what they are not, and that binary oppositions are mutually constitutive, he must believe that evil is necessary to the existence of good. It is also empirically true: a good man will use his knowledge of bad books as material by which to augment his virtue. The startlingly counterintuitive but inescapable conclusion is that good and evil are actually *the same thing*:

> Good and evil we know in the field of this world grow up together almost inseparably; and the knowledge of good is so involved and interwoven with the knowledge of evil, and in so many cunning resemblances hardly to be discerned, that those confused seeds which were imposed upon Psyche as an incessant labour to cull out, and sort asunder, were not more intermixed. It was from out the rind of one apple tasted, that the knowledge of good and evil, as two twins cleaving together, leaped forth into the world. And perhaps this is that doom which Adam fell into of knowing good and evil, that is to say of knowing good by evil. (2:514)

This truly is a quantum advance in the history of thought. It would not be matched until the nineteenth century, when Nietzsche applied dialectics to morality in works like *Beyond Good and Evil*. But Milton's thought is far superior to Nietzsche's puerile and simplistic devil-worship. Milton accomplished the strenuous task of reconciling the identity of good and evil with the existence of a benign Creator. He did not fully achieve this goal until the crowning glory of *Paradise Lost*, but he makes important advances toward it in *Areopagitica*. All Milton's ideas develop throughout his career, but the essential basis of his concerns remains remarkably constant. Not only does *Areopagitica* anticipate the conclusions that come to fruition in *Paradise Lost*, it also looks back to his very earliest published writing, the Elegies to Diodati. In those verse letters he describes arousing himself with the sight of girls passing by, but only in pursuit of the heightened pleasure and moral virtue of denying himself satisfaction. At the age of eighteen he was already certain that virtue is manufactured in the battle against vice, and that temptation is therefore a constant necessity in the life of a truly moral man. *Areopagitica* applies the same reasoning to the reading of books:

> He that can apprehend and consider vice with all her baits and seeming pleasures, and yet abstain, and yet distinguish, and yet prefer that which is truly better, he is the true wayfaring Christian. I cannot praise a fugitive and cloistered virtue, unexercised and unbreathed, that never sallies out and sees her adversary but slinks out of the race, where that immortal garland is to be run for, not without dust and heat. Assuredly we bring not innocence into the world, we bring impurity much rather; that which purifies us is trial, and trial is by what is contrary. That virtue therefore which is but a youngling in the contemplation of evil, and knows

not the utmost that vice promises to her followers, and rejects it, is
but a blank virtue, not a pure; her whiteness is but an excremental
whiteness. (2:514–5)

The argument for reading evil and potentially corrupting books is
identical to the argument for tolerating erroneous religious sects, and here
it develops into a general guide for living. Because virtue is vice's opposite, virtue can only be manufactured through conflict with vice. Without
vice, virtue could not exist. Vice is therefore a necessary component of
virtue. Human beings will certainly experience vice and virtue as distinct
and opposite from one another, but logically, as Milton has now come
to realize, they are actually the same thing: "Suppose we could expel sin
by this means; look how much we thus expel of sin, so much we expel
of virtue: for the matter of them both is the same" (2:527). He therefore
rejects the monkish policy of simply secluding oneself from temptation as
a cowardly refusal to offer battle to vice. Milton has arrived at a position
he will maintain throughout his mature theodicy. A theodicy attempts, as
Milton puts it in *Paradise Lost*, "to justify the ways of God to men." It
endeavors to answer the most profound dilemma raised by monotheism:
How can a being who is both omnipotent and beneficent allow evil to
exist? Milton stumbles across the answer quite fortuitously, in the course
of his topical and self-interested argument against Parliament's licensing
order. What appears evil to human beings is not evil in itself. What human
beings experience as evil is, if they can muster the intellectual fortitude to
perceive it as such, the necessary prerequisite of good. Milton's mind has
moved beyond good and evil not, like Nietzsche, by fatuously preferring
evil but by demonstrating the mutually determining nature of this opposition. As if carried away by the excitement of his discovery, Milton heartily embraces its vastly profound theological implications:

Many there be that complain of divine Providence for suffering Adam
to transgress; foolish tongues! When God gave him reason, he gave
him freedom to choose, for reason is but choosing; he had been
else a mere artificial Adam, such an Adam as he is in the motions.
We ourselves esteem not of that obedience, or love, or gift, which
is of force: God therefore left him free, set before him a provoking
object, ever almost in his eyes; herein consisted his merit, herein the
right of his reward, the praise of his abstinence. Wherefore did he
create passions within us, pleasures round about us, but that these
rightly tempered are the very ingredients of virtue? (2:527)

Milton here endorses the ancient doctrine of *felix culpa*, the "fortunate fall." God tempted Adam and Eve with the "provoking object" of
the tree, just as the teenage Milton used the female body as a "provoking object" to tempt himself. Resistance to temptation constitutes virtue.
Such resistance would be impossible without the Fall, and the Fall itself
is good, because it introduces the faculty of reason into the human soul.
After the Fall, human life became an endless series of choices between
good and evil, which is to say that it became a ceaseless exercise of the
rational faculty. In Milton's theology, the rational faculty was divine, both
in the sense that it was the immortal element within the soul, and also in
that reason is God's representative within us. Insofar as he is knowable
by human beings, Milton believed, God is reason. Reason is the form in
which God manifests himself to human beings. Reason is God incarnate.
The Greek word *logos*, which is used in John 1:1 ("In the beginning was
the Word, and the Word was with God and the Word was God"), is usually translated as "word," but "reason" is an equally valid rendition. This
is the concept that Christians identify with the "Son" of God who took

incarnate form as Jesus of Nazareth. By making the exercise of reason a constant element of human experience, then, the Fall introduces the Son of God into the human soul, thus making possible its redemption.

As Milton notes, "reason is but choosing." It consists of the selection of some alternatives over others. Reason is thus a process of constant mental and social change; hence Milton concludes that God makes himself manifest in the ever-changing movement of human history. At a microcosmic, individual level, God makes himself known through a person's ceaseless selection of certain courses of action over the myriad available alternatives, and so he ensures that we are all constantly presented with alternatives to choose between. Virtue consists in the ability to make our choices in accordance with the dictates of reason, rather than the demands of passion or appetite, and the absence of that ability is vice. In order for virtue to exist, therefore, vice must also exist as a viable alternative choice. Those who seek to remove this alternative by banning evil books, closing brothels and theaters, forcing women to cover their faces, or forbidding any of vice's raw materials are attempting to leave people no choice. They are trying to make the exercise of reason superfluous, thus in effect working to erase the divine image from the human soul. They are doing the work of the devil.

III

PERHAPS THE MOST striking element of Milton's argument for us today is that he associates the decline of reason with the growth of a market economy, a process in which he was himself deeply implicated. In a famous passage, Milton describes what we would call the "alienation" of the rational faculty as a form of commodification:

> A wealthy man, addicted to his pleasure and to his profits, finds religion to be a traffic so entangled, and of so many piddling accounts, that of all mysteries he cannot skill to keep a stock going upon that trade. What should he do? Fain he would have the name to be religious, fain he would bear up with his neighbours in that. What does he therefore, but resolves to give over toiling, and to find himself out some factor, to whose care and credit he may commit the whole managing of his religious affairs; some divine of note and estimation that must be. To him he adheres, resigns the whole warehouse of his religion, with all the locks and keys, into his custody; and indeed makes the very person of that man his religion; esteems his associating with him a sufficient evidence and commendatory of his own piety. So that a man may say his religion is now no more within himself, but is become a dividual movable, and goes and comes near him, according as that good man frequents the house. (2:544)

Milton does not condemn commodification per se here, but he does find it disgracefully inappropriate when applied to religion. Other forms of labor can be alienated without severe consequences to the health of the soul, but to alienate the psychological labor which, for Milton, true religious belief must always involve is scandalously blasphemous. The pattern of alienated labor, which English people were learning to embrace in many aspects of their lives, must not be allowed to impose itself on religion. Thus do proto-economic debates converge with metaphysical conflicts between supernatural forces, with military clashes between opposing armies, and with the psycho-sexual agonies suffered by an individual mind to produce *Areopagitica*, a work of revolutionary prophecy to rival Jeremiah but which places the city of London rather than Jerusalem at the epicenter of divine and human history. Addressing us across the ages from the very middle of that center, having wrought himself to the utmost pitch of revolutionary ardor, Milton cannot refrain from rejoicing at the fortuity of his circumstances:

> Behold now this vast city: a city of refuge, the mansion house of liberty, encompassed and surrounded with his protection; the shop of war hath not there more anvils and hammers waking, to fashion out the plates and instruments of armed justice in defence of beleaguered truth, than there be pens and heads there, sitting by their studious lamps, musing, searching, revolving new notions and ideas wherewith to present, as with their homage and their fealty, the approaching Reformation: others as fast reading, trying all things, assenting to the force of reason and convincement. What could a man require more from a nation so pliant and so prone to seek after knowledge? What wants there to such a towardly and pregnant soil, but wise and faithful labourers, to make a knowing people, a nation of prophets, of sages, and of worthies? (2:553–4)

Such ecstasies are always fleeting. By the end of his life Milton's opinion of his countrymen had effectively been reversed, and his greatest works would consist of attempts to come to terms with the crushing sequence of disillusioning events that he would have to face over his life's last two decades. In 1644, however, England stood poised on the brink of revolution, and Milton's dawning consciousness of that fact must have mitigated the pain and fury induced by his wife's desertion. He was in any case not the kind of man to take such desertion lying down, and he seems to have engaged in some healthily enthusiastic pursuit of female companionship. Edward Phillips remembers that

> now as it were a single man again, [he] made it his chief diversion
> now and then in an evening to visit the Lady Margaret Ley. This
> lady, being a woman of great wit and ingenuity, had a particular
> honour for him, and took much delight in his company; as likewise
> her husband, Captain Hobson, a very accomplished gentleman.[5]

Presumably Captain Hobson's accomplishments included such confidence in his wife's affections as to allow her to be regularly visited by a
handsome, intelligent and recently separated man, who was sufficiently
enamored of her to compose a sonnet in her praise. Apart from the fact
that Phillips describes Milton's visits as the result of his now being single,
however, there are no grounds for suspecting any amorous interaction
between the poet and Margaret Ley. The same cannot be said of Mary
Davis, a doctor's daughter described by Phillips as "a very handsome
and Witty Gentlewoman,"[6] to whom Milton actually proposed marriage.
This was a bold and highly illegal idea; Milton was suggesting that the
lady become an accomplice to bigamy, and it is not surprising to learn
from Phillips that she was "averse" to the plan. But she was clearly interested enough to have allowed the courtship to progress to the point where
Milton believed success was possible.

In his long theological treatise *Of Christian Doctrine* Milton makes a
persuasive case for polygamy, and we can assume he was equally persuasive in person. Although his efforts to seduce Mary Davis into marriage
were unsuccessful, political revolutions often produce sexual experimentation among their partisans, and antinomian sects like the Ranters certainly took full advantage of this circumstance. There is no reason to
doubt that, despite his marriage, Milton was considered an eligible man
among his regular circle of acquaintances, many of whom must have

been impressed by his doubtless frequent and impassioned conversations on the subject, and he has left us ample evidence of his strong susceptibility to female beauty. If he ever engaged in sexual relations during the three years of separation from his wife, however, posterity has no knowledge of it.

We do know, however, that during the mid-1640s Milton surrounded himself with a circle of avant-garde artists and thinkers of the kind often attracted to revolutionary situations. By the late twentieth century the world would grow weary of such madcap enthusiasts who generally herald the disastrous collapse of the causes they attempt to espouse, but the intellectuals of London in the 1640s were not nearly so jaded. The half-Polish polymath Samuel Hartlib was buzzing around town, full of schemes for the "reformation" of every sphere of life, public and private. He attached himself to Milton and elicited from him a privately published epistle, *Of Education,* in which Milton laid out detailed plans for the production of good Commonwealth-men. He notes the lack of systematic program of ideological "endoctrinating," "for the want whereof this Nation perishes" (2:363), and he announces his conviction that a "compleat and generous Education [is] that which fits a man to perform justly, skilfully and magnanimously all the offices both private and publick of Peace and War" (2:378–9). Milton's tone throughout the tract is notably republican rather than Puritan: he wants to train the youth for full participation in the *res publica,* not merely for the contemplation of divinity. Virtue is for Milton always a positive, active quality, never the mere absence of vice. And this tract makes it clear that Milton perceived a worrying absence of virtue in England as he wrote. After describing what he considers a necessary regime of military training in his ideal academy, he inserts a jibe at the recent military failures of the pre-Cromwellian parliamentary armies:

They would not then, if they were trusted with fair and hopeful armies, suffer them for want of just and wise discipline to shed away from about them like sick feathers, though they be never so oft suppli'd: they would not suffer their empty and unrecruitable Colonels of twenty men in a Company to quaff out, or convey into secret hoards, the wages of a delusive list, and a miserable remnant: yet in the mean while to be over-master'd with a score or two of drunkards, the only souldery left about them, or else to comply with all rapines and violences. No certainly, if they knew ought of that knowledge that belongs to good men or good Governours, they would not suffer these things. (2:412)

It was precisely this sort of cowardice and corruption that Cromwell was engaged in rooting out as he shaped the New Model Army into the most powerful fighting force since ancient Rome, and Milton evidently finds it impossible to avoid introducing such topical issues into his tract. He would certainly have discussed them, as well as the copious moral and practical challenges wrought by the revolution, with the coterie that gathered regularly at his houses in Petty France and, later, High Holborn. Hartlib was noisily prominent, but the circle also included John Dury, Robert Boyle, Charles Culpeper, the great Bohemian philosopher Comenius and, unusually, a significant number of learned women, including Lady Ranelagh. Milton was also augmenting the size of his own school, adding such scions of the nobility as the Earl of Barrymore and Sir Thomas Gardiner, as well as Cyriack Skinner, the grandson of Sir Edward Coke, and three or four others whom his nephew remembers as "the sons of some gentlemen that were his intimate friends" (1,032). Throughout the mid-1640s the Milton household must have throbbed with intellectual debates as vigorous as any of the battles in which the

English nation was tearing itself apart on the fields of Marston Moor, Naseby and Worcester.

It was a time and a place when quite literally anything seemed possible, up to and including the Second Coming. London remained in ferment as gangs of iconoclasts roamed the streets, engaging in pitched battles with the defenders of images as they attempted to reform the city's physical appearance by direct action. Many, though not all, of their destructive offensives were officially sanctioned. On April 24, 1643, the House of Commons sent a working party into Westminster Abbey to smash the most obnoxious of the icons. The previous month a mob had hurled the priceless Rubens altarpiece of Somerset House into the river Thames. Soldiers publicly wiped their bottoms with pages torn from the Book of Common Prayer. In May 1643 the great cross that stood in Cheapside, long the site of regular brawls between iconoclasts and iconodules, was finally pulled down by order of the Parliamentary Committee for the Demolition of Monuments of Superstition and Idolatry. People on both sides were fully cognizant of the decisive impact of images on the mind, and the battles that raged around London's icons and statues was arguably as important in deciding the war's outcome as the military campaigns waged throughout the country.

Civil wars are often fratricidal, and the Powells were not Milton's only Royalist relatives. His brother Christopher, a convert to Catholicism, was a musketeer in the King's army stationed in Reading, where he lived with his family and Milton's eighty-year-old father. When the Parliamentarians took the city in April 1643, Christopher's family moved to London, while Christopher himself escaped to continue his support for the Royalists. But the brothers do not appear to have allowed their political differences to affect their personal relationship. As far as we know they remained close throughout their lives, and at the height of hostilities in June 1643,

Christopher Milton baptized his new son John. Christopher peers out of
the historical record as more of a private, family man than his brother,
and certainly less fanatical in his devotion to political or religious causes.
In 1646 he found no difficulty in taking the covenant, thereby expressing allegiance to Parliament and Presbyterianism, against both of which
he had recently been in arms. Nor was he unusual in this. Thousands of
Englishmen did the same, and Christopher certainly appears the more
human, though the less heroic, of the brothers Milton.

Relations with the Powells were not so smooth. Throughout the early
1640s Milton's struggles against his Royalist in-laws merged and combined with Parliament's war against the king. In 1644 Richard Powell
ceased paying the interest on his loan from Milton. If he hoped for indulgence from his hostile son-in-law he was grievously disappointed, and it is
more probable that his default was a deliberate act of provocation. Perhaps
by this stage Powell no longer cared for the opinion of the strange, book-
ish, Puritan usurer who happened to be married to his daughter. Milton
immediately began proceedings aimed at literally removing the roof from
over his wife's head: he tried to levy his debts against Powell's real estate.
The families were now locked in combat on multiple fronts, but it was
military events that determined the outcome. The Powells emerge from
the story as an amiably unprincipled, jollily blundering, cheerfully oppor-
tunistic family. Like most people in any age, they were ready to trim their
politics to the prevailing winds. In 1642 these had seemed to be blowing
strongly against Parliament, and the Powells took steps to distance their
daughter from the company of its adherents. Until the battle of Marston
Moor in July 1644, Richard Powell's relations with his son-in-law were
distant and cool. After that, however, the tide began to turn, and by the
middle of 1645 it was obvious that some kind of parliamentary rule
would soon be established.

It was at this juncture that the Powells learned of Milton's marriage proposal to Mary Davis. Of course such a match would be illegal, but there was no telling what strange new laws might be introduced by a revolutionary government. Like all other Royalist "malignants," Richard Powell was now suffering the sequestration of much of his property. He badly needed friends among the nation's new governors, and the prospect of permanently losing a prospective ally in Milton must have worried him. He happened to be on friendly terms with a family named Blackborough, who were related to Milton, and through them he engineered a scenario that must have been as traumatic as it sounds dramatic. According to Edward Phillips:

> he [Milton] making the usual visit [to his relative Blackborough], the Wife was ready in another Room, and on a sudden he was surprised to see one whom he thought to have never seen more, making Submission and begging Pardon on her Knees before him; he might probably at first make some shew of aversion and rejection; but partly his own generous nature, more inclinable to Reconciliation than to perseverance in Anger and Revenge; and partly the strong intercession of Friends on both sides, soon brought him to an Act of Oblivion, and a firm League of Peace for the future.[7]

Milton's willing reconciliation with his wife shows a remarkably magnanimous spirit. Perhaps, having so recently been rejected by Mary Davis, and entertaining no hope that his project for legalizing divorce could make any headway, he simply felt that he had no choice. Or perhaps he really was a saintly, forgiving, tender-hearted gentleman. The rebarbartive tone he adopts in his pamphlets does not necessarily exclude that possibility. In any case, there followed a period of domestic upheaval that must have tested his generosity to its limits, as well as made it virtually impossible for him to pursue any serious literary projects. He already shared his house in the Barbican with his father and several of his pupils. In May 1646 Oxford was besieged and the Powells' lands seized. Fleeing their conquered home-town, Mary's parents and five of their other children now moved in with the Miltons at the Barbican. Richard Powell died on January 1, 1647, still owing Milton £1,372, for which he was unsuccessfully sued in court by Powell's other debtors. In August 1647 Powell's holdings in Wheatley were appraised, seized by Parliament and, in November, awarded to Milton as collateral for his debt. Meanwhile in March, Powell had been followed to the grave by John Milton senior, aged eighty-four, which must have been a far more profound loss to his devoted son. He did not have the chance to mourn in solitude; Powell's widow and children remained in Milton's home until August, and on July 29, 1647, this noisy household received the new addition of Milton's first child, Anne.

One wonders how much contact Milton had with the baby; fathers were not usually much involved in the nursing of infants, and Anne was surrounded by seven energetic matrilineal relatives. It gradually became clear that the child was both mentally and physically disabled. It is just possible that she had been healthy at birth; Edward Phillips comments that "whether by ill constitution, or want of care, she grew more and more decrepit,"[8] which would appear to imply that a disappointingly female baby did not rank very high among the priorities of any resident of the Barbican household. We do not know the exact nature of her malady, but it was severe enough to quench any hopes Milton may have had of her developing into the kind of intellectual "help-meet" he so desperately desired. The atmosphere of the family residence even before the birth of the baby is captured in a gloomy letter Milton wrote to his old Florentine friend Carlo Dati in April 1647:

Soon an even heavier mood creeps over me, a mood in which I am
accustomed often to bewail my lot, to lament that those whom perhaps proximity or some unprofitable tie has bound to me, whether
by accident or by law, those, commendable in no other way, daily
sit beside me, weary me, even exhaust me, in fact—as often as
they please; whereas those whom character, temperament, interests had so finely united are so nearly all grudged me by death
or most hostile distance are for the most part so quickly torn from
my sight that I am forced to live in almost perpetual solitude.
(2:762–3)

Surrounded by private and public chaos, Milton secluded himself as
best he could, plugging dutifully away at what today would be considered
the workaday tasks of a middle-ranking academic. He labored over treatises on grammar and rhetoric, as well as histories of Russia and Britain,
but these worthy works would not appear in print for decades. Milton's
ambition evidently felt the need for some more immediate source of literary repute, and in October 1645 he assembled the many, disparate and
various poems he had composed since his youth and registered this collection for publication by Humphrey Moseley. Moseley was a Royalist
and had also published Waller, Carew and Suckling, all of whom were
associated with the Cavalier cause and all of whose work sold far better
than Milton's. The choice of publisher suggests that Milton was trying to
put some distance between his reputation as a radical pamphleteer and
any renown he might earn as a largely apolitical poet.

It is an odd volume is many ways. Scorning any other attempt at formal or thematic coherence than the personality of its author, it contains
a bewildering variety of verses written for widely divergent occasions
over a twenty-year period, in both Latin and English, including many

epistles formally designed as private correspondence. Many of its con-
tents, like "L'Allegro," "Il Penseroso" and "Lycidas," rank among the
finest ever compositions in any language, but the book lacks all unity.
All that links these poems together is the fact that they were written by
Milton. Once again we get the strong sense that his real purpose was
to put down a marker for posterity. These poems tell his interior biography in verse, detailing his pubescent lusts, his adolescent dalliances,
his mature romances, the varied public figures who attracted his admiration, conversations with revered older men, and theological mediations
on virtue, heroism and death. The author is referred to as "John Milton,
Londoner," proudly affirming the revolutionary city's formative influence
on his soul, but there are few other indications that the poet would soon
be among the most renowned political radicals in Europe.

The impression that the book's true subject is its author is reinforced
by the comic controversy that developed around the engraving of Milton
on the volume's frontispiece. An artist named William Marshall had been
engaged for the task, but, whether through temporary incompetence or
deliberate malice (for Milton now had many enemies likely to be associated with a publishing house of Royalist sympathies), the engraver produced a picture of a hideously deformed, bug-eyed, drooling buffoon.
It looks nothing whatsoever like the other pictures we have of Milton,
which show him to have been (as he did not neglect to remind us) an
unusually handsome man. Perhaps there was no time or money to find
another engraver, or perhaps Milton saw a chance to display his wit in
response to Marshall's insulting portrait. It remained in the printed version, but Milton asked the artist to append a verse in Greek, a language
that he evidently did not know. An English translation reads: "You, who
really know my face, / Fail to find me in this place. / Portraiture the fool
pretends; / Laugh at the result, my friends."[9] As throughout his prose

pamphlets, Milton responds to misrepresentation with learned mockery that only he and his intended "fit audience though few" will understand. The best part of the joke is that its butt fails to understand the humor, but an unmistakable vanity also adheres to its author. Neither is this impression vitiated by the inclusion of sundry commendatory verses from Milton's English and Italian friends attesting to his brilliance and erudition.

But the 1645 *Poems* fell on deaf ears. The volume sold badly, and so far as we know, it was entirely ignored outside the close circle of Milton's personal acquaintances. Disappointment must have combined with domestic disruption to quell Milton's muse, and between 1645 and 1648 he wrote very little. The major reason for this temporary silence, however, was presumably far more serious. Milton, whose life from childhood had been entirely made up of more or less constant reading and writing, and who had always conceived of his skill in these endeavors as a sacred, inviolable gift from God, was gradually, painfully, but by 1645 undeniably going blind. Since he was old enough to hold a book he had been reading, by flickering candlelight, until the early hours of the morning, and although his father had read without spectacles until his death, his mother had suffered serious problems with her vision. Milton's eye pain started in August 1644, as he labored feverishly over *Areopagitica,* and over the next five years his view of the world was steadily, inexorably obscured by a cloudy, creamy whiteness that filled first one eye, then the other, ultimately becoming the blankly invariant prospect that greeted him every morning and remained with him all day, every day.

Going blind is an agonizing ordeal for anybody at any time. I do not think, however, that it is too much to claim that for John Milton in 1644, blindness was an even more devastating fate than usual. This was partly due to the nature of his vocation: a man who lives by reading and writing can deal with any other physical disability, but hardly with blindness. Milton's suffering was doubtless exacerbated, and may well have been caused, by the nervous strain he must have suffered during the separation and reconciliation with his wife and her family. Worst of all, however, must have been the nagging suspicion that his encroaching blindness was a message from God. Physical sight and its absence were constantly used, then as now, as metaphors for intellectual insight and its opposite. Milton himself had frequently drawn on this tropological device. In his very first published pamphlet, *Of Reformation*, he had used it to suggest that human understanding is systematically inadequate to the apprehension of truth:

> The very essence of Truth is plainnesse, and brightnes; the darknes and crookednesse is our own. The Wisdom of God created understanding, fit and proportionable to Truth the object, and end of it, as the eye to the thing visible. If our understanding have a film of ignorance over it, or be blear with gazing on other false glisterings, what is that to Truth? (1:566)

At this early stage of his career, Milton still believed it might be possible to "purge with sovrain eyesalve that intellectual ray which God hath planted in us" (ibid.), to reform people's minds through political revolution. Later he would conclude that error is an ineradicable condition of fallen humanity, although it never occurred to him that the error might be his own. Milton's confidence in his own powers of reasoning was always absolute. It needed to be: his use of the metaphor of eyesight for insight would return to plague him once his own sight had failed. He later recalled that in late 1644:

I noticed my sight becoming weak and growing dim, and at the
same time my spleen and all my viscera burdened and shaken with
flatulence. And even in the morning, if I began as usual to read, I
noticed that my eyes felt immediate pain deep within and turned
from reading, though later refreshed after moderate bodily exercise; as often as I looked at a lamp, a sort of rainbow seemed
to obscure it. Soon a mist appearing in the left part of the left
eye (for that eye became clouded some years before the other)
removed from my sight everything on that side.[10]

The process of going blind was gradual for Milton and must have
been yet more tortuous for that reason. His enemies frequently seized on
it as evidence of divine retribution for his heresies, but Milton responded
with magnificent aplomb. From his very earliest work he had been preoccupied by the concept of the "blind seer" and had always envisioned
himself as the inheritor of the reputedly blind prophet-poets of classical
mythology. His affliction struck him as confirmation of his prophetic status and redoubled his already prodigious confidence in his divine vocation.
He announced this to the public by adopting the defiant motto "in weakness my strength is made perfect."

IV

WHILE MILTON WRESTLED with the physical and psychological demons
that afflicted him and stilled his pen during these years, the fate of the
nation was being decided in dramatic, theatrical fashion. In January 1647
the Scots finally wearied of King Charles's intransigent duplicity and
handed him over to the English Parliament. In so doing they unwittingly

signed his death warrant, for the balance of power in England was about to change. The Presbyterian-dominated Parliamentarians were comfortable in the assumption that they would be able to cut a deal with Charles. All that remained was to disband the army, which had by this time outlived its usefulness by achieving its spectacularly glorious and courageous victories. It was true that the soldiers had not been paid, but never in the past had that presented much of a problem in dispersing the disorderly and drunken rabble that had always made up earlier English armies.

The New Model Army was very different. They were not drunk; in fact they were often fanatically sober. They were not motivated by plunder or rapine; they marched into battle singing Psalms and amused themselves around the campfire by debating the nature of the Holy Ghost or the correct location of church altar rails. Through tracts like Milton's, as well as many others, they had absorbed the principles of classical republicanism, which taught that active participation in government was a necessary component of personal virtue. Their religion frequently took an antinomian form, leaving them poorly disposed toward earthly authority in general and advocates of a Presbyterian state-church in particular. The deposition of the King had raised doubts in many minds about the general legitimacy of inherited power, or even inherited wealth. Communistic groups like the Diggers began taking matters into their own hands, setting up camp on common land and advocating the reclamation of all land from private ownership, which they interpreted as the same kind of tyrannical usurpation that characterized monarchy in the republican view. Furthermore, radicals within the army had used the period since the cessation of hostilities to organize themselves; several individual regiments had elected Agitators to represent their interests, and these tended to form alliances with the emergent political grouping known as the Levellers. Although not quite outright democrats (generally they favored household, as opposed

to manhood, suffrage), the Levellers were by some distance the most radically egalitarian political force England had ever witnessed. As the breadth
and depth of their support among a large and well-disciplined body of
armed men became clear, the Presbyterian aristocrats took serious, well-
justified alarm.

The New Model Army began bombarding Parliament with petitions
for the redress of grievances. In June 1647 they assembled at Newmarket
to pass the Solemn Engagement, vowing not to disband until their demands
for religious tolerance and an extended franchise had been met. On June
3 the lowly officer Cornet Joyce personally abducted King Charles from
the custody of Parliament and placed him under the control of the army.
In August the army marched into London and set up camp at Putney. The
situation was now unmistakably revolutionary, and swift, decisive action
by the Levellers might well have changed the course of English and world
history. Instead, in archetypically English fashion, they held a debate. The
Levellers formulated a republican, quasi-democratic manifesto known
as the *Agreement of the People,* which included the remarkably and, to
some, terrifyingly radical declaration that "all power is originally and
essentially in the whole body of the people."

The political logic behind this claim was to eliminate the need for representatives mediating between the people and government. The people, it
suggested, needed no representatives; they could govern themselves. This
is the same logic that inspired religious iconoclasm, which seeks to remove
representational intermediaries between the human mind and its Creator.
It is also the logic that guided the witch hunts and the semi-official campaign against magic that was being conducted throughout Europe. Magic
is the use of representation to achieve objective ends, and like political
democrats and religious iconoclasts, the witch hunters were dedicated
to tearing down the power of representation. Between October 28 and

November 11, 1647, the army debated the *Agreement of the People* at
Putney, just outside (but threateningly close to) London. The Leveller
leader Thomas Rainsborough famously insisted that "the poorest he that
is in England has a life to live, as the greatest he: and therefore truly, sir,
I think it's clear, that every man that is to live under a government ought
first by his own consent to put himself under that government."[11] But
the army "Grandees" led by Cromwell retorted that only those with a
material stake in the country deserved a voice in its government and so
demanded that any new constitution must include a property qualification for the franchise and a permanent stake in power for both the House
of Lords and the King. Cromwell understood the severity of the threat
posed by the Levellers very well. As he declared, pounding on the table
during a meeting of the Council of State: "[Y]ou have no other way to
deal with these men but to break them in pieces. If you do not break them,
they will break you."[12]

There was a real possibility that England might become a democracy
in 1649. But on November 11 a dramatic and suspicious event took place
that abruptly put an end to the increasingly acrimonious Putney debates.
King Charles escaped from army custody to Carisbrooke Castle on the
Isle of Wight, where he was promptly imprisoned again by its governor.
The King had apparently been induced to this extremity by being given
to understand that certain violent radicals among the Levellers intended
to assassinate him. But the apparent irrationality of his behavior, combined with his erroneous belief that the governor of Carisbrooke would
be sympathetic to his cause, led many to perceive the hand of Cromwell
behind the escape. The Grandees' position was now immensely strengthened, since they rather than the Agitators had control over the King's body.
Andrew Marvell captured the public mood of skepticism when he wrote
of Cromwell: "twining subtle fears with hope, / He wove a net of such

a scope / That Charles himself might chase / To Caresbrooke's narrow case."[13] At this point Royalist risings, now allied with the English and Scots Presbyterians, broke out in Wales and the west country, and the army was ordered into what became the "second civil war" with its demands still unmet. Several regiments mutinied, but their protests were suppressed by force, and the battle against the Royalists recommenced. The English revolutionary moment had passed, never to return. After prolonged and bloody fighting, particularly in South Wales, Cromwell finally crushed the Royalists and the Scots, thus firmly establishing himself as the preeminent power in the realm. This time he was in no mood for clemency. In December 1648 Colonel Pride forcibly purged Parliament of its Presbyterian members, leaving only a "Rump" of Cromwell's Independent supporters, who now had all of England, including its King, firmly at their mercy.

Milton had not been directly involved in these events, although he had composed several occasional poems reflecting upon them. In 1648, while the Parliamentary general Sir Thomas Fairfax was besieging Colchester, Milton dedicated, and probably sent, a sonnet to him. It is notable for its assumption that the English revolution was merely the precursor of a worldwide republican movement; Fairfax's martial exploits are said to "daunt remotest kings."[14] The sestet makes the more detailed point that the only way to put an end to the apparently ceaseless round of rebellion and revolt is to firmly and conclusively establish the separation of church and state:

> O yet a nobler task awaites thy hand;
> For what can Warrs, but endless Warr still breed,
> Till Truth, & Right from Violence be freed,
> And Public Faith cleard from the shamefull brand
> Of Public Fraud. In vain doth Valour bleed
> While Avarice, & Rapine share the land. (9–14) (Sonnet XV, 159)

The "violence" to which Milton refers is the state's attempt to coerce its subjects into accepting a single religion. This is the "public fraud" that will inevitably permit "avarice and rapine" to pillage England, since the events of the past eight years had made it perfectly clear that many English people would resist to the death any attempt at coercive conformity. The only way to peace, Milton informs Fairfax (whose own opinions on the matter were very different), is to allow people to pursue their "public faith" unmolested by civil or ecclesiastical authority.

In early 1648 Milton translated Psalms 80 though 88, with their reflections on moral and physical "darkness" and its relation to physical struggle against earthly enemies. He continued work on his *History of Britain,* to which he appended a stinging criticism of the Long Parliament's betrayal of the revolution. It is interesting to note that Milton connects the alleged lack of principle displayed by many of the Presbyterian Members of Parliament with the commercial background from which they sprang: "Some who had bin calld from shops & warehouses without other merit to sit in supreme councel[s] and committees, as thir breeding was, fell to huckster the common-wealth" (5:445). This is rather rich coming from a professional usurer, and Milton somewhat undermines his case by proceeding to lament the financial misfortune he has himself suffered: "They in the meane while who were ever faithfullest to thir cause, and freely aided them in person, or with thir substance [were] . . . slighted soone after and quite bereav'd of thir just debts by greedy sequestration" (5:447). He complains here that Richard Powell's estate, which Milton had acquired through unabashed and ruthless usury, had been sequestered for the purposes of Parliament rather than transferred to Milton personally. This is not the poet's most public-spirited or attractive moment, but it can perhaps be excused by the continuing domestic turmoil surrounding him as his sight continued to fail. The birth of his second daughter, Mary, in October 1648 indicates that relations with his wife were by now reasonably harmonious, but in general Milton seems to have been kept out of active political involvement by personal travails between 1645 and 1648. In that year, however, as the revolution approached its most critical moment, Milton returned to the fray. And this time his intervention was to make him world famous forever.

6

KILLING NO MURDER

I

COLONEL PRIDE'S PURGE of Parliament attempted to secure the gains of the radicals by limiting England's government to a single "party," although that term was not yet being used in the modern sense. It expelled the Presbyterians, leaving the Independents as the effective government of England. On January 4, 1649, the "Rump" Parliament declared itself the supreme power in the realm. As with the French Jacobins or the Russian Bolsheviks, the group of English revolutionaries now in power had ideas and a program far more radical than those desired, or even imagined, by the general population. Two days later the Rump signaled the arts by which it intended to maintain its power by appointing a commission of 135 members to place King Charles on trial for treason. The very idea was inconceivably counterintuitive to many people. Since the centralization of state power begun by the Tudors, English people had grown accustomed to identifying the state with the person of the monarch, and this notion had sunk deep psychological roots throughout the populace. In literary texts like Shakespeare's *Macbeth*, regicide is treated as a form of suicide:

killing the King is like a man's severing his own head. Nor did the microcosmic social implications of the King's trial escape perceptive observers;
if the King was the "father" of the nation, then rebellion against him was
analogous to, and quite possibly causative of, a breakdown of patriarchal
authority in general. Shakespeare's *King Lear* depicts the degeneration
of monarchical power as inseparable from the dissolution of a father's
authority over his children. For many seventeenth-century English people,
including many of the rebels who had fought against him, King Charles
was a divinely anointed ruler. It was one thing to force him to negotiate and compromise, but to depose him was nothing short of rebellion
against God himself. To kill the King was to commit an unthinkable,
unforgivable sin.

Unwilling to stain their hands with royal blood, eighty of the appointed
commissioners immediately resigned their positions. This was a damaging
blow to the Rump's legitimacy, particularly in view of the fact that many
of the army's most prominent leaders, including Thomas Fairfax himself,
were among the resigners. It was clear that any legal moves against the
King would have to be immediate and irrevocable, for such support as
remained for putting him on trial would soon evaporate entirely. During
his increasingly lengthy private prayer sessions, Oliver Cromwell was
being led to the conclusion that Charles was a tyrant and a traitor and,
more surprisingly, that these were capital offences in a monarch. The trial
began on January 20, and the presiding judge was Milton's personal lawyer, John Bradshaw. Bradshaw was a close friend of the poet's (in 1654
Milton would describe him as "the friend whom I most revere") (4.i.676)
and had acted on his behalf during his endless disputes with the Powell
family. As a member of the intimate circle of radical London intellectuals,
Milton now found that many of his close acquaintances were suddenly
wielding power of life and death over their monarch. We can presume

that some among them encouraged him to return to literary pursuits, this time employing his pen in the service of political revolution rather than domestic or religious liberation.

During the King's ten-day trial London was awash in furious propaganda pouring forth from every direction. The Presbyterians were campaigning ferociously to save the King's life, inveighing against the authority of the Rump, which they regarded as simple usurpation. The Royalists, many of whom were now in exile, were hatching plots of violent desperation. The Levellers, defeated within the army but still powerful on the streets, raised tumults to hasten what they saw as divine vengeance on a tyrant. Yet more radical groups such as the Fifth Monarchists were emerging, intoxicated with the faith that judgment on the King heralded the return of King Jesus promised in the Book of Revelation. We must recall again that Milton's contemporaries lacked our experience of political revolutions; they were living through events so unprecedented that most people could understand them only as the direct hand of the Almighty.

The King conducted himself at his trial with such resolution and sagacity as might have saved his crown had he displayed them earlier. He declined to recognize the court's legitimacy, refused to remove his hat during its sessions and responded to all questioning by demanding by what authority he was being tried. It was an excellent question, to which the Rumpers had no convincing answer. It was a question that had never even been asked before, let alone answered. In such situations dangerously radical minds—minds innovative to the point of eccentricity, minds original to a degree that in ordinary times makes them look absurd—can, for a while, make themselves important. Milton's time had come, and in this atmosphere of turmoil and panic, he finally managed to forget his domestic difficulties and return to serious work. Throughout the trial he toiled feverishly at a tract aiming at its vindication. Whether he undertook the task at his own initiative or was prompted by his friends among the judges, the result of his efforts, published in February 1649 as *The Tenure of Kings and Magistrates,* certainly reads like an official justification of the revolutionary government's action.

By the time it was published, Charles was already dead. His head was severed on January 30, 1649, in front of a large crowd outside the banqueting hall at Westminster. Reports agree that, at the moment the axe fell, an eerie keening emanated from the stunned throng. As one observer reported: "The blow I saw given, and can truly say with a sad heart, at the instant whereof, I remember well, there was such a groan by the thousands than present as I never heard before and desire I may never hear again."[1] Almost no one had foreseen this, hardly anyone approved of it, and most people were left absolutely terrified at the action's enormity. A less noble mind than Milton's might have produced a querulous, half-hearted, guilty rationalization of this awe-inspiring deed. To defend such an act was to become complicit in it and permanently to earn the deadly enmity of highly dangerous men. It was to endorse an event that had shocked the world, including the people who had carried it out. It was to set oneself up as a symbol of the revolution and a tempting, easy target for its enemies, who would soon begin assassinating those involved in the King's trial. Isaac Dorislaus, who had helped draw up the charges against Charles, was murdered in the Hague by exiled Royalists in May 1649. Anthony Ascham, the Commonwealth's ambassador to Spain, met a similar fate a year later. To justify in print the trial and execution of a reigning monarch was, in short, an act of astonishing bravery.

Milton did not merely justify the regicide. He celebrated it. He believed it to be a momentous step forward on the road of human progress. In *The Tenure,* the execution of a tyrant is not presented as a dire necessity or a regrettably unavoidable exigency. It is called a deed of "majesty and grandeur." It is claimed as a heroic act, an "impartial and noble piece of justice" (3:311). The radicalism of this claim was not approached by other revolutionaries for over a century, and it has never been surpassed. The breathtaking daring of Milton's argument can be gleaned from the title of the book's 1650 edition:

> The Tenure of Kings and Magistrates: Proving, That it is Lawfull, and hath been held so through all Ages, for any, who have the Power, to call to account a Tyrant, or wicked King, and after due conviction, to depose, and put him to death; if the ordinary Magistrate have neglected, or deny'd to doe it. (3:189)

The key phrase here is "for any." Milton is not arguing that a representative body, or a properly constituted authority, or even a revolutionary vanguard has the right to kill a tyrant. He argues that anyone has that right, albeit "after due conviction." Some form of legal process is necessary, but the objective fact of a ruler's tyranny in itself justifies revolution. The authority of "the ordinary Magistrate" can be swept aside if it fails to put an end to tyranny. What this argument clearly demands is an unambiguous, objective definition of a tyrant. Many political theorists of the day connected tyranny with usurpation; thus if a King had inherited the crown legitimately he could not possibly be a tyrant. Obviously such an understanding of tyranny was of no use in justifying Charles's execution. Milton therefore looks back to Aristotle for his definition: "A Tyrant whether by wrong or by right comming to the Crown, is he who regarding neither Law nor the common good, reigns onely for himself and his faction" (3:212).

Milton's reasoning here, as throughout his life, is teleological. For Aristotle, any thing's identity is defined by its end or purpose, its *telos* in Greek. So in order to explain what a king is, Milton first asks what a king is *for*: what is the purpose of monarch, of a monarchy? He answers that the purpose of a king, as of any government, is the good of the people as a whole. Once again, Milton extrapolates from the rights of an individual man, the most fundamental of which, he declares, is "self-defence and preservation." The purpose of centralized political authority is simply, and only, to expand this right to society as a whole. Milton approaches the anarchistic when he declares that there can be no other possible justification for political authority: "[T]o him that shall consider well why among free Persons, one man by civil right should beare autority and jurisdiction over another, no other end or reason can be imaginable" (3:199). This leads him into an egalitarian scorn for the quasi-idolatrous bowing, scraping and flattering that inevitably constitute court culture:

> It being thus manifest that the power of Kings and Magistrates is nothing else, but what is only derivative, transferr'd and committed to them in trust from the People, to the Common good of them all, in whom the power yet remaines fundamentally, and cannot be tak'n from them, without a violation of thir natural birthright, and seeing that from hence *Aristotle* and the best of Political writers have defin'd a King, him who governs to the good and profit of his People, and not for his own ends, it follows from necessary causes, that the Titles of Sov'ran Lord, natural Lord, and the like, are either arrogancies, or flatteries. (3:202)

This repudiation of aristocratic culture played an important role in emboldening the revolutionaries in their struggle against the King. Milton had rehearsed it as far back as 1634, in *Comus*, where the Lady accepts what appears to be a shepherd's "honest offer'd courtesy, / Which oft is sooner found in lowly sheds / With smoky rafters, than in tap'stry Halls / And courts of Princes, where it first was nam'd, / And yet is most pretended" (322–6). In such passages Milton lays the basis for the republican cultural attitudes that, after intermittent periods of hibernation, would revive to trouble the courts of James II and, later, Louis XVII and George III. The American Revolution was particularly Miltonic in inspiration, and despite the intellectual content of Milton's prose, it breathes a democratic spirit that has led many modern Americans to claim him as one of their own. The author of Milton's first American biography went so far as to assert that "religious and political America sprang from [Milton's] brain."[2] And certainly the disdain for pomp, deference and ceremony that Milton always displays has historically been regarded as characteristic of the American psyche. Milton's political writing is engaged in manufacturing a republican culture, as well as in arguing for republican politics. When he declares that political authority is "transferr'd and committed to [Kings] in trust from the People," he makes a point that is as much social as directly political. He does not only oppose monarchy, he protests against the attitudes of social deference that monarchy promotes. This is an attitude that would, over the succeeding generations, seep gradually into the minds of ordinary people whose forefathers had been tugging their forelocks to their social superiors for millennia.

In other words, *The Tenure* is an attempt to convince people to stop behaving slavishly. This is no easy matter, since throughout most of civilized human history, most people have been slaves. The habits and thought processes of slavery have become so deeply ingrained as almost to be part of human nature itself. In *Eikonoklastes* Milton describes this servile mentality as deliberately cultivated by Royalist politicians, who work "by subduing first the Consciences of Vulgar men, with the insensible poyson of thir slavish Doctrin . . ." (3:578). But slavish doctrines often fell on fertile soil. Even today, when legal slavery is abolished, most people remain slaves in the sense that they must sell part of their time,

every day, in order to survive. Milton would have found confirmation
of their servile status in the fact that they see nothing amiss in this situation; most people probably accept that selling their life to another, and
spending their life serving the purposes of another, is their natural and
inevitable fate. Economic slavery brings psychological slavery along with
it, and for most people slavery appears as nothing less than the human
condition itself. To be human is to be a slave. It is this situation that
Milton seeks to challenge in passages such as this:

> to say, as is usual, the King hath as good right to his Crown and
> dignitie, as any man to his inheritance, is to make the Subject no
> better then the Kings slave, his chattell, or his possession that may
> be bought and sould. And doubtless if hereditary title were suffi-
> ciently inquir'd, the best foundation of it would be found either but
> in courtesie or convenience. But suppose it to be of right heredita-
> rie, what can be more just and legal, if a subject for certain crimes
> be to forfet by Law from himself, and posterity, all his inheritance
> to the King, then that a King for crimes proportional, should forfet
> all his title and inheritance to the people: unless the people must
> be thought created all for him, he not for them, and they all in one
> body inferior to him single, which were a kinde of treason against
> the dignitie of mankind to affirm. (3:203–4)

Again the reasoning is teleological: the people were not created for
the King, but the King was created for the people. If the King fails to fulfill the role for which he was created, he has already ceased to be a King.
There is no need to depose him—he has deposed himself. All the people
have to do is call him to account for his crimes, and since he is no longer
a king but a private person, there should be no legal impediment to doing
so. This probably seems perfectly logical to most readers today, but we

should guard against the arrogant assumption that we have eradicated the slavish mentality that made the trial and execution of a reigning monarch seem so horrific to most seventeenth-century English people. The most startlingly modern, or rather postmodern, aspect of *The Tenure of Kings and Magistrates* is its serene certainty of a direct correlation between the personal and the political. The tract's opening sentences make this point, while also alluding to Milton's own domestic arrangements and their relation to his political opinions:

> If men within themselves would be govern'd by reason, and not generally give up thir understanding to a double tyranny of Custom from without, and blind affections within, they would discerne better, what it is to favour and uphold the Tyrant of a Nation. But being slaves within doors, no wonder that they strive so much to have the public State conformably govern'd to the inward vitious rule, by which they govern themselves. For indeed none can love freedom heartilie, but good men; the rest love not freedom, but licence; which never hath more scope or more indulgence then under Tyrants. Hence is it that Tyrants are not oft offended, nor stand much in doubt of bad men, as being all naturally servile; but in whom vertue and true worth most is eminent, them they feare in earnest, as by right thir Maisters, against them lies all thir hatred and suspicion. (3:190)

The connection between the two revolutionary ideologies on which Milton is drawing here—classical republicanism and radical Protestantism—is clear and explicit. The right to mastery is conferred by virtue, not birth. Only a good man can know true liberty; a bad man will abuse his freedom by directing it toward the licentious pursuit of physical pleasures. Those who build their lives on the pursuit of physical pleasure enslave themselves, for such pleasures are shared with beasts and lack the definitively human element of rationality. A legal slave is one who serves the ends of another; a psychological slave is one who serves his appetite rather than his reason. In both cases, their servility is defined by their pursuit of an end other than that for which they are naturally designed. It is therefore in the interest of tyrants to foster sinful behavior as a means to enslave their subjects because sin, as the Bible also repeatedly stresses,[3] is slavery. Milton's contemporaries had only to think of the scandalous libertinism practiced at the Stuart courts to confirm the truth of his charges that sin, and therefore slavery, were deliberately fostered by tyrannical rulers. In *Eikonoklastes* he describes Charles's followers as "the ragged infantry of stews and brothels; the spawn and shipwreck of taverns and dicing houses . . ." (3:380–81). This was a view of ruling-class decadence that would be heartily endorsed by subsequent revolutionary Puritans well into the twentieth century. But the connection between individual moral rectitude and political liberation faded from popular view in the Western world during the 1960s, when libidinal excess and leftist politics were often associated, or rather confused. Today, when the tyranny of money over humanity forcibly demands incessant consumption and indulgence, so that it effectively becomes a duty, internalized through ubiquitous advertisement, the rationale behind Milton's ascetic radicalism may be clearer than it was a generation ago.

II

The Tenure of Kings and Magistrates is directed primarily against the Presbyterians. Milton felt personally aggrieved at their party, members of which had been most prominent in mocking and stigmatizing him as "the Divorcer." Here he exposes the alleged grief for Charles's fate, which

Presbyterians bewailed in hundreds of tracts during and after the trial, as rank hypocrisy. In a brilliant logical maneuver, Milton proves that Charles had already been deposed before his execution and that it had been the purportedly mournful Presbyterians who deposed him. Milton's argument depends upon the assumption that identity is relational. No man is an island; people become what they are by virtue of their relations to other people:

> We know that King and Subject are relatives, and relatives have no longer being then in the relation; the relation between King and Subject can be no other then regal autority and subjection. Hence I inferr past their defending, that if the Subject who is one relative, take away the relation, of force he takes away also the other relative; but the Presbyterians who were one relative, that is to say Subjects, have for this sev'n years tak'n away the relation, that is to say the Kings autority, and thir subjection to it, therfore the Presbyterians for these sev'n years have remov'd and extinguishd the other relative, that is to say the King, or to speak more in brief have depos'd him. (3:229–30)

A King and his subjects form a mutually definitive relationship. A King without subjects is no king at all; the subjects make the King what he is. The Presbyterians severed this relationship when they took up arms against the King, for a subject, by definition, does not fight against his ruler. If he does so, he is no longer a subject, and the ruler is no longer a ruler. The Presbyterians instituted divorce proceedings against Charles, but as they had already demonstrated by their blundering misreading of Milton's own divorce pamphlets, the Presbyterians understood neither the need for nor the nature of divorce. They made a fetish, an idol, of monarchy just as they did of marriage, and just as they did of God himself in their liturgical religious practices. Milton's advocacy of iconoclasm as a way of life emerges in religious form in the anti-episcopal tracts and expands into the private sphere in his writings on divorce. In his political tracts of the 1650s, it arrives at its logical destination as a theory of state politics. Even in the *Commonplace Book* Milton cites Augustine to show that "[i]f in governmental rule there is any servitude, actually the one in authority is the slave, rather than he who is subject to him" (1:417). He employs what today's philosophers would call a dialectical mode of reasoning to deconstruct existing power relations, by demonstrating that each element in the relation of ruler and ruled depends upon the other for its existence. This was an idea with a long and vigorous life ahead of it, a breakthrough in political thought that would be echoed in Hegel's master-slave dialectic, and eventually taken up by Karl Marx in his demonstration that capital is merely labor power in alienated, symbolic form.

From the moment of *The Tenure of Kings and Magistrates*'s publication two weeks after the King's death, Milton's personal fate was inextricably linked to the revolution. It was the first lengthy defense of the King's execution, and it took most people by surprise with its utterly unrepentant, even celebratory tone. The shell-shocked members of the Rump doubtless took heart from Milton's enthusiasm as they attempted to institute their program of political and religious reforms, reforms so radical that they have not been fully implemented in England to this day. The House of Lords was abolished on March 19, with the Commons declaring that this body had no right to exercise power "over the people whom they did not at all represent."[4] That summer the Royalist newspaper *Mercurius Pragmaticus* lamented that "these new Christians have taken care, that old things must pass away, and all things become new . . . by which means old England is now grown perfectly new, and we in another world."[5] Even before the King's death a new Great Seal representing the

Commonwealth had been struck; it featured an engraving of the House of Commons surrounded by the words "In the First Year of Freedom by God's blessing restored."[6]

The year 1649 was intended to be the English equivalent of Pol Pot's "year zero": a moment of total transformation of state and individual alike. The specter of Apocalypse haunts all Milton's prose from that year. Although he was far too level-headed to join the Fifth Monarchists or Quakers in their excited expectation of King Jesus's imminent accession, Milton's republicanism did clear the theoretical way for Christ's return by removing the antichristian rulers whose downfall was universally agreed to be a necessary precursor of the Second Coming. Yet more remarkable than Milton's ability to think such thoughts is the fact that the English government enthusiastically endorsed them. In fact *The Tenure of Kings and Magistrates* so impressed the revolutionary leaders that they were moved to offer Milton the only real job he ever held. On March 20, 1649, he took up the appointment of Secretary for Foreign Tongues to the Council of State.

The Council of State was the governing executive body of England, hastily assembled out of those Rumpers and army officers not held in panicked paralysis by the enormity of what they were doing. *The Tenure* may well have been privately commissioned by some of its members, with many of whom Milton had been personally acquainted for years: the Council's President John Bradshaw was his private lawyer, and another member, Luke Robinson, had been his contemporary at Christ's College, Cambridge. As Secretary for Foreign Tongues, Milton was charged with employing his prodigious linguistic gifts to translate and interpret correspondence from foreign powers, and also to compose the English government's responses. Many of the documents issued by the Council in the early 1650s have a Miltonic tone about them, and it is quite probable that the poet had a hand in formulating policy as well as transmitting it. The United Provinces of the Netherlands apart, all the states of Europe were ruled by monarchs, and they were naturally reluctant to recognize the Rump as England's legitimate government. The Council was fortunate indeed to find a man of Milton's linguistic talent to represent its case. Historically it is very unusual for a man of such intellectual gifts to find himself so close to the center of political power. It is remarkable that the English revolution was able to achieve any success at all, given how far in advance of common political assumptions its actions were, and Milton surely bears much of the credit for that success. He moved into new apartments in Whitehall, physically at the heart of the state, and one of the first tasks he was assigned involved the examination of the former king's private books and papers. It seems that he discovered ample confirmation of the ethically degenerate effects of royalty in the course of this duty, and his demeanor during his years in power is that of a man determined to put into practice his theories about the relation between the personal and the political, and above all to ensure that never again would the people of England suffer under the rule of a moral weakling.

Of course, the practical business of governing is far more morally delicate than the composition of abstract theoretical declarations. One of the fascinating spectacles of Milton in political power is the prospect of a man of rigid, inflexible principles coming to terms with the messy realities of practical politics. In particular, the advocacy of a relatively free press that Milton espoused in *Areopagitica* was difficult to sustain as a member of a government beset by furiously hostile adversaries, who now aimed at nothing less than the death of its members, Milton very much included. On May 12 John Bradshaw, in his capacity as Lord President of the Council, was asked by his colleagues to "prepare and bring in an Act concerning the prohibiting of the printing of invective and scandalous pamphlets against the Commonwealth:"[7] in other words, to introduce the kind of government censorship against which Milton had protested in 1644. The Press Act was eventually passed in September, and Milton left no public record of any objection. During 1649 he investigated the papers of several people suspected of treason against the new regime, acting as what we would now call an agent of the security state apparatus, or secret police. One of his targets was the continually incandescent William Prynne; another was Clement Walker, whose *Anarchia Anglicana* (1649) painted a woeful picture of England as a nation in chaos. In contrast to the Sex Pistols song that its title uncannily prefigures, Walker's tract is a conservative protest against what the author views as the dangerously novel and eccentric opinions that were sweeping the land in the revolution's wake. The Council ordered Milton to investigate this work in October, and the Secretary's eyebrows must have twitched as he perused Walker's litany of barking heresies:

> There is lately come forth a book of John Melton's (a Libertine, that thinketh his Wife a Manacle, and his very Garters to be Shackles and Fetters to him; one that (after the Independent fashion) will be tied by no obligation to God or Man), wherein he undertaketh to prove, That it is lawfull for any that have power to call to account, Depose, and put to Death wicked Kings and Tyrants (after due conviction) if the ordinary Magistrate neglect it. (199–200)[8]

The reference is to *The Tenure of Kings and Magistrates*, but it is interesting to note how Walker automatically connects Milton's "Libertine" attitude to marriage, and his "Independent" approach to religious discipline, to both his republicanism and his advocacy of violent means to republican ends. This was a chain of reasoning that Milton himself had described in his divorce pamphlets. All sides were aware that the issues

at stake in England's travails included ecclesiastical, civil and sexual politics, and even a more general attitude toward life as a whole. The terms
"Puritan" and "Cavalier" had, until recently, fallen from favor among
historians as ways of describing seventeenth-century psychologies, but
they were frequently used by contemporaries, and they capture the broad,
inclusive nature of the dispute with admirable acuity. For Milton and
Walker alike, Independent religion, republican politics and revolutionary
methods were interlinked aspects of an empirically indentifiable personality type. Milton would probably have accepted the title "Puritan," while
indignantly rejecting Walker's labeling of him as a "Libertine," but both
men recognized that their political views were part of a far wider spec-
trum of practices and beliefs combining to form a particular species of
character. Today the exigencies of postmodern, consumer capitalism are
encouraging an identity politics that in many ways recalls the seventeenth-
century warfare between Puritans and Cavaliers.

III

As a SENSATIONAL glorification of Charles I's execution, *The Tenure* automatically became notorious. It was also a commercial success and went
into a second edition by September. Milton was now too deeply implicated in the revolution to recant or retreat. Having celebrated the death of
the King as an act of noble heroism, to be repeated if possible throughout
the entire world, Milton was involved up to his neck, which stood every
chance of being severed if the fickle tide of political fortune should ever
turn. From now on he was writing for his life, and this shows in the frantic erudition, the panicky grasping for precedent and rationale and above
all in the savage, frightened ferocity that characterizes his prose from the
1650s. The stress cannot have been alleviated by his rapidly and painfully

declining eyesight. By the time he accepted his government post he was already completely blind in one eye, and in a letter of 1654, he recalls the travails he suffered over the next three or four years:

> Everything which I distinguished when I myself was still seemed to swim, now to the right, now to the left. Certain permanent vapors seem to have settled upon my entire forehead and temples, which press and oppress my eyes with a sort of sleepy heaviness, especially from mealtime to evening. . . . While considerable sight still remained, when I would first go to bed and lie on one side or the other, abundant light would dart from my closed eyes; then, as sight daily diminished, colors proportionately darker would burst forth with violence and a sort of crash from within. (4.ii.869)

Seventeenth-century treatments for what sounds like glaucoma were themselves horrifically painful, involving passing red-hot needles between the skin and skull, along with copious bouts of induced bleeding and purging. But Milton was always physically brave, and he needed his eyes. His entire life had consisted of little more than reading and writing, and such pursuits were not easily available to a blind man in the seventeenth century. His defiant attitude to the deterioration of his sight is evident from the biblical maxim that, from 1651 onward, he began prefixing to his autograph: "[M]y strength is made perfect in weakness." Perhaps blindness was a blessing and not a curse? Visions of the blind seers of the past, of Homer and Tiresias, were flashing through his mind, as the conception consolidated within him that he might prove to be among them. For his invitation to join the government of "the saints," as many were now referring to the Rumpers with varying degrees of irony, was more than a means to earthly fame. It seemed to him final confirmation of his calling from God, so that to reject it would be to jeopardize his immortal soul. He therefore continued his literary campaign against the enemies of the republic while undergoing the most exquisite physical tortures, and what often seems a needlessly vehement intemperance in his prose can surely be excused under the circumstances.

According to William Riley Parker, "[I]t is likely that his first assignment was to provide a Latin translation of the Parliament's official *Declaration* establishing the new government and justifying its recent actions."[9] Just as Milton's greatest poetic work was to be a theodicy, a justification of the ways of God to man, so his first job as a civil servant was to justify the apparently arbitrary and cruel actions of England's new rulers. An equally urgent task facing him was the composition of a reply to the *Eikon Basilike*: the "King's image" or, as it was popularly known throughout Europe, the "King's book." This was allegedly a series of reflections written by Charles himself as he awaited execution, but in fact it is more likely to have been composed by John Gauden, one of the personal chaplains who attended the captive monarch. There is, however, no reason to doubt that it reflects actual conversations between the two men, or that it represents the real views of Charles himself. It is one of the most successful pieces of political propaganda in history; vastly popular and enormously widely read, it did much to regain posthumously for Charles the public sympathy he had squandered by his foolishness and duplicity while alive. In fact, with the military wing of organized Royalism in complete disarray, the *Eikon Basilike* was the greatest practical threat the young republic had to face. In an epidemic of guilt and recrimination, large sections of the population had seized upon it as a surrogate scripture; it was rapidly translated into every major language, and it went into sixty editions. To Milton it appeared as the veritable apotheosis of literature as idolatry. He describes it as utterly worthless, "save only that a king is said to be the author, a name than which there needs no more among he blocish vulgar, to make it wise, and excellent, and admired, nay to set it next the Bible" (3:339).

The book's technique is apparent from the frontispiece, which is an engraving by William Marshall, the same artist who had portrayed Milton as a hideously deformed monster on the front of his 1645 *Poems*. It depicts Charles as a holy martyr, grasping a crown of thorns while his earthly crown, labeled "vanity," lies on the ground and he fixes his eyes on a heavenly crown inscribed "glory." Before even beginning its argument, the *Eikon Basilike* makes an idol of the King twice. Its title announces itself as the "King's image," while its iconic frontispiece blasphemously appropriates the role of martyr for the deposed monarch. As Milton admits in his response, *Eikonoklastes*: "In one thing I must commend his op'nness who gave the title to this book, *Eikon Basilike* (in Greek), that is to say, the Kings Image; and by the Shrine he dresses out for him, certainly would have the people come and worship him" (3:343). The iconic medium through which the King's book conveys its message is part of that message itself; the *Eikon Basilike* is concerned with suggesting that visual images and sensory icons are ethically sound, religiously sanctioned ways of experiencing the world. The implicit suggestion is that the Puritans' religious and political iconoclasm is excessively fanatical and likely to produce even more extreme fanaticism in its adherents.

By entitling his reply *Eikonoklastes*, Milton acknowledged the centrality of images to the dispute. In it he reminds his readers that "*Iconoclastes* [was] the famous Surname of Many Greek Emperors, who in thir zeal to the command of God, after long tradition of Idolatry in the Church, took courage, and broke all superstitious Images to peeces" (3:343). The various differences between the Puritans and the Cavaliers can all, finally, be reduced to questions of signification, with each side putting forward its own ethic of representation as the basis of its political, religious and social attitudes. In 1645 Milton had taken his revenge on William Marshall by having him mock his own engraving in Greek, a language he evidently did not know. Words neatly trumped visual images in that case, and Milton sought to repeat the victory in *Eikonoklastes*. He points out that the Latin motto, which the ordinary people will not understand, is a hint to the educated of the King's true intentions:

> by those Latin words after the end, *Vota dabunt quœ Bella negar-*
> *unt;* intimating, That what hee could not compass by Warr, he
> should atchieve by his Meditations. . . . heer may be well observ'd
> the loose and negligent curiosity of those who took upon them
> to adorn the setting out of the Book: for though the Picture sett
> in Front would Martyr him and Saint him to befool the people,
> yet the Latin Motto in the end, which they understand not, leave
> him, as it were a politic contriver to bring about that interest by
> faire and plausible words, which the force of Armes deny'd him.
> (ibid.)

Reason, not visual images or aesthetically "faire" words, is the proper medium for political debate. Images are used in politics only to deceive and mislead, and *Eikonoklastes* is perhaps the earliest critique of the "aestheticization of politics" that was to culminate in the searchlight rallies of Nuremberg, and to be more subtly perfected in the image-based political campaigns of our own day. Milton mocks Marshall's frontis-piece as consisting of "quaint Emblems and devices begg'd from the old Pageantry of some Twelf-nights entertainments at Whitehall" (3:342–3). Charles's saintly image is dismissed as "Stage-work," "drawn out to the full measure of a Masking Scene," a "conceited portraiture . . . set there to catch fools and silly gazers" (3:530). Using techniques that have been honed to perfection by the spin doctors of postmodern politics, Charles and his advisors understood that, in politics and perhaps in life as a whole, perception matters more than reality. Milton discovered that a prayer presented in the King's book as Charles's own thoughts was actually plagiarized from Phillip Sidney's *Arcadia*. Charles thus literally "put tyranny into an art," and Milton vows "to throw contempt and disgrace in the sight of all men upon this his idolized book" by revealing this trickery. It is not so much the plagiarism to which Milton objects but the employment of fiction in the alleged pursuit of truth:

> a Prayer stol'n word for word from the mouth of a Heathen fiction praying to a heathen God; & that in no serious Book, but the vain amatorious Poem of *Sr Philip Sidney's Arcadia*; a book in that kind full of worth and wit, but among religious thoughts, and duties not worthy to be nam'd. (3:356)

The fact that Charles does not understand that a fiction, which works by the manipulation of emotion, has no place in a rational argument is further evidence of the basically idolatrous nature of his understanding: "if only but to tast wittingly of meat or drink offered to an Idol, be in the doctrine of St. Paul judg'd a pollution, much more must be his sin who takes a prayer, so dedicated into his mouth, and offers it to God" (3:363–4). Charles's idolatrous mental habits are signaled by his inability to distinguish his own thoughts from those of a fictional character. Again, Milton is protesting against a tendency that has reached undreamed-of levels in our own day, when many people unabashedly construct their personalities after the pattern of celebrities, and when some individuals have actually lost the ability to distinguish between fictional characters in soap operas and real people. *Eikonoklastes* argues passionately against the incursion of iconic representation into political debate, defending logic against rhetoric, advancing the claims of essence over appearance and noting the connections between the King's addiction to images and his religious and political positions. Milton laments that "[t]he people, exorbitant and excessive in all their motions, are prone ofttimes not to a religious only, but to a civil kind of idolatry in idolizing their kings" (3:343).

Charles's strongest argument, which he uses at great length, is that all his efforts to resolve England's problems were undermined by the "tumults" on the streets of London. This was the first occasion in modern times that the Western ruling classes encountered the power of another new phenomenon with a great future ahead of it: the urban mob. Cities on the scale of mid-seventeenth-century London had not been seen in northern Europe since the Roman Empire, and the rabble-rousers and street orators of the day were only just beginning to grasp the political utility of what would become known as "King Mob." During the early debates of the Long Parliament, conservative defenders of episcopacy and the royal prerogative had often found themselves harassed on the streets or in their homes by gangs of rioters. The *Eikon Basilike* begins by reminding its readers of this fact, which, Charles alleges, eventually made it impossible for him to govern:

> Which those Tumults did to so high degrees of Insolence, that they
> spared not to invade the Honour and Freedome of the two Houses,
> menacing, reproaching, shaking, yea, & assaulting some Members
> of both Houses, as they fancyed, or disliked them: Nor did they
> forbear most rude and unseemly deportments both in contemptu-
> ous words and actions, to My selfe and My Court.[10]

The King warns the aristocratic wing of his enemies that they risk unleashing forces that they will not be able to control. His fear, which by 1649 was shared by large numbers of the Presbyterians who had led the

Parliamentary struggle against him, was that having abandoned the notion that the King represents the nation as a whole, the people will cease to see why they should be governed by any representative at all. Why should they not govern themselves: "[N]othing was more to be feared and lesse to be used by wise men, then those tumultuary confluxes of meane and rude people, who are taught first to petition, then to protect, then to dictate, at last to command and overawe the Parliament" (ibid. 7). Although he attributes part of their motives to a simple desire "to see their betters shamefully outraged, and abused," Charles is also certain that the mob had been manipulated by reckless and unscrupulous Parliamentarians, in order to force their desired measures through the Houses without proper debate or consideration:

> Generally, who ever had most mind to bring forth confusion and ruine upon Church and State, used the midwifery of those Tumults: whose riot and impatience was such, that they would not stay the ripening and season of Counsels, or fair production of Acts, in the order, gravity, and deliberatenesse befitting a Parliament; but ripped up with barbarous cruelty, and forcibly cut out abortive Votes, such as their Inviters and Incouragers most fancyed. (ibid.)

In fact, the King threateningly announces, he is aware of the identity of those pulling the strings that manipulated the mob: "impudent Incendiaries, who boasted of the influence they had, and used to convoke those Tumults as their advantages served." He protests that "some (who should have been wiser Statesmen) owned them as friends, commending their Courage, Zeale, & Industry. . . ." In *Eikonoklastes*, Milton responds to this most cogent of Charles's points by noting that the arbitrary government by which the King had reigned between 1629 and 1640 was just as extra-legal as the "tumults." He points out that the King has misread the

"signs" of the riots and so failed to understand what they meant: "Those
Tumults were . . . not signes of mischiefs to come, but seeking relief for
mischiefs past."[11] There is, according to Milton, a species of law that is
above all human government and that can take any earthly manifestation
it pleases. He is not afraid to claim that, under certain circumstances, the
urban mob can become the vehicle for divine justice. We know today the
dangers inherent in such claims, but Milton was witnessing the first modern expression of the political power that can be wielded by an armed and
angry populace. As long as it was used for purposes with which he agreed,
he found that power both inspiring and inspired.

Charles goes on to claim that he abandoned London, not because he
wanted to raise an army to use against his rebellious subjects but because
the "tumults" made him afraid for his personal safety, being unwilling
to "skuffle with an undisciplined rabble."[12] He begins this portion of his
argument with an unwieldy metaphor: "With what unwillingnesse I with-
drew from *Westminster*, let them judge, who, unprovided of tackling,
and victuall, are forced by Sea to a storm; yet better do so, then venture
splitting or sinking on a Lee shore." In his reply, Milton scorns to criticize
Charles's literary methods, pointing out instead the inherent impropriety
of employing style at the expense of substance in a rational debate. The
Eikon Basilike uses rhetorical methods of emotional manipulation that
are appropriate to fiction, not to politics:

> The Simily wherewith he begins I was about to have found fault
> with, as in a garb more Poetical then for a Statist: but meeting
> with many straines of like dress in other of his Essaies, and hearing
> him reported a more diligent reader of Poets than of Politicians, I
> begun to think that the whole Book might perhaps be intended a
> peece of Poetrie. (3:406)

But Milton senses what the politics of our own day amply confirm: that the use of images to political ends, idolatrous and evil as it may be, is highly effective. He worries that the *Eikon Basilike*, while obviously no threat to the intellectual integrity of an educated person, may easily infect ordinary people accustomed to hearing "the doctrine and perpetual infusion of servility" from the pulpit every Sunday. The emotional public reaction to the King's death has already made Milton nervous that the English people may:

> show themselves to be by nature slaves and arrant beasts—not fit for that liberty which they cried out and bellowed for, but fitter to be led back again into their old servitude like a sort of clamoring and fighting brutes, broke loose from their copyholds, that know not how to use or possess the liberty which they fought for, but with the fair words and promises of an old exasperated foe are ready to be stroked and tamed again into the wonted and well-pleasing state of their true Norman villeinage, to them best agreeable. (3:483)

Eikonoklastes ends with a prescient warning that, although a sound minority of convinced republicans are presently in power, the kind of campaign represented by the *Eikon Basilike* may prove successful in winning "the worthless approbation of an inconstant, irrational, and image-doting rabble; that like a credulous and hapless herd, begotten to servility and enchanted with a new device of the king's picture at his prayers, hold out both their ears with such delight and ravishment to be stigmatized and bored through in witness of their own voluntary and beloved baseness" (3:601). Ironically, Charles has much the same concerns as Milton about what he refers to as "the people" or "the multitude." Independents like Milton claimed that the Presbyterian system of church-government amounted to nothing more than "a Pope in every parish." Charles takes this argument to its logical conclusion, claiming that if left to their own devices regarding religious belief, "every man soone growes his owne Pope, and easily absolves himselfe of those ties, which, not the commands of Gods word, or the Lawes of the Land, but onely the subtilty and terrour of a Party casts upon him" (89). The King believes that most people have a natural need for authority and will impose it on themselves if it is not imposed from outside. This is virtually identical to Milton's position; the difference between them is really over whether those people sufficiently virtuous to successfully resist their own internal popery should be free of the constraints that the mass of natural slaves willingly accept.

Charles argues that, if such people assert their freedom from the law, the "multitude" will turn antinomian by example. He prays that God will "[r]ebuke those beasts of the people, and deliver Me from the rudenesse and strivings of the multitude." Seventeenth-century writers often use the word "multitude" to denote the people considered as a single, corporate body, a power that they were just beginning to identify. In *Religio Medici*, published in 1642, Thomas Browne sneers at "that great enemy of reason, virtue, and religion, the multitude; that numerous piece of monstrosity, which, taken asunder, seem men, and the reasonable creatures of God, but, confused together, make but one great beast, and a monstrosity more prodigious than Hydra."[13] Furthermore, for Browne "the multitude" does not necessarily refer to a particular group of people; it designates, rather, an attitude of mind that can be found in anyone: "Neither in the name of multitude do I only include the base and minor sort of people: there is a rabble even amongst the gentry; a sort of plebeian heads, whose fancy moves with the same wheel as these; men in the same level with mechanicks, though their fortunes do somewhat gild their infirmities. . . ." (ibid.)

The years of civil war and interregnum saw a complicated debate about the nature of the "people" and the "multitude." In Thomas Hobbes's *Leviathan*, also first published in 1642, the "multitude" is the sum total of individuals represented in a single body. The state's governing power was an accurate representative of the "multitude." According to Hobbes, a "multitude of men, are made one person, when they are by one man, or one person, represented."[14] This replacement of the actual multitude by a "representative" of the multitude is, Hobbes argues, absolutely necessary if the multitude are to be governed successfully and so kept from falling back into the condition of the *bellum omnia contra omnes*: the "war of all against all," which Hobbes believed characterized pre-civilized human life. Milton was no more sanguine than Browne or Hobbes about the intellectual capacities of the majority of the population. But during his brief moment of political optimism in 1649–50, Milton portrays the multitude as the scourge of God's vengeance against tyrannical rulers. This position is implicit in his defense of the "tumults" in *Eikonklastes* and explicit in *The Tenure*'s approbation of the "extraordinary" but nonetheless divinely-sanctioned means of the King's removal: "if all human power to execute, not accidentally but intendedly, the wrath of God upon evil doers without exception, be of God; then that power, whether ordinary, or if that faile, extraordinary so executing that intent of God, is lawfull, and not to be resisted" (3:198).

All parties understood that the issue of government was part of a discussion about the nature of representation. In the *Eikon Basilike* Charles denounces the Parliament as an inaccurate representation of his personal will, "[w]hose agreeing Votes were not by any Law or reason conclusive to My Judgment; nor can they include, or carry with them My consent, whom they represent not in any kind" (8). In response, Milton asserts that Parliament is not supposed to represent the will of the monarch: "[I]f the

Parlament represent the whole Kingdom, as is sure anough they doe, then doth the King represent only himself; and if a King without a Kingdom be in a civil sense nothing, then without or against the Representative of his whole Kingdom he himself represents nothing...." (3:414). A page later he narrows the representative still further, to the House of Commons alone: "[Charles] and the Peers represent but themselves, the Commons are the whole Kingdom" (3:415). In fact the Parliament, properly understood as the governing representative of the whole nation, is the sovereign power in the realm and, in this sense, the King: "Where the Parlament sits, there inseparably sitts the King . . . who fought for the King divided from his Parlament, fought for the shadow of a King . . . and for things that were not . . ." (3:530). Parliament is the essence of political authority; the King is merely its image, its visual symbol, its icon. The royalists were fighting for a chimera, an idol. As Milton would soon come to realize, however, the problem with this argument is that, having been elected on a strictly limited property franchise, the House of Commons itself represented only a small section of the nation. It was arguable, and in the 1650s it was often argued, that the New Model Army, being drawn from all levels of society, was more genuinely representative than the Parliament and thus better qualified to rule the country.

The issue of sexuality also looms large in this dispute. It was not necessarily scandalous to have homosexual inclinations or experiences, as both Charles and Milton seem to have done, but what was deemed inappropriate in a ruler was to be what we would now call sexually submissive. Milton unabashedly interprets Charles's preference for style over substance as a womanly trait, scorning the King's love of "unmaskuline Rhetorick," claiming that he is domestically "govern'd by a Woman" (3:538) and that his expostulations to his wife amount "almost to Sonnetting" (3:420). This is not a matter of gender: Milton believes that people who are sexually submissive are unfit to govern a nation, no matter to which gender they belong. We should recall here his insistence during the divorce controversy that there are circumstances under which female domination is perfectly acceptable: "if she exceed her husband in prudence and dexterity, and he contentedly yeeld; for then a superior and more naturall law comes in, that the wiser should govern the lesse wise, whether male or female" (2:589). In the household as in the state, the most rational and virtuous elements should rule, and those who neglect this imperative in their domestic lives will ignore it in public affairs. As Milton puts it elsewhere: "He in vain makes a vaunt of liberty in the senate or in the forum, who languishes under the vilest servitude, to an inferior at home" (4.i.233). He dismisses Charles among "the Government of effeminate and Uxorious Magistrates. Who being themselves govern'd and overswaid at home under a Feminine usurpation, cannot but be farr short of spirit and authority without dores, to govern a whole Nation" (3:421). Milton's micropolitics lead him to assume that someone not in charge "within doors" will be a natural slave and thus unfit to rule others "without dores."

Eikonoklastes was published in October 1649. The following month the propaganda war intensified with the publication of the *Defensio Regio* by Claude Salmasius, an irreproachably Protestant and undeniably brilliant sage, whose multifarious publications on an enormous variety of issues had won him a prominent position among the most famous thinkers in the world. The backing of such an illustrious figure provided the Royalists with powerful intellectual ammunition, and the Council of State testified to their continued faith in the relatively unknown Milton by asking him to compose their reply. The decision to accept cannot have been easy; in fact it was reckless in many ways. In 1654 Milton recalled:

and with the apprehension of soon losing the sight of my remaining eye, and when my medical attendants clearly announced, that
if I did engage in the work, it would be irreparably lost, their pre-
monitions caused no hesitation, and inspired no dismay. I would
not have listened to the voice even of Esculapius himself from the
shrine of Epidauris, in preference to the suggestions of the heavenly monitor within my breast; my resolution was unshaken, though
the alternative was either the loss of my sight or the desertion of
my duty. (4.ii.869)

Looking back on his decision, Milton was in no doubt that his pamphlet war with Salmasius had cost him his eyesight. In 1655 he wrote a
sonnet to his friend and former pupil Cyriack Skinner, lamenting the loss
of his eyes and describing the source of his continued determination to
persevere:

What supports me, dost thou ask?
The conscience, Friend, to have lost them overply'd
In libertyes defence, my noble task,
Of which all Europe talks from side to side. (9–12) (Sonnet XXII,
170)

Milton cannot resist a touch of vanity here, and it was quite justified;
his controversy with Salmasius was indeed the talk of intellectual Europe
in the early 1650s, and this was the height of the fame that Milton so passionately desired. Nevertheless, his obviously conscious, fully informed
decision to sacrifice his eyesight seems remarkable in a middle-aged
man who had still not nearly achieved his life's ambition of composing
England's national epic poem. It was a sacrifice which would in all probability put that aim forever beyond his power. Why did he do it?

7

UXORIOUS USURERS

I

IN ALL PROBABILITY it was the identity of his opponent that compelled Milton to this battle, despite the physical disaster it presaged. It seemed to most people likely to be a one-sided fight, even a mismatch; the erudition of Salmasius was renowned throughout Europe, while Milton was unknown outside his native land, and little known even within it. Milton knew that bettering such an adversary would win him universal fame. But there is more to it than that. As a radical iconoclast who had always lived by usury, Milton was in an extremely paradoxical position. He was particularly well placed to observe the practical, objective effects of images when manipulated in financial form. And yet it is this very efficacious power of images that he inveighs against as "idolatry" in its liturgical and political manifestations. This contradiction in his thought expresses itself in his revealingly furious, almost manic verbal warfare with Salmasius.

Early modern Europeans debated the question of usury with a frequency and an intensity that bespeak their keen knowledge of the issue's widespread ramifications. As Robert Filmer noted in 1653, "the valuation of the use of money is the foundation and rule which govern the valuation of all other sorts of bargains."[1] Milton was fully aware that usury involves the production of wealth by the manipulation of images, by treating images as efficacious in a way that can be, and regularly was being, described as magical and idolatrous. And yet Milton the usurer was also the greatest iconoclast of his day. This does not necessarily imply hypocrisy. The people of seventeenth-century England were used to having experiences and feelings that they understood as simultaneously natural and sinful. The Christian dialectic of temptation and repentance itself testifies to the existence of contradictory forces within the psyche, as does Plato's famous metaphor of the soul as a chariot driven by two horses, one representing reason and the other desire. The fact that usury was widely practiced did not necessarily make it morally acceptable to its practitioners, any more than visiting the brothel or the tavern was necessarily acceptable to those who practiced those vices.

So I think we are justified in perceiving the almost unbelievably vitriolic abuse that Milton heaps on Salmasius as neurotic in nature. It is as if he is purging a tendency within himself, by projecting it upon his adversary. For Salmasius had first won his fame a decade before his dispute with Milton with a series of brilliantly innovative defenses of usury, including *De Usuria* (1638), *De Modo Usurarum* (1639) and *De Foenore Trapezitico* (1640). For Milton's contemporaries, these superbly persuasive rationalizations of interest would have been the most prominent part of Salmasius's reputation, and their historical importance cannot be exaggerated. Max Weber called *De Usuria* "the first theoretical justification of interest"[2] and recognized the Protestant legitimation of interest as "the achievement of Salmasius."[3] Eugen von Böhm-Bawerk declared that Salmasius's works "almost by themselves determined the direction and substance of the theory of interest for more than a hundred years."[4] The "credit crunches" and sundry financial crises that are convulsing the global economy as I write these lines in 2009 can be traced directly to the theories of Salmasius. Their roots can also be discerned in Milton's ambiguous, conflicted responses to his opponent's claims. Not only was Milton a usurer's son, not only had usury provided him with the leisure to study and write rather than work for a living, not only had usury earned him his bride—his political and polemical nemesis was internationally renowned as usury's greatest champion. He never devoted a thoroughgoing, sustained analysis to the issue, but Milton must have spent a significant portion of his life in consideration of usury. What were his conclusions on this most controversial of all topics?

The fact that he rarely discusses the matter explicitly must not blind us to the ways in which the usury controversy insistently insinuates itself into Milton's work. His figurative associations and logical procedures are frequently drawn from the debate around usury, and the formal pattern of that argument stamped itself indelibly on his mind. Milton spent much of the early 1650s in furious denunciation of Salmasius, wallowing in the ad hominem and arguing that the personal vices of the Frenchman and his allies were the direct causes of their political folly. He even picks apart Salmasius's private life, carefully explaining its causal relation to his Royalist theories of state. It is therefore striking that he avoids mentioning the highly dubious issue on which Salmasius's reputation had been made, and the most plausible explanation for this uncharacteristic reticence is that, at one level, he agreed with Salmasius's pro-usury argument. In fact Milton's differences with Salmasius are generally caused by the Frenchman's failure to see the implications of his ideas, or to apply the logic of his economic insights to the realm of politics.

Salmasius's epochal breakthrough was to acknowledge, explain and justify the fact that money was a commodity. It was a substantial essence

that could be rented and traded just like any other thing. Since Aristotle
the conventional position had been that usury was unnatural because
money was not a commodity itself but the measure of other commodities,
and a medium of expression for their value. In the words of Aquinas:

> All other things from themselves have some utility; not so, however,
> money. But it is the measure of utility of other things, as is clear ac-
> cording to the Philosopher in the Ethics V:9. And therefore the use
> of money does not have its utility from this money itself, but from
> the things which are measured by money.[5]

Money was not a quality but a quantity. It had no use-value: it was
exchange-value. To treat money as if it were a thing of value in itself,
rather than as the abstract standard of value, was held to be an egregious
violation of nature. The commodification of exchange-value was recognized as the definitive characteristic of usury by Gerard Malynes in *A
Treatise of Tripartite Exchange* (1610): "In [Henry VII's] tyme the bank-
ers had their begininge who did invente the merchanisynge exchange,
makynge of money a merchandise" (17). Usury's opponents claimed that
such behavior evinced magical thinking, for it granted practical, efficacious power to something that did not exist in nature. To make money
breed was to effect a re-creation, to displace God's creation by a human
concept, to override nature by custom. It was regarded as morally vital
to maintain the distinction between use-value and exchange-value and as
ethically deleterious to treat the latter as though it were the former. As
Thomas Pie explained in *Usuries spright coniured*:

> if I lend you ten faire Soueraignes to carie in your purse for a
> shew, or to decoct them in a medicine for Physicke, it is commodat-
> ing; for which use if I take anything, it is letting and hiring: but if I

lend you the same ten Soueraignes to spend or lay out, it is mutu-
ating, for which use, if I take any thing, it is usurie.[6]

Pie differentiates between the material objects of the gold coins,
which had practical use-value and therefore could legitimately be rented,
and their exchange-value. Exchange-value was the measure of use-value;
it was not itself a use-value. It therefore could not be rented except fraudulently and usuriously. All these objections Salmasius brushed aside:
Was not money, he asked, a useful commodity that could and should be
rented out like land or a house? Income received from moneylending was
a "fee" (*merces*) for the use of a commodity, not "profit" (*lucrum*) out
of nothing:

> Money that is given out at interest is treated no differently from a
> building or a field or works for which a fee is required from those
> who have rented them . . . Usury is properly not a profit, but a fee.
> Nor is it taken on account of the business of exchange, but rather
> on account of the use of the money. For a fee is one thing, profit
> another. The latter is an additional acquisition, over and above
> the matter; the former comes from the matter itself.[7]

Milton himself echoed this argument in *Of Christian Doctrine*, using
terms similar enough to suggest familiarity with Salmasius's argument:
"Usury, then, is no more reprehensible in itself than any other kind of
lawful commerce. . . . [I]f we may make a profit out of cattle, land, houses
and the like, why should we not out of money?" (6:776–7). Salmasius
was the first thinker to give theoretical expression to the transformation
of the medium of exchange into an object of exchange. He collapsed the
distinction between use-value and exchange-value by declaring that the
exchange-value of money was its use-value. On this momentous insight

was raised the entire edifice of capital that dominates the world to this day. Salmasius gave substantial being and efficacious power to what had previously been understood as an impotent, merely referential sign. He made money come alive.

Once again, we must remember that the people of the seventeenth century did not view usury as an "economic" problem, for they lacked our conception of an "economy." Usury was a philosophical and ethical matter, and Salmasius challenged his culture's most fundamental assumptions when, in the course of this debate, he deconstructed the polarity between the Aristotelian notions of "quality" and "quantity." The economic valence of these concepts has been aptly explained by Karl Marx, who describes the difficulties suffered by the pre-capitalist mind attempting to grasp the counter-intuitive proposition that exchange-value could be a substantial thing:

> Every useful thing, as iron, paper, &c., may be looked at from the two points of view of quality and quantity. . . . The utility of a thing makes it a use value. But this utility is not a thing of air. Being limited by the physical properties of the commodity, it has no existence apart from that commodity. . . . Use values become a reality only by use or consumption: they also constitute the substance of all wealth, whatever may be the social form of that wealth. . . . Exchange value, at first sight, presents itself as a quantitative relation, as the proportion in which values in use of one sort are exchanged for those of another sort, a relation constantly changing with time and place. Hence exchange value appears to be something accidental and purely relative, and consequently an intrinsic value, i.e., an exchange value that is inseparably connected with, inherent in commodities, seems a contradiction in terms.[8]

But Salmasius abolished this contradiction by expressing the abstract principle of quantity (exchange-value) in the form of a qualitative thing (a use-value). He claimed that exchange-value is itself a substantial essence, not merely a quantitative expression of other substantial essences. Hence it was perfectly logical and legitimate to retain ownership of money while allowing someone else the use of it. Money was not the same as the use of money. Shakespeare, like Milton a usurer's son, deftly employs this distinction when the male speaker of his Sonnets decides to loan his homosexual lover out to the female sex while retaining propriety rights over him: "Mine be thy love, and thy love's use their treasure."[9] Milton understood the implications of Salmasius's thought for non-economic matters, in a way that the modern mind does not immediately grasp (although the financial crises of the twenty-first century seem to be driving the ethical and social implications of unrestricted moneylending back into popular consciousness). Although he understood them, however, Milton also knew how deeply implicated he himself was in the destructive effects of usury on the psyche. Perhaps this explains the otherwise incomprehensible vehemence with which Milton verbally assaulted this particular opponent, as well as his willingness to sacrifice his eyesight in the process.

There is no proof that Milton read Salmasius on usury, but it is surely implausible that he would have neglected to do so. A resounding vindication of his family business by one of the most famous Protestant scholars in Europe cannot have escaped his attention. Even if Milton did not read the tracts when they first appeared, he would surely have familiarized himself with Salmasius's oeuvre once he had been selected as Parliament's champion against the *Royal Defence*. Milton had no choice but to endorse usury, having always lived by it. Although he does not cite Salmasius, Milton follows his reasoning closely, dutifully condemning excessive

interest and interest taken from the poor, but arguing that there is nothing wrong with usury per se. It is significant that usury seems to have
preyed on his mind most persistently during the divorce controversy. *Of
Christian Doctrine* apart, his every mention of the word "usury" occurs
in the divorce tracts, and it appears likely that the ancient and medieval
conception of usury as a sexual vice, a "sodomy in nature," was forcing
its way into his thoughts. He never actually praises it, as Salmasius had,
but he does point out the paradox whereby usury is legal while the much
less harmful practice of divorce is outlawed:

> Seeing Christ did not condemn whatever it was that Moses suffer'd,
> and that thereupon the Christian Magistrate permits usury and
> open stews . . . why we should strain thus at the matter of divorce,
> which may stand so much with charity to permit, and make no
> scruple to allow usury, esteem'd to be so much against charity.
> (2:320)

As if automatically, Milton repeats the pro forma popular association of usury with sexual impropriety, the "open stews" of prostitution.
But shortly afterward he makes clear his disagreement with the popular
estimation that usury is uncharitable:

> The example of usury, which is commonly alleg'd makes against
> the allegation which it brings, as I touch'd before. Besides that
> usury, so much as is permitted by the Magistrate, and demand-
> ed with common equity, is neither against the word of God, nor
> the rule of charity, as hath been often discurst by men of eminent
> learning and judgement. (2:322)

He repeats the point in *The Judgement of Martin Bucer*: "As for what
they instance of usury, let them first prove usury to be wholly unlawfull,

as the law allows it; which learned men as numerous on the other side will deny them" (2:425). In 1644 everyone would have identified these "learned men" with Salmasius, and this is the closest Milton comes to acknowledging his intellectual debt to his future foe. But Milton's mention of usury here actually militates against his own argument. In the previously quoted paragraph, he notes that to allow usury while forbidding divorce is inequitable because usury is widely regarded as uncharitable, but in the above paragraph he denies that usury is uncharitable, thus removing the grounds for the alleged inequity of permitting it while forbidding divorce. This rare logical contradiction suggests that Milton was experimenting with different definitions of "usury" and attempting to draw a moral distinction between them.

Certainly his first mention of usury in *The Doctrine and Discipline* assumes a negative evaluation of the practice. He employs it to counter the argument that, because Jesus says that the Jews were granted the right to divorce only due to "the hardness of [their] hearts," divorce is therefore forbidden to Christians. Milton points out that "[The Jews'] hearts were set upon usury, and are to this day, no Nation more; yet that which was the endammaging only of their estates, was narrowly forbid" (2:289). He alludes here to Deuteronomy 23:20: "Unto a stranger thou mayest lend upon usury; but unto thy brother thou shalt not lend upon usury: that the Lord thy God may bless thee in all that thou settest thine hand to in the land whither thou goest to possess it." Milton interprets this in a narrowly economic sense, a modern sense. He emphasizes the practical, material advantages to the Jews of practicing usury only against aliens, and the "endammaging . . . of their estates" that would result from charging interest from their "brothers."

He pointedly refrains from endorsing any ethical objection to usury as such. But Milton does tacitly concede that charging interest was an act of aggression, as Deuteronomy implies, because it was calculated to damage the estate of the borrower. As Paul Johnson observes, in biblical times "[i]nterest was . . . synonymous with hostility."[10] Both Cato and Seneca compared it to homicide. In *The History of Britain* Milton gives an example of usury as war by other means, recalling how Seneca, "having drawn the British unwillingly to borrow of him vast sums upon false promises of easy loan, and for repayment to take their own time, on a sudden compels them to pay in all at once with great extortion" (5:77). Milton's *Commonplace Book* records several applications of usury theory to the definition of monarchy. He notes an observation from Thuanus's *Historia*: "[T]he king is merely the usufructuary of the property of the realm in his possession" (1:441). A "usufructuary" is the beneficiary of a loan, but the loan is not necessarily one of money. Thuanus defines a usufructuary as "one having the right of using and enjoying the fruits or profits of an estate or other thing belonging to another, without impairing the substance." (ibid.). Milton readily employs this argument in his anti-monarchical tracts. In *Observations on the Articles of Peace* (1649) he approvingly recalls that King John had been informed that "a King in no case, though of extreamest necessity, might alienate the Patrimony of his Crown, whereof he is onely Usu-fructuary, as Civilians terme it, the propriety remaining ever to the Kingdome, not to the King" (3:306). In his *Defence of the English People* (1651), Milton rhetorically demands: "Shall he then who enjoys only the usufruct of the crown, as it is said, and of crown property by the grant of the people, be able to claim title to that people itself?" (4.i.307). He is pointing out and exploiting the contradiction between Salmasius's economics and his politics, between his justification of usury and his rationalization of monarchy.

The people of seventeenth-century England conceived of both economics and politics as issues of representation. Political debate regarding the possible make-up of a future Parliament referred to it as "the new representative." Oliver Cromwell pointed out that the army was more genuinely representative of the English people than Parliament, but this served to raise the more radical question of whether Parliament should represent people or property. Neither Cromwell himself nor any of his allies managed to reach the democratic conclusion that Parliament should represent every individual adult in the nation, but the question was at least being raised. Before the trial of the King, Cromwell presciently asked his colleagues to "let us resolve here what answer we shall give the King when he comes before us, for the first question that he will ask us will be by what authority and commission we do try him."[11] Who or what, in other words, did the court represent? An eloquent silence descended until the radical, secular Member of Parliament Henry Marten commenced: "In the name of the Commons and Parliament assembled and all the good people of England . . ." (ibid.) The qualifier "good" indicates that Marten, like many other Parliamentarians, believed that they represented only people of a certain kind, a certain quality. But later, when John Bradshaw called on Charles to answer a charge brought "in behalf of the Commons assembled in Parliament and the good people of England," Lady Fairfax cried from the gallery, "It's a lie, not half, nor a quarter of the people!"[12] Her expostulation expresses the alternative view, that government should represent a quantitative majority of the people.

Matters were easier for the Royalists, because the notion of the King as a true and accurate representative of the whole people was already familiar. For Milton, and the brand of radical Protestantism he espoused, this was an idolatrous argument because it identified an image with what the image represented. His iconoclastic approach to images, which differentiated them from what they represent, led Milton to argue that, if the King was merely the "image" of the nation, there could be no harm in replacing him by a different kind of image. But the Royalists argued that images were "emanations" from what they represented, that signs were organically connected to their referents, so that to destroy the image of something was also to damage the thing itself. To kill the King was to inflict a potentially mortal wound on England as a whole. We can see here how Milton's insistence on the separation between sign and refer-ent in the usury debate, in which he asserted that money, a mere sign, could legitimately reproduce in the absence of the substantial commodi-ties it represented, closely parallels his argument about the people's right to alter their representative. Salmasius's failure to draw this connection between his economic and his political theories enraged Milton, driving him to new heights of raging invective.

Partly because of his encroaching blindness, with its attendant physi-cal indignities (he explained that "in the precarious health I still enjoy I must work at intervals and hardly for an hour at a time, though the task calls for continuous study and composition") (4.i.307), partly due to his copious other responsibilities as a government servant, but mostly because he knew that he now had the ear of all Europe and was deter-mined to permanently cement his fame with a glorious victory, Milton spent over a year composing his reply to Salmasius. It was eventually published as the *Defence of the English People* in February 1651. Milton addressed the question of representation with Apocalyptic confidence, boldly asserting that the English people were functioning as God's earthly delegates: "But why do I proclaim as if performed by the people these deeds which, as I may say, in their very nature send forth a voice and bear witness to the presence of God in every place?" (4.i.305). There is, how-ever, no suggestion that Milton intends here a numerical majority of the people. Rather he has in mind a politicized version of Calvin's concept of the predestined elect or "saints": "[t]he people furthermore do with

God's approval judge their guilty rulers: for He conferred this office on his chosen ones . . ." (4.i.359). In 1654's sequel, the *Second Defence*, he expresses his understanding of "the people" succinctly. He identifies the "people" with the *representative* of the people. Referring to Parliament. he asks:

> if, after receiving supreme power to decide on the gravest mat-
> ters, they were forced once more to refer those questions, which
> especially exceed the comprehension of the masses, I do not say
> to the people (for with this power they are themselves now the
> people), but to the mob, which conscious of its own inexperience,
> has originally referred things to them, what would be the end of
> this referring back and forth? (4.i.634–5)

By 1651 Milton's advocacy of revolutionary justice had surpassed even that of *The Tenure*, which had at least allowed for legal due process. In the first *Defence*, Milton's identification of "the people" with God's "chosen ones" leads him to dismiss the need for legal niceties altogether: "[I]t is right for a people to do away with a tyrant either before or after trial, in whatever way they can" (4.i.469). This presumably includes what we would call acts of terrorism, provided they are carried out by God's "chosen ones." Furthermore, although the "people" does not refer to the entire population, its limits are set by moral virtue and emphatically not by social class: "[B]y people we mean all citizens of every degree" (4.i.471). It may be hard to accept, but it seems clear that Milton is saying that God may select any righteous person to carry out political violence in his name. In our time such proclamations are almost never heard in the West among even the most fanatic of Leftist groupuscles, but they emanate with increasing vehemence from the radical elements within the Muslim world. Reading Milton may help us understand their terrible logic, for he provides an instance of a manifestly humane, extraordinarily learned and intelligent human being who was perfectly prepared to advocate terrorism for political ends.

The "people," for Milton, were defined by quality rather than by quantity. They were God's "chosen ones," identified by their special virtue; they were not a numerical majority. In fact Milton's politics always show great scorn for the majority. He remains convinced that the citizens of even his home country are mostly natural slaves: "[T]here are a few, and those of great wisdom and courage, that either desire or deserve liberty. Most men by far prefer just masters—masters, note, but just ones" (4.i.375). But what is truly degrading about Salmasius's argument is his insistence that the English have a duty to obey even *unjust* masters such as Charles I. Milton unleashes his fury against such ideas in a gleeful, shameless torrent of abuse. He begins from the fact that Salmasius is a "hireling," who has accepted money for his work. His own ideas have thus become alien to him, their ownership transferred to those who have purchased them: "[Y]ou called it a "Royal" Defence: for after you had sold it the defence was no longer yours but rightly royal, bought indeed for a hundred sovereigns" (4.i.308–9). Milton was a proud member of the commercial classes, but that does not prevent him from declaring that commodified arguments are worthless. "Your discourse is hired then" (4.i.308), he remarks, before haughtily declaring that, having sold his work, Salmasius is no longer even worth addressing: "I suppose that crew of renegades paid you a few pennies to write this; and so I must direct my answer not to you who prate of things you quite fail to understand, but to those who hired you" (4.i.457). Milton finds it quite inconceivable that commodified discourse can be sincere; the process of commodification introduces an extraneous profit motive, a market-driven imperative to appeal to the masses that inevitably corrupts the argument. He denounces his opponent for acting "like some brazen hawker at a country fair . . . that you might peddle your faded dyes and lye-filled vials to as many readers as possible" (4.i.326).

Milton is probably the greatest master of invective in the English language, and he unleashes the full, sadistic force of his most violent power against the unfortunate Salmasius, who never responded, fell ill and, much to Milton's delight, shortly afterward died. It is hilarious fun to read at this historical distance, but we should not allow ourselves the impression that Milton's insults are random or arbitrary. On the contrary, they dwell almost obsessively on the single concept of slavery. Salmasius's arguments are "not to be borne by the vilest of slaves" (4.i.306), claims Milton. Salmasius is himself a "slave to the whim or purse of a master" (4.i.319). He had been careless enough to refer to Charles as the "master" of the nation; for Milton this is proof of the unmitigated servility of his character: "Learn now, you rascal house-born slave, that unless you remove the master, you destroy the state, for it is some private property, and not a commonwealth, that owns a master" (4.i.334). He rhetorically wonders how any free man "could have written books so slavish in spirit and design that they seem rather to emanate from some slave factory or auction block" (4.i.341). He declares that Salmasius is "smeared . . . with the slave-market slime" (4.i.347), recommends him "as a candidate for slavery to replace an ass in a mill" (ibid.), and addresses him thus: "You knight of the lash, concealer of slavery's blemishes . . . you are so foul a procurer and hireling pimp of slavery that even the lowest slaves on any auction block should hate and despise you" (4.i.461). Once again, political servility is inseparable from sexual submissiveness, and Milton makes endless references to the rumors that Salmasius was dominated by his wife: "[Y]ou are yourself a Gallic cock and said to be rather cocky, but instead of commanding your mate, she commands and hen-pecks you;

and if the cock is king of many hens while you are the slave of yours, you must be no cock of the roost but a mere dung-hill Frenchman!" (4.i.428). As if it were the most obvious, natural connection in the world, Milton draws the link between Salmasius's alleged submission to his wife and his advocacy of monarchy in state politics: "[N]aturally you want to force royal tyranny on others after being used to suffer so slavishly a woman's tyranny at home" (4.i.380).

Salmasius is, in short, what the modern world knows as a sexual masochist: "A man would sooner tire of thrashing him than he of presenting his back to the lash" (4.i.399). In fact, Milton claims that the Frenchman's fetish for slavery has undermined his own argument, by demonstrating that to support the King is inevitably to advocate slavery. At moments of heightened excitement such as this, Milton foresees the prospect of a worldwide revolution against monarchy:

> In raising royal power immeasurably above the law, you manage to warn men far and wide of their unsuspected slavery, and you spur them on more sharply to awake with all speed from that hibernation in which they used to dream that they were free; you have warned them of what they had not known, that they are slaves of kings. (4.i.399–400)

By 1654 he dared to imagine that "from the Pillars of Hercules all the way to the farthest boundaries of Father Liber, I seem to be leading home again everywhere in the world, after a vast space of time, Liberty herself, so long expelled and exiled" (4.i.555). Such an international uprising would not actually take place for well over a century, but Milton was by no means alone in envisioning Cromwell's England as the vanguard of a pan-European republicanism. Within months of *Eikonoklastes*'s publication Andrew Marvell, Milton's friend and junior colleague in the government's service, composed "An Horatian Ode upon Cromwell's Return From Ireland," which foresees the hero's conquests spreading from the Celtic fringe to the heart of Antichrist in Rome itself: "a Caesar he, ere long, to Gaul / To Italy an Hannibal / And to all states not free / Shall climacteric be."[13] But even at this heady moment of revolutionary fervor, Milton is concerned that the natural human attraction to slavery may reassert itself among the English people. His deep knowledge of the Old Testament, as well as his keen observation of human nature, had taught him the tenacity of the human desire to play a servile role. Thus even in *Eikonoklastes* he is careful to caution his countrymen:

> All slavery indeed is a stain upon any freeborn man, but for you to wish to resist your destiny and return to slavery after your freedom had been won by God's assistance and your own valor . . .would be not simply a shameful act, but an ungodly and criminal act! Your sin would equal the sin of those who were overcome with longing for their former captivity in Egypt and were at length destroyed by God in countless disasters of all sorts, thus paying to their divine deliverer the penalty for their slavish thoughts. (3:532)

Milton is well aware that most people must be forced to be free and that the New Model Army is the only power in the realm capable of achieving such coercion. Anticipating the Bolshevik concept of the "dictatorship of the proletariat," he believes that a period of dictatorial, military rule will be necessary before the English people learn to love liberty. Although he claims that the army has "fought and conquered not only their enemies in arms, but the inwardly hostile or superstitious beliefs of the mob as well" (4.i.336), Milton had been sufficiently shocked by the backsliding of the Parliamentary Presbyterians to hint that a military coup might prove necessary: "[M]y belief is, though I hesitate to express it, that our troops were wiser than our legislators, and saved the commonwealth by arms when the others had nearly destroyed it by their votes" (4.i.332–3). He was coming to experience first-hand the truth of a maxim he had noted in his *Commonplace Book*: "Against a bad ruler there is no other enemy than the sword" (1:456).

II

THROUGHOUT 1651 THE fame of Milton's *Defence* swept across Europe, and it appeared in ten separate editions within a year. Its demolition of Salmasius's arguments was conclusive enough to cause serious concern among the continent's crowned heads, although the most progressive among them were intrigued. Salmasius was employed at the court of Queen Christiana of Sweden, who was counted among the most learned and liberal of monarchs. We catch the flavor of her response to Milton's tract from the private correspondence of one of his colleagues, Isaac Vossius, who remarks that "I had expected nothing of such quality from an Englishman" and reports that the Queen herself was impressed by the author: "In the presence of many, she [Christina] spoke highly of the genius of the man, and his manner of writing."[14] This cannot have pleased Salmasius, who reportedly grew despondent and sickly. As Milton reported it, Christiana "had invited Salmasius or Salmasia (for to which sex he belonged is a matter of uncertainty) to her court," but the androgynous sage was "disgraced" when "my defence suddenly surprised him in the midst of his security" (4.i.557). He allows that the Queen was too gracious to actually expel Salmasius but claims that she lost all respect for him, so that he slunk away in shame, dying in misery shortly thereafter. Milton happily reports:

[T]here are some who impute his death to the penetrating severity of my strictures, which he rendered only the more sharp by his
endeavours to resist. When he saw the work which he had in hand
proceed slowly and the time of reply elapsed, the public curiosity
subsided, his fame marred and his reputation lost; the favour of
the princes, whose cause he had so ill-defended, alienated, he was
destroyed after three years of grief rather by the force of depres-
sion than disease. (4.i.559)

Milton was thrilled to think that he had murdered Salmasius: "I
met him in single combat and plunged in his reviling throat this pen, the
weapon of his own choice" (4.i.556). And it undoubtedly must have dis-
turbed the poor Frenchman to find himself answered with such homicidal
ferocity by an opponent of such astounding brilliance. *Eikonoklastes* was
soon translated into French and Dutch, and the government of the United
Provinces ordered twenty-five copies for the perusal of its members. The
King of France immediately recognized Milton as a revolutionary threat.
In June, a correspondent to the English government newspaper *Mercurius
Politicus* reported that the *Defence* was to be "burnt in Toulouse and
Paris for fear of making state-heretics. The truth is, that doctrine begines
to be studied and disputed more of late, and is pretty taking among such
people as they, who, like Issachar's ass, sink under their burdens . . ."[15]
In July, a reader in Paris wrote to the same newssheet that Milton's book
"is so farr liked and approved by the ingenuous sort of men, that all the
Copies, sent hither out of the Low-Countries were long-since dispersed,
and it was designed here for the Press, whereof notice being taken, it is
made Treason for any to print, vend, or have it in possession . . ." (ibid.)
As Blair Worden has recently noted, Milton was the official licencer
of the *Mercurius*, and from January 1651 he appears to have played a

prominent role in producing it, alongside its official editor Marchamont
Nedham. Worden describes the newssheet as a "literary partnership"
between the two men. An ebullient, chimerical character, Nedham
had first come to Milton's attention as the editor of the Royalist newssheet *Mercurius Pragmaticus*. The Council of State ordered Milton to
investigate Nedham's views, and finding them nebulous and malleable,
the Secretary for Foreign Tongues evidently decided that the young jour-
nalist's copious talents could be put to good use in the service of the
revolution. Throughout 1651 the two men cooperated closely in producing a vastly entertaining journal that must have done much to palliate the
austere ambience surrounding many of the republic's leaders. The first
issue announces its intent to create a specifically republican culture of
merriment and wit, pointing out that there is no reason these should be
the preserve of the Cavaliers:

> Why should not the Commonwealth have a fool, as well as the
> king had? . . . But you'll say, I am out of fashion, because I make
> neither Rimes nor Faces, for Fiddlers pay, like the Royal Mercuries;
> yet you shall know I have authority enough to create a fashion of
> my own, and make all the world to follow the humour.[16]

This is a call for cultural revolution. The Miltonic notion that political revolution demands, and even enforces, micro-revolutions in personal conduct is prevalent in the journal's pages. In October it recalled
admiringly how the people of republican Rome "observed every man's
looks, his very nods, his garb and his gait; whether he walked, con-
versed, and lived as a friend of freedom among his neighbours" (ibid.).
There was naturally also a great deal of hard news to be relayed, much
of it military. In late 1649 and early 1650 Cromwell had crushed the
Irish rebellion with extreme brutality, including wholesale massacres of

civilians at Wexford and Drogheda. In June 1650 the son of the late king, styling himself Charles II, took the Presbyterian covenant, thus facilitating an alliance of convenience with the Scots, who remained determined to impose their state religion on their southern neighbors. The series of campaigns continued until September 2, 1651, when Cromwell finally defeated the pretender's military ambitions at the battle of Worcester. Many people, including Cromwell himself, perceived the hand of God in his dramatic victories, and Milton was moved to compose one of his occasional political sonnets in his praise. It was his first work of poetry in four years, and he communicates his interpretation of the remarkable events of the time in his description of how Cromwell "on the neck of crowned Fortune proud / Hast rear'd God's trophies" (5–6) (Sonnet XXVI, 160). By comparing monarchy to "Fortune" Milton shows his disdain for the arbitrary, unprincipled, whimsical rule of a single man; by announcing Cromwell's triumphs to be "God's trophies" he signals his continuing faith that the revolution was a divinely ordained, providential sequence of events. But the poem ends with a caution and an appeal for a different kind of assistance from "our chief of men":

> New foes arise
> Threat'ning to bind our souls with secular chains:
> Help us to save free Conscience from the paw
> Of hireling wolves whose gospel is their maw. (11–14)

The specific reference is to the Presbyterians, but more generally Milton is recommending the permanent separation of church and state as a matter of principle. This was an issue of growing prominence, as many members of the Rump were advocating the reimposition of some form of official state religion. In the same year Milton composed another sonnet to Henry Vane, which praised the young Member of Parliament's ability "to know / Both spirituall powre & civill, what each meanes, / What severs each . . ." (8–10). The separation of church and state was for Milton the most vital gain of the revolution, to be preserved at all costs. A state church will always attract insincere "hirelings," and the remuneration of the priesthood by wage-labor will naturally encourage such priests to suppress competitors. Milton was certainly, as A.N. Wilson has put it, "among the most beautiful of capitalism's first fruits,"[17] and he was the most actively capitalist of any English poet. Nevertheless he was well aware of the morally enervating effects of capital, as we saw in his troubled, ambiguous attitude to usury, and here he evinces a shrewd awareness of the psychological distortions produced by wage-labor. It was a theme to which he would return later in *The Likeliest Means to Remove Hirelings*, and despite his own implication in dubious financial affairs, we can discern an unmistakable suspicion of capital and its effects in such passing remarks.

Milton's domestic affairs also continued to be problematic. In 1647 the Powells' Wheatley property had been awarded to Milton as the fruit of his usury. Since the death of her husband, Milton's mother-in-law, Mary Powell, was entitled to a share of the income known as the "widow's thirds," which Milton scrupulously paid until 1650. In that year, however, Parliament demanded fines from those who had been awarded the properties of former Royalists, in order to put a stop to the common practice of fraudulent transfers of ownership aimed at avoiding the payment of penalties. Milton now considered himself legally exonerated of the duty to pay his mother-in-law her share of the property's profits, and he abruptly ceased to do so. Mary Powell's opinion of her son-in-law is revealed by the fact that she evidently blamed him personally for this deprivation. She declared, with undue confidence:

By the law she might recover her thirds without doubt, but she is so extreme poor she hath nor wherewithal to prosecute, and besides, Mr. Milton is a harsh and choleric man, and married Mrs. Powell's daughter, who would be undone if any such course were taken against him by Mrs. Powell, he having turned away his wife heretofore for a long space upon some other occasion.[18]

Someone was being disingenuous here. Had Milton really "turned away his wife" in 1642, or had she left him at the urging of her Royalist family? Most early biographies of Milton suggest the latter, but they were composed by his close friends and relations. And did Mrs. Powell really fear that Milton would kick her daughter into the street in retaliation for any legal action against him? If so, why had he accepted her back into his home in the first place? In any case, it seems that his mother-in-law succeeded in souring relations between Milton and the rest of his family. A third daughter was born in April 1652, and as happened so frequently in the seventeenth century, the birth proved dramatically deleterious to the mother's health. Mary Milton died three weeks after giving birth to the child, whom Milton rather strangely named Deborah. This was an unusual name at the time, and it belonged to the biblical prophetess who had liberated the Israelites from their Philistine oppressors. It would have been typical of Milton to send a message to posterity by such means, announcing the true state of his marital relations. In any case the family was never destined for happiness. Milton's only son, also named John, followed his mother to the grave later in 1652, aged just fifteen months, and Milton's nephew Edward Phillips later blamed "the ill usage or bad constitution of an ill-chosen nurse."[19] Since deaths in early childhood were very common, Phillips's comment suggests that the tragedy was the subject of some controversy within the Milton household, much like his suggestion that the disability of Milton's first daughter had been caused by neglect. In any case, his mid-forties found Milton blind and surrounded by female relatives who gave every appearance of loyalty to the maternal side of the family rather than to its patriarch.

He cannot be called lonely, however. During these years Milton gathered around him a circle of mostly younger men, who appear to have filled the role of surrogate sons. They included Nedham, whom the early biographer Anthony Wood described as his "great crony," the poet Andrew Marvell, the Phillips brothers and other former pupils like Cyriack Skinner and Edward Lawrence. The early biographies emphasize Milton's sociability. Aubrey calls him possessed "of a very cheerful humour . . . extremely pleasant in his conversation, and at dinner and supper," and remarks that as he aged "he would be cheerful even in his gout-fits, and sing."[20] Toland reports his "equal and cheerful temper," although Aubrey qualifies his praise of Milton's good humor by noting that it was "satirical," and Anthony Wood claims he was "of a very sharp, biting and satirical wit."[21] It is easy to sympathize with Milton's servant, who apparently followed some of London's more outrageous sectarian preachers. According to Jonathan Richardson's *Life* this unfortunate was

> a very honest, silly fellow, and a zealous and constant follower of these teachers; when he came from the meeting, his master would frequently ask him what he had heard, and divert himself with ridiculing their fooleries, or (it may be) the poor fellow's understanding; both one and t'other probably; however, this was so grievous to the good creature, that he left his service upon it.[22]

But even his daughter Deborah admitted he had been "delightful company, the life of the conversation" and mentioned his "unaffected cheerfulness and civility."[23] He was a likeable man, and most people liked him, even if those closest to him did not. In any case, he had more than enough work to distract him from his domestic griefs. Relations with the United Provinces of the Netherlands were at an especially crucial stage, and they reveal an intriguing contradiction between ideological sympathy and economic self-interest. In political, religious and cultural terms the two nations shared much in common, and in 1651 Cromwell actually made overtures aimed at integrating their governments, in order to conquer and divide the crumbling but lucrative Spanish empire between them. In many ways, including the physical, the Netherlands were far closer to England's government than was Scotland, and Cromwell's idea was both rational and visionary. It foundered on the rocks of more immediate commercial rivalries, however, and in 1652 the neighbors found themselves at war. Milton was instrumental in the various stages of negotiations and studied Dutch under the aegis of his friend Roger Williams, the former governor of Rhode Island. Williams was an enthusiastic advocate of Milton's ideas and wrote to friends encouraging them to read his work. But the reputation of a sexual libertine was hard to shake, and one lady wrote in reply: "If I be not mistaken that is he that has wrote a book of the lawfulness of divorce, and if report says true, he had at that time two or three wives living. This perhaps were good doctrine in New England, but it is most abominable in old England."[24]

It is interesting to learn that Milton had the popular reputation of being a polygamist. He did in fact defend polygamy in *Of Christian Doctrine*, and although he did not publish that work during his lifetime, one wonders how often, and in what company, Milton espoused such views. One even wonders whether he ever translated them into practice, at least to the extent of engaging in extramarital sexual intercourse. In 1656 he wrote to the son of Lady Ranelagh, who was separated from her husband, informing him that "to me also she has stood in the place of all kith and kin."[25] This would of course include the role of wife, Mary Milton having died four years previously, and William Riley Parker is correct to observe that "[t]he meager facts of this relationship are most tantalizing . . . Lady Ranelagh was an intimate friend, almost like a younger sister, to Milton. . . . Was she anything more?. . . . We shall probably never know" (ibid.). True enough, but we can surely assume that the connoisseur of female beauty whom we meet in the early Elegies, the passionate admirer of Charles Diodati whom we encounter in the *Epithaphium Damonis*, the proposer of a bigamous marriage to Mary Davis, the haughty disdainer of convention and petty morality, would not have been averse in principle to an extra-marital liaison. There were plenty of libertines among the republicans: Henry Marten, one of the most radical of the Rumpers, was among the most unabashed whoremongers of the age. In 1656 Milton's nephew John Phillips, who had lived with and been educated by his uncle, published a compilation of racy literature entitled *Sportive Wit: The Muses' Merriment*, which was condemned as obscene in Parliament and publicly burned. His other nephew Edward, also educated by Milton, published a handbook of erotic chat-up lines entitled *The Arts of Wooing*, which included such phrases as "Will you ambrosiac kisses bathe my lips?," "Midnight would blush at this," and "You walk in artificial clouds and bathe your silken limbs in wanton dalliance."[26] Perhaps Milton was not quite a Lothario, but he was certainly no prude when it came to the pleasures of the flesh. To fully enjoy those pleasures, however, they must be kept in their appropriate place as the servant, not the master, of the mind's rational faculties. It was the reversal of this relationship, not the indulgence in carnality itself, that Milton condemned in the morality of the Cavaliers.

As his reputation as a public relations man for the Commonwealth grew, and especially following his vicious destruction of the hapless

Salmasius, Milton's own morality was subjected to increasingly virulent attacks, which often focused on his sexuality. Salmasius himself was reduced to asserting that Milton had supported himself in Italy by "selling his buttocks for a few pence," while the former Bishop Bramhall claimed he had been expelled from Cambridge for "unnatural" sexual practices. In 1652 came the anonymous publication of *The Cry of the Royal Blood to Heaven against the English Parricides*, which cast numerous aspersions on Milton personally, as well as on the government he served. It was obviously not written by Salmasius, who was by now in badly failing health brought on, as Milton contentedly assumed, by the damage *The Defence of the English People* had done to his reputation, but it returned with interest the abuse Milton had dished out, accusing him of being a "worm voided from the dung pit" and threatening him with violence and death: "Seize him! Quick! Quick! Bind him hands and feet! I owe him the sacred rites of the scourge. First, prod with a goad, this future disciple to a gallows, this great bulwark of the people, this prop of Parliament."[27]

This was no joke; this was exactly the fate that Milton could expect if King Charles II should ever come to power. Milton admits that he is unsure of the precise identity of the author of *The Cry of the Royal Blood*, but he is certain that he must be "some skulking and drivelling miscreant. . . . Certainly one of the dregs of men, for even slaves are not without a name" (4.i.560). The tract's true author, who wisely declined to reveal himself, was one Pierre du Moulin, but Milton chose instead to believe the rumors that a Scots-French clergyman named Alexander More was the guilty party. This was a convenient belief, because the scandalous nature of More's personal life allowed Milton ample scope for the invective he so relished. His reply, known as *The Second Defence of the English People* and published in 1654, is yet more abandonedly scurrilous than its predecessor. Making diligent inquiries,

Milton discovered that, while a Presbyterian minister in Geneva, More had "conceived a violent passion for the maid-servant of his host, and even after she was married to another, did not cease to solicit the gratification of his lust" (4.i.591). Having lost his job by this scandal, More decamped to the Netherlands and "went to pay his respects to Salmasius; where he immediately cast his libidinous looks on his wife's maid, whose name was Pontia; for the fellow's lust is always inflamed by cooks and waiting-maids" (ibid.). This provided endless scope for Milton's customary reflections on the relations between sexual and political servility. He even descends to hinting that More enjoyed sexual practices that were regarded as perverted and servile, so that his "breath is steaming with the effluvia of venereal putrescence." Like Salmasius, More was understandably distressed on finding himself the target of such abuse, and he made every effort to suppress Milton's book, even going to the lengths of personally buying up all 500 copies that had been delivered to one bookseller. He was also bemused, since his role in the production of *The Cry of the Royal Blood* had been limited to writing a short preface and delivering the manuscript to the publisher. He made inquiries among his friends as to what he might have done to deserve Milton's fury, and he must have been confused to learn from one correspondent that no major offence was necessary:

> This man [i.e. Milton] hath been told that you were not the author
> of the book which he refuted; to which he answered that he was
> at least assured that you had writ the preface and, he believes,
> some of the verses that are in it, and that that is enough to justify
> him for setting upon you.[28]

One is forced to conclude that by this stage his various personal and political travails had driven Milton beyond the point of reason. He

lashed out wildly at every adversary in sight, including the tract's publisher Vlacq, who had contributed a brief forward to *The Cry*. Displaying
sound business sense, Vlacq had also offered to publish Milton's work,
but Milton is outraged that commercial considerations should have been
allowed to influence the man's conscience:

> But lo! He, who had lately made me such an officious proffer of his
> services, soon appears, not only as the printer, but the (suborned)
> author of a most scandalous libel upon my character. My friends
> express their indignation; he replies with unabashed effrontery,
> that he is quite astonished at their simplicity and ignorance of the
> world, in supposing that he should suffer any notions of right or
> wrong to disturb his calculations of profit, and his speculations of
> gain. (4.i.593)

The pattern of logic that always guides Milton's thought is asserting itself here: Royalists are slaves, and since servility follows appetite
rather than reason, the defenders of the King will naturally be monsters
of financial and sexual incontinence: "[S]uch a cause was not likely to
procure adversaries of a different stamp." Milton's opinion, confirmed by
long experience, of the connection between the personal and the political removes any shame he might have felt at descending to this level. To
defend himself was to defend his nation for, he demands, "[W]ho is there
who does not identify the honor of his country with his own?" (ibid.). It
is fortunate for posterity's knowledge of Milton that he held such views,
for they impel him into the most revealing autobiographical revelations of
his career. He had been attacked for alleged physical ugliness (an impression that would have been reinforced by anyone who took the engraving
on the frontispiece of his book of poems as a true likeness). He finds even
such silly accusations worthy of rebuttal:

I do not believe that I was ever once noted for deformity . . . My
stature certainly is not tall, but it rather approaches the middle
than the diminutive . . . Nor, though very thin, was I ever deficient
in courage or in strength; and I was wont constantly to exercise
myself in the use of the broadsword as long as it comported with
my habit and my years. Armed with this weapon, as I usually was,
I should have thought myself quite a match for any one, though
much stronger than myself; and I felt perfectly secure against the
assault of any open enemy. At this moment I have the same courage, the same strength, though not the same eyes; yet so little do
they betray any external appearance of injury that they are as
unclouded and bright as the eyes of those who most distinctly see
. . . though I am more than forty years old, there is scarcely anyone
to whom I do not appear ten years younger than I am; and the
smoothness of my skin is not in the least affected by the wrinkles
of age. (4.i.603)

And in what is surely a deliberately humorous gesture, Milton bitch-
ily derides his opponent's appearance in the act of announcing that such
tactics are beneath his dignity: "Respecting yours, though I have been
informed that it is most insignificant and contemptible, a perfect mirror of
the worthlessness of your character and the malevolence of your heart, I
say nothing" (ibid.). This kind of viciousness would be unbecoming were
it not for the historical context in which it was composed, and Milton
makes it clear that he considers his pamphleteering as war conducted by
other means:

For though I did not participate in the toils or dangers of the war,
yet I was at the same time engaged in a service not less hazardous

to myself, and more beneficial to my fellow-citizens; nor, in the adverse turns of our affairs, did I ever betray any symptoms of pusillanimity and dejection; or show myself more afraid than became me, of malice or of death. (4.i.604)

The personal and the political are inseparable. Therefore, just as Milton defames the character of the Commonwealth's enemies, he praises at length the personal virtues of its leaders, particularly Cromwell, and his personal friend John Bradshaw. He explains his long-held view that a virtuous character is the best qualification for political power. The English civil war had been won and lost within the minds of the combatants:

Other camps are the scenes of gambling, swearing, riot, and debauchery; in ours, the troops employ what leisure they have in searching the Scriptures and hearing the word; nor is there one, who thinks it more honourable to vanquish the enemy than to propagate the truth; and they not only carry on a military warfare against their enemies, but an evangelical one against themselves. (4.i.606)

This internal holy war against slavish desires determined the outcome of the external holy war against the advocates of political slavery. Before seizing the government of England, Milton declares that Cromwell "first acquired the government of himself, and over himself acquired the most signal victories; so that on the first day he took the field against the external enemy, he was a veteran in arms, consummately practised in the toils and exigencies of war" (4.i.608). Addressing Thomas Fairfax, Cromwell's predecessor as commander of the parliamentary forces, Milton exults: "Nor was it only the enemy whom you subdued; but you have triumphed over that flame of ambition and that lust of glory, which are wont to make the best and the greatest of men their slaves" (4.i.610). Although he would have disdained the term, Milton was anticipating the tactics of future revolutions by constructing personality cults around England's liberators. It is interesting to find a particularly warm reference to the Leveller leader Richard Overton, and the terms in which Milton expresses his admiration suggest that their views may have been surprisingly close: "O Overton! Who hast been most endeared to me now for so many years by the similitude of our studies, the suavity of your manners, and the more than fraternal sympathy of our hearts" (ibid.). In spite of its exultant tone, however, the content of *The Second Defence* is notably more pessimistic than that of the first. In 1651 Milton had expressed the hope that, although the "good" people of England were presently in a minority, they would eventually grow to numerical as well as moral superiority. By 1654 this hope appears to have evaporated, and Milton presents the virtuous as a struggling, beleaguered minority:

> Who denies, that there may be times, in which the vicious may constitute the majority of the citizens, who would rather follow Cataline or Antony, than the more virtuous part of the senate? But are not good citizens on this account to oppose the bad with vigour and decision? Ought they not to be less deterred by the smallness of their numbers, than they are animated by the goodness of their cause? (4.i.612)

Milton distrusted democracy for the same reason he distrusted the market: They both led to the rule of quantity over quality. The fact that he was himself a lifelong beneficiary of the market goes some way to explaining the stunningly splenetic tone of his prose in the 1650s. Like his heroes Cromwell and Fairfax, he was not only battling external enemies, he was also fighting against himself.

III

THERE WERE ALSO good political reasons for pessimism, for by 1654 the republican principles for which Milton had believed himself to be fighting were under significant threat, this time from within the revolution. In yet another uncanny parallel with its French and Russian successors, the English revolution could survive only by replicating the tyranny it had aspired to abolish. Inexperienced and factious, the Rump Parliament quickly degenerated into an impotent and corrupt talking shop; many of its members feared the power of the army and refused to address its grievances. By April 1653 Cromwell had reached the end of his short tether. In an ironic but far more successful echo of Charles I's attempt to arrest the five members, he personally strode into the House accompanied by armed men. "[P]erceiving the spirit of God so strong upon me,"[29] as he later explained, he decided, apparently on the spot, to dissolve the assembly altogether. "Come, come," he exclaimed, "I will put an end to your prating. You are no Parliament. I say you are no Parliament. I will put an end to your sitting." Milton's friend Henry Vane rose to protest: "This is not honest, yea it is against morality and common honesty," which completed Cromwell's exasperation: "O Sir Henry Vane, Sir Henry Vane, the Lord deliver me from Sir Henry Vane." A detailed account of events is provided by an early eighteenth-century history:

> [Cromwell] commanded the Speaker to leave the Chair, and told them they had sat long enough, unless they had done more good, crying out You are no longer a Parliament, I say you are no Parliament. He told Sir Henry Vane was a Jugler; Henry Martin and Sir Peter Wentworth that they were Whoremasters; Thomas Chaloner, he was a Drunkard; and Allen the Goldsmith that he cheated the Publick: Then he bid one of his Soldiers take away that

Fool's Bauble the mace and Thomas Harrison pulled the Speaker

of the Chair; and in short Cromwell haveing turned them all out of

the House, lock'd up the Doors and returned to Whitehall.[30]

The facade of representative government survived a little while longer. The Independent churches were asked to nominate Members of Parliament, and the resulting assembly of incompetent visionaries, made up of what the Earl of Clarendon would call "inferior persons of no quality or name, artificers of the meanest trades," became known as "Barebones' Parliament," after one of its more enthusiastic members, Praise-God Barbon (in a delicious historical irony his son Nicholas would later become one of the earliest capitalist economists, building his theories on the foundations of Salmasius's rationalization of usury). These men bickered and quarreled to little practical effect for a few months until Cromwell saw no alternative but to take power into his own hands. In December 1653 he was declared "Lord Protector" of England.

We might expect Milton to have been dismayed by such developments, which were clearly tending toward the concentration of power in the hands of one man. As many among the republicans remarked, this was to transform the vaunted "new representative" of Parliament into something closely resembling the old representative of monarchy. Milton's closest friends certainly noticed the way things were going. John Bradshaw resigned as head of the Council of State in November 1651, and John Dury reported that Cromwell "alone holds the direction of political and military affairs in his hands. He is ONE equivalent to all, and, in effect, King."[31] But Milton remained in the government's service, and in 1654's *Second Defence* he extols Cromwellian rule in the most exalted of terms. Following the dissolution of Barebones' Parliament:

you, O Cromwell! alone remained to conduct the government, and
to save the country. We all willingly yield the palm of sovereignty
to your unrivalled ability and virtue, except the few among us,
who, either ambitious of honours which they have not the capacity to sustain, or who envy those which are conferred on one more
worthy than themselves, or else who do not know that nothing
in the world is more pleasing to God, more agreeable to reason,
more politically just, or more generally useful, than that the supreme power should be vested in the best and the wisest of men.
Such, O Cromwell, all acknowledge you to be . . . (4.i.615)

This was not inconsistent with Milton's lifelong conviction that
power should be vested in the most virtuous citizens. Cromwell had
indeed distinguished himself by his heroic fortitude in battle and the
strict rectitude of his personal morality. But the fact remained that the
Protectorship assumed that the people of England could be represented by
a single individual, and this was a principle to which Milton had recently
declared himself irreconcilably opposed. He solaces himself by noting
that Cromwell had been offered, and had refused, the crown itself: "[T]he
title of king was unworthy the transcendant majesty of your character."
He bravely reminds the Protector of his duty to to keep his power within
strictly limited bounds:

You cannot be truly free, unless we are free too; for such is the
nature of things, that he who entrenches on the liberty of others
is the first to lose his own and become a slave. But, if you, who
have hitherto been the patron and tutelary genius of liberty, if you
who are exceeded by no one in justice, in piety, and in goodness,
should hereafter invade that liberty which you have defended,

your conduct must be fatally operative, not only against the cause
of liberty, but the general interests of piety and virtue. Your integrity and virtue will appear to have evaporated, your faith in
religion to have been small; your character with posterity will
dwindle into insignificance, by which a most destructive blow will
be levelled against the happiness of mankind. (ibid.)

He even goes so far as to urge Cromwell to share power with other,
equally virtuous army leaders. But he did not go so far as to resign his
position as a government servant, which he retained throughout the
Protectorate. Milton did not need the money, and he was hardly the
man to sacrifice principle to political ambition. He continued to serve the
Protector because of his conviction that true liberty, and real oppression,
was internal rather than external. The purpose of the revolution had been
to make the English people psychologically free, and finally, as he reminds
them in *The Second Defence*, the achievement of such freedom lies within
their power alone:

Unless you will subjugate the propensity to avarice, to ambition,
and sensuality, and expel all luxury from yourselves and from your
families, you will find that you have cherished a more stubborn
and intractable despot at home, than you ever encountered in the
field; and even your very bowels will be continually teeming with
an intolerable progeny of tyrants. (ibid.)

The imagery here anticipates *Paradise Lost*'s allegorical portrayal of
Sin as unceasingly giving birth to hell-hounds that constantly gnaw their
way back into her entrails. It also reveals a significant shift in Milton's
politics. In his first regicidal tracts, tyranny is presented as imposed on
the people by external force. Under the Protectorate, however, tyranny

is produced within the minds of the people themselves. This is an idea that he would bring to fruition in *Paradise Lost*, but already in 1654 Milton argues that royalism and republicanism are finally internal, moral issues. To be enslaved by psychological appetites is to be a royalist, no matter what political persuasion one formally adopts. It was by subduing such lusts, as Milton informs his countrymen, that "you obtained the ascendant over the royalists. If you plunge into the same depravity, if you imitate their excesses, and hanker after the same vanities, you will become royalists as well as they . . ." (4.i.617).

His worry is not that Cromwell is personally admirable enough to rule—of that he has no doubt. Rather, his concern is that he may have been selected to rule for royalist rather than republican reasons. Milton is afraid that their adoration of the Protector may be revealing the English people's natural propensity to idolatry and slavery. Noting that licentious and avaricious people continue to feature prominently among the citizenry, he warns: "It is not agreeable to the nature of things, that such persons ever should be free. However much they may brawl about liberty, they are slaves, both at home and abroad, but without perceiving it" (4.i.618). Milton can have taken little comfort from the rule of the Major-Generals, whom Cromwell appointed in 1655 to rule over the provinces of England and who dramatically eroded the government's popularity by attempting to suppress alehouses, horse racing, dancing, even the celebration of Christmas. He must have felt that the message of his *Areopagitica*—"[L]ook how much we thus expel of sin, so much we expel of virtue: for the matter of them both is the same" (2:527)—had fallen on stone-deaf ears.

Milton may also have believed that his involvement might exert a salutary influence on government policy. In early 1655 news reached England of the horrific massacre of the Waldenses, a religious sect that claimed to have preserved themselves continuously from Papist idolatry since apostolic times. Milton agreed with their self-evaluation and was appalled to hear that the Duke of Piedmont had determined to root these heretics out of his domain with atrocious violence. The Council of State dispatched an ambassador to investigate the affair and sent endless missives to foreign powers protesting against this persecution. They may well have been composed by Milton himself; his indignation certainly impelled him to write one of his most impassioned political sonnets, calling on God to "Avenge, O Lord, thy slaughter'd saints," and once again looking forward to a pan-European revolution against the "Babylonian woe" imposed by the Papal "triple tyrant" (Sonnet XVIII). Clearly the hope that the English revolution might prove a harbinger of the Apocalypse itself was not yet entirely extinguished in Milton's breast.

But he was now approaching fifty, the threshold of old age in the seventeenth century, and being completely blind, he was in constant need of the care and attention of others. The vibrant young men with whom he surrounded himself were doubtless a great help, but he also felt the need of more intimate assistance. Accordingly, in November 1656, he remarried, naturally in a civil ceremony. His bride, twenty years his junior, was Katherine Woodcock, the daughter of a bookseller turned soldier who had been killed in the war against the Scots. The couple lost no time in consummating the match, and in October 1657 Milton's fifth child, a daughter named after her mother, was born. But Milton was destined to a tragic personal life. The new mother rapidly sickened and died, and the baby followed shortly afterward. This drew from Milton his most moving and personal poem, the sonnet beginning "Methought I saw my late espoused saint." In a dream, the poet recounts seeing the veiled face of the wife on whose real features he had been unable to gaze in life. The sonnet's final lines suggest that the invisible world of dreams, in which Milton received visitations from unearthly spirits, was already more real to him than the fallen world of sensual experience: "But Oh! as to embrace me she inclin'd, / I wak'd, she fled, and day brought back my night" (13–14).

These personal sorrows were soon followed by bitter political disappointment. In September 1658, quite suddenly, Oliver Cromwell died. The Commonwealth was thrown into confusion, as the question of political representation reasserted itself with dramatic force. Parliamentary representation having been seen to fail, the political nation could conceive no alternative but a return to the monarchical model. Cromwell's son Richard inherited the Protectorship. But Milton's strictures against the representation of a nation by a single individual were soon amply vindicated. Richard Cromwell, known to contemporaries as "Tumbledown Dick," was possessed of a character diametrically opposed to that of his father. Amiable, easygoing and indolent, he had neither the taste nor the capacity for political power, and he wisely abdicated in May 1659. The army once again took control, restoring a tiny, nominal group of Members of Parliament to provide the facade of a Parliament: the rump of the Rump.

In the early 1650s Milton had been absolutely certain that the course of the revolution was being guided directly by the hand of Providence. This belief now died slowly within him. Or rather, perhaps, it remained alive, but altered his opinion of Providence itself. How could a deity who was both benign and omnipotent allow the defeat of so righteous a cause? He had, furthermore, ample reason to take God's actions personally. Not only had he lost two wives and two children, not only had he been struck blind at the height of his powers; he now faced the prospect of a traitor's death, if the increasingly eager Charles II should manage to seize the throne. For a whole year he stubbornly refused to believe it possible. In February 1659 he published *Of Civil Power in Ecclesiastical Causes*, followed in August by *The Likeliest Means to Remove Hirelings*. These tracts returned to the theme of his earliest prose publications, the mode of church government. They vehemently insist on the need to keep church and state separate, and they argue forcefully against the remuneration of priests by tithes. Milton conceived of tithes as a form of wage-labor, and he recognized wage-labor as a piecemeal form of slavery. The liturgical form of slavery was idolatry, just as its political form was monarchy, so Milton was convinced that a "hireling" priest must inevitably be both an idolator and a royalist. *The Likeliest Means* also contains the nearest Milton ever came to a recantation of his earlier opinions. It applauds the reassembling of the Rump after a "short but scandalous night of interruption." This can only refer to the Protectorship, which Milton had supported in print and served in practice. But we need not convict him of error. It is true that in *The Second Defence* he had defended Cromwell's personal rule, on the grounds of his unparalleled personal virtue. In the same tract, however, he had warned of disaster should the Protector prove personally unworthy of the responsibility bestowed upon him. The succession of Oliver Cromwell by Richard resoundingly confirmed this opinion, and *The Likeliest Means* deplores the practical consequences of the Protectorship rather than the principle of rule by the most virtuous.

Milton still refused to give up hope; he remained in government service when many others were abandoning a manifestly sinking ship, and he continued to receive his government salary until the end of 1659. In January of the following year, however, the end began to approach, slowly but inexorably. General "Silent George" Monk had grown disgusted at the chaotic condition of England's ever-changing governments. He led his army out of Scotland and marched on London, prudently keeping his intentions to himself. Most people managed to guess what they were, but Milton either mistook or, more likely, defied them. His many enemies were already licking their lips in anticipation of vengeance, and Milton once again found himself the subject of public mockery. He was derided in such tracts as *The Outcry of London Prentices* and Roger L'Estrange's cruelly titled *No Blind Guides*. The anonymous *Character of the Rump* described him as

> an old heretic both in religion and manners, that by his will would shake off his governours as he doth his wives, four in a fortnight. . . . He is so much an enemy to usual practices that I believe, when he is condemned to travel to Tyburn in a cart, he will petition to be the first man that ever was driven thither in a wheelbarrow.[32]

As disturbing as such threats must have been, this description at least does Milton the service of recognizing the thoroughgoing, all-inclusive nature of his political, sexual and social iconoclasm. But the day of the iconoclasts was drawing to its close. Arriving in the capital, Monk recalled the original Long Parliament that had been elected in 1640. This body was obviously royalist in orientation, but still Milton struggled against the tide of history. In an act of truly suicidal bravery he published *The Readie and Easie Way to Establish a Free Commonwealth*, bringing out an augmented second edition within three weeks of the monarchy's restoration. He had no hope of changing the collective minds of either the Parliament or the people, and he knew it. He was, as always, writing for posterity, recording his implacable resolution for the inspiration of future generations:

> Thus much I should perhaps have said though I were sure I should have spoken only to trees and stones; and had none to cry to, but with the Prophet, *O earth, earth, earth,* to tell the very soil itself what its perverse inhabitants are deaf to. (7:462–3)

The tract is clearly written in sorrow, in anger, and in haste. Observing that most English people now clearly desired the restoration of monarchy, Milton robustly reiterates his conviction that the qualities of reason and virtue, rather than a quantitative majority, ought to decide the form and nature of government. The inherent purpose of government, he repeats, is to ensure the liberty of the people:

> They who past reason and recoverie are devoted to kingship, per-
> haps will answer, that a greater part by far of the Nation will have
> it so; the rest therefor must yield. . . . Suppose they be; yet of free-
> dom they partake all alike, one main end of government: which if
> the greater part value not, but will degeneratly forgoe, is it just or
> reasonable, that most voices against the main end of government
> should enslave the less number that would be free? More just it is
> doubtless, if it com to force, that a less number compell a greater
> to retain, which can be no wrong to them, thir libertie, then that
> a greater number for the pleasure of thir baseness, compell a less
> most injuriously to be thir fellow slaves. (7:455)

Milton is arguing for what Robespierre, over a century later, would call a "dictatorship of virtue." Those who have liberated themselves internally, who have freed themselves from their own lusts and desires, have the right, even the duty, to force those who remain "slaves within doors" to follow their example, no matter how disproportionate their numbers may be. This is familiar Miltonic doctrine. But *The Readie and Easie Way* also contains a very new idea, an idea that seems far more readily and easily applicable to our time than to Milton's: a prophetic idea. Milton now attributes the people's impulse to servility not to human nature, but to a quite specific economic formation. He blames their desire for slavery on the market economy. It is consumerism that fosters servile sensuality;

it is the process of commodification that debases government, morality and religion. Milton protests against the vulgar argument that monarchy is good for business:

> if trade be grown so craving and importunate through the pro-
> fuse living of tradsmen that nothing can support it, but the luxu-
> rious expences of a nation upon trifles or superfluities, so as if
> the people generally should betake themselves to frugalitie, it
> might prove a dangerous matter, least tradesmen should mutinie
> for want of trading, and that therefor we must forgoe and set
> to sale religion, libertie, honour, safetie, all concernments divine
> or human to keep up trading, if lastly, after all this light among
> us, the same reason shall pass for current to put our necks again
> under kingship, as was made use of by the Jews to return back to
> Egypt and to the worship of thir idol queen, because they falsly
> imagind that they then lived in more plenty and prosperitie, our
> condition is not sound but rotten, both in religion and all civil
> prudence. (7:386)

These are words that speak to us today, but they were neither addressed nor attended to by the people of Milton's time. On May 29, 1660, Charles II entered London to the triumphant applause of the masses. Those Commonwealth men who had not prudently made their peace with the new regime were imprisoned, fled the country or went into hiding. Milton chose the last course. A warrant for his arrest was issued in June, and in August a royal proclamation erroneously declared him "fled." All his books were called in and burned publicly by the hangman at the Old Bailey. But the Providence that must by now have appeared to Milton as a remorseless persecutor showed him an unexpected mercy. With prudent though reluctant clemency, Charles issued an Act of Free and General Pardon, which, while generous in general, condemned to death those directly responsible for his father's execution. Although Milton had been the loudest public celebrant of Charles I's death, and indeed had composed the revolutionary regime's official justification of the regicide, his name was not on the list. He came out of hiding to suffer arrest and a brief imprisonment for the final two months of 1660. Then he was let go.

Nobody knows exactly why he was spared. It is likely that his royalist brother interceded for him; it is probable that his many friends who found themselves able to live with the new regime, such as Andrew Marvell, pleaded his case. Marvell certainly protested in Parliament that Milton had been overcharged for his stay in jail. But it seems most reasonable to suppose that he was allowed to live on, in humiliation, blindness, poverty and obscurity, as an example to any who might be tempted to follow in his footsteps. As one anonymous rhyme from the early 1670s put it: "That thou escap'st that vengeance which o'ertook, / Milton, thy regicides, and thy own book, / Was clemency in Charles beyond compare. / And yet thy doom doth prove more grievous far: / Old, sickly, poor, stark blind, thou writ'st for bread / So for to live thou'dst call Salmasius from the dead."[33] Milton most certainly did provide an example to posterity, but in a manner quite the reverse of what his enemies had expected. Permanently banned from any further involvement in political affairs, he was finally free to complete what he had always seen as the work to which his life was consecrated. He returned to the composition of *Paradise Lost*.

8

BLIND MAN'S BLUFF

I

CHARLES II'S DECISION to spare Milton's life proved, in the long term, to be one of history's gravest blunders. The crowned heads of Europe would be paying the price of this mistake for centuries. For Charles's clemency made possible the composition of *Paradise Lost,* which would become an inspiration for many and various subsequent anti-monarchical revolts. It inspired many of the ideas and actors behind the Glorious Revolution of 1688, in which the English people expelled Charles II's brother James II and selected for themselves a new monarch, on terms that Milton would have found far more congenial than the reactionary settlement of the Restoration. Since then Milton's epic has functioned as kind of literary time bomb, exploding into life in the minds of the eighteenth-century American patriots, fanning the flames of republicanism in revolutionary France, setting fire in the bellies of the Romantic and Socialist insurrectionaries of the nineteenth and twentieth centuries. It is not inconceivable that Milton's poetic prophecy may yet help awaken the presently dormant aspirations to liberty that, as he would have argued, lie within the breasts of virtuous men and women in every epoch.

Forbidden to take any further part in public life, Milton spent his fifties as he had spent his twenties, shut away in private contemplation and composition. Until his late middle age his poetry, while it would certainly stand alone as a brilliant corpus, falls short of the epic aspirations that Milton had been putting on record since earliest adulthood. He had dedicated the best twenty years of his life to politics, and his poetry up until the Restoration can best be characterized as he himself described it: the "buds" and "blossoms" of promise rather than fulfillment. This time, however, his labors bore very ripe fruit. It is incomprehensible, almost incredible, that a blind man should have composed a work of such verbal complexity and technical brilliance as *Paradise Lost*. Some critics suppose that it must have been written earlier than the 1660s. It is true that Milton showed a small finished section to his nephew in 1642, and as we have seen, he mentions a surprisingly well-developed plan to compose an epic describing the councils of heaven and hell in his very earliest poems. It is probable that *Paradise Lost* was in some sense his whole life's work.

But while it might have been started, it was evidently far from completed before the Restoration, for it consists in large part of an effort to come to terms with Milton's circumstances following that most bitter of defeats. *Paradise Lost* is a "theodicy," an attempt, as Milton puts it, to "justify the ways of God to men."[1] From Milton's perspective, they were in bad need of justification. The most pressing personal grievance he had against God was his blindness. The defeat of his cause and the deaths of his wives and children were misfortunes shared by many others, but blindness must have seemed an affliction aimed at him personally, cruelly and specifically designed to prevent him from achieving what he had always assumed was his purpose on this earth: the composition of the greatest poem ever written. What sort of God would do such a thing?

Either an evil god, or a God whose actions are not to be taken literally but interpreted in a symbolic, or "mysterious," manner. Either a malicious enemy of the human race or a being whose nature is not to be understood from mere appearances. Although in *Paradise Lost* he often seems tempted to endorse the concept of an evil god, Milton ultimately rejects it. He chooses instead to reinterpret his physical blindness, locating its true significance behind its seemingly obvious meaning. Before the Restoration, defending himself against one of the many literary attacks he suffered because of his disability, Milton had told his opponent: "I would, Sir, prefer my blindness to yours: yours is a cloud spread over the mind, which darkens both the light of reason and of conscience; mine keeps from my view only the coloured surfaces of things" (4.i.589). Physical blindness removes the world of appearances, giving instead direct access to the essential, underlying reality that that world merely represents. In fact Milton proclaims that his affliction is actually a blessing: "[I]ndeed, in my blindness, I enjoy in no inconsiderable degree the favour of the Deity; who regards me with more tenderness and compassion in proportion as I am able to behold nothing but himself" (ibid.). He expands on this point in *Paradise Lost,* where, in a remarkably bold gesture, he reconciles his blindness with God's justice by claiming that the deity has compensated his loss of his sensory sight with the far more exalted gift of superhuman insight. He asserts that his poem is quite literally a divinely inspired work of prophecy.

Milton sincerely believed that he received nightly visitations from a divine spirit, which dictated to him directly, so that on waking in the morning he would call for his daughters, who labored as his amanuenses, demanding to be "milked" of the lines he had received during sleep. In one autobiographical passage he confidently anticipates the posthumous fame his work will win, "unless an age too late, or cold / Climate, or years damp my intended wing / Depressed, and much they may, if all be mine / Not hers who brings it nightly to my ear" (9:44–7). Milton points out that it would be effectively impossible for someone as old, obscure, ill, freezing and sad as himself to write a poem like this one. He advances this as proof that these cannot be his own words, but must rather be the Word of God, or perhaps the words of gods. For he calls the deity he invokes here his "celestial patroness," and he describes her in terms more reminiscent of the classical Muses than of the Christian God. The polytheistic culture of the Greco-Roman world had by no means been purged from his imagination by the sterner inheritance of the monotheistic Judeo-Christian tradition.

The conflicts and contradictions between Athens and Jerusalem had troubled Milton throughout his life. He was born and bred a Christian, but his capacious, tolerant mind would not allow him to dismiss pagan beliefs out of hand, as many of his Puritan contemporaries did. At the age of twenty-one, in the "Hymn on the Morning of Christ's Nativity," he had attempted to exult that the birth of Christ expelled the pagan gods, so that "Apollo from his shrine / Can no more divine / With hollow shriek the steep of Delphos leaving" (176–8). But one gets the impression that even that early in his career, his heart wasn't really in it. Milton's iconoclasm was directed against the internal idols of the mind, not the external icons of wood and stone. He was perfectly prepared to use the classical deities as symbolic tools to explore psychological states and experiences, much as Freud employed the myth of Oedipus. The really interesting, and truly subversive, point about *Paradise Lost* is that it treats Christianity in the same way.

It would hardly be surprising if Milton had repudiated Christianity altogether. The cause to which he had devoted his life's most energetic years, and which he had firmly believed to be God's, had been utterly defeated. He had suffered emotional and physical deprivations that would have crushed the spirit of virtually any man. To these were added, as a final insult to his old age, the exquisitely painful tortures of severe gout. Who would not turn his back on the power that had inflicted such calamities? And Milton did stop attending public church services, having concluded that any attempt to discipline or control the individual's relation to God was apostasy. In a poem published as a preface to *Paradise Lost,* Milton's close friend Andrew Marvell records his fear that the old man might be preparing to demolish the Christian faith altogether:

When I beheld the poet blind, yet bold,

In slender book his vast design unfold,

Messiah crowned, God's reconciled decree,

Rebelling angels, the forbidden tree,

Heaven, hell, earth, chaos, all; the argument

Held me a while misdoubting his intent,

That he would ruin (for I saw him strong)

The sacred truths to fable and old song

(So Sampson groped the Temple's post in spite)

The world o'erwhelming to revenge his sight. (*On Mr. Milton's Paradise Lost,* 1–10)

Marvell had been concerned that Milton's epic might "ruin," or reduce, the "sacred truths" of Christian scripture to the level of "fable" or mythology. The manifold tragedies of his biography, so the younger man worried, might have embittered Milton against God so badly that he would treat the biblical story in a manner akin to a Homeric or Virgilian epic, as a work of literary fiction rather than as the uniquely holy and inspired Word of God. As Marvell's verse goes on to admit, *Paradise Lost* does not quite do that. But Milton certainly does blend pagan, polytheistic

literature into the Judeo-Christian stories, and he also alters and extrapolates from the biblical narrative to suit his own purposes. *Paradise Lost*
is not a rejection of the Bible, but it is a supersession. Milton's bold and
unambiguous claim to divine inspiration confirms that he conceived of
his greatest work as a third Testament, assimilating but surpassing the
first two, and revising them in accordance with the dramatic, seemingly
incomprehensible history of his own life and times.

The key riddle that must we must solve in order to understand
Paradise Lost is the identity of the spirit that inspired it. If not Milton's,
then whose words, exactly, are we hearing as we read the poem? The
issue is raised directly in a series of invocations, strategically located at
the beginnings of books one, three, seven and nine. In book three Milton
calls upon a "holy Light" (3:1), which cannot, of course, be physical and
must therefore refer to a spiritual power. Although he cannot see, he
claims to "feel" (3:22) its influence and to "revisit" (3:21) it regularly.
Given the fact that his enemies had adduced his blindness as evidence of
divine disfavor, Milton could be forgiven for avoiding reference to his
disability altogether. But instead he tackles the issue head-on, following
the logic of his motto, "[I]n weakness my strength is made perfect," to
dig beneath the apparent, surface meaning of his loss of sight to uncover
its deeper significance. He allows himself a degree of pathos when,
addressing the "Light," he complains: "[T]hou / Revisit'st not these eyes,
that roll in vain / To find thy piercing ray" (3:22–4). Having engaged
the reader's sympathy, however, he employs it to draw a bold analogy between himself and the ancient tradition of sightless seers: "Blind
Thamyris, and blind Maeonides [Homer], / And Tiresias and Phineus
prophets old" (3:35–6).

Milton's selection of prophetic forbears is, as usual, highly significant.
According to a legend quoted by Milton in the *Second Defence,* Zeus

blinded Phineus as a punishment for the prophet's unerring insight into the affairs of the gods. He then condemned him to be forever tormented by three Harpies. Milton had three daughters; is he now suggesting that some malign deity has punished him in the same way, and for the same cause? Tiresias was famous for having magically spent time as both a woman and a man. Zeus therefore selected him to settle an argument he had been having with Hera about whether the male or female received greater pleasure from sexual intercourse. Tiresias answered that women enjoyed sex ten times more than men and, enraged at the prophet's public revelation of this female secret, Hera blinded him in revenge. Zeus then compensated him with the gift of foresight. Is Milton leaving us a clue as to his own sexual preferences? There is in any case no doubt that Milton had devoted lengthy consideration to the lineage of blind seers. Repudiating the mockery of his foes in the *Second Defence* he rhetorically asks:

> Shall I mention those wise and ancient bards whose misfortunes the gods are said to have compensated by superior endowments, and whom men so much revered that they chose rather to impute their want of sight to the injustice of heaven than to their own want of innocence or virtue? (4.i.584)

The people of the classical past chose to blame the gods for striking their seers blind. In this intriguing conflict between the virtue of men and "the injustice of heaven" we can discern a strong suggestion that the deity itself is hostile to humanity. The question arises again: Does Milton actually believe that God is evil? Is he in effect cursing divinity itself? Or is he, perhaps, suggesting that God has more than one aspect, many modes of manifestation? The ancient heresy of the Manicheans, which continually reasserts itself throughout Christian history, resolves the contradiction between belief in a benign deity and the manifest existence of evil by suggesting that there are actually two gods, one good and one evil, who are continually battling for control over the human soul. In *Paradise Lost* Milton frequently appears tempted to adopt this position. But as the poem's drama unfolds, we come to understand why he is tempted by Manicheansim: it is the theological position held by the Tempter. Satan's great mistake, the error that both causes and constitutes his alienation, is the belief that he acts independently of God, that he is an autonomous agent who is not under God's control but is somehow fighting or rebelling against Him. And this is where we find the poem's relevance to our situation today, for Satan falls into this fatal illusion because of the same misunderstanding of representation, the same political, economic, and sexual misconstrual of the relation between sign and thing—in short the same idolatry—that distorts the human mind in the twenty-first century.

II

MILTON'S LAST YEARS were not utterly devoid of comforts. In 1662 his doctor Nathan Paget introduced the fifty-four-year-old retiree to Paget's twenty-four-year old cousin, Elizabeth Minshull, and the couple soon married. As far as we know they were entirely happy, and "Betty," as Milton called her, spoke nothing but good of her husband after his death. She was less well disposed toward his daughters, and perhaps not without reason. Milton evidently did not even bother to tell his daughters of his plans to remarry. When she heard of them from another source, Mary Milton replied that it "was no news, to hear of his wedding; but if she could hear of his death, *that* was something!"[2] It would appear that what was uppermost in the minds of Milton's daughters was not his welfare but his inheritance, of which they would be deprived by his new wife.

They needed the money quite badly. Milton had lost thousands of pounds
in money loaned to the Commonwealth government, debts that were naturally not honored by the new regime, and Parker asserts that "in his
latter years Milton lived in considerable poverty" (ibid. 226). That may
be an exaggeration, but he was certainly living far less comfortably than
at any previous stage of his life. The house in Chalfont St. Giles, to which
he moved temporarily to avoid the plague in 1665, was described as a
"pretty box." The following year the family house on Bread Street was
destroyed in the Great Fire, and although Milton was not resident there
at the time, this cannot have helped his finances. By 1670 his daughters
had had enough of the tense atmosphere pervading the Milton residence,
and in a dramatic indication of the decline in the family's economic fortunes, they left home in order to learn their own trades. Edward Phillips
recounts that they found the task of assisting in the composition of the
greatest poem in the English language rather tedious:

> The irksomeness of this imployment could not always be concealed,
> but broke out more and more into expressions of uneasiness; so
> that at length they were all (even the Eldest also) sent out to learn
> some Curious and Ingenious sorts of Manufacture, that are proper
> for Women to learn, particularly Imbroideries in Gold or Silver.[3]

It is doubtful that Milton himself cared greatly about his reduced
circumstances. He was already inured by choice to frugality, being convinced of its spiritual benefits, and he was in any case engaged in one
of the most extraordinary intellectual adventures ever undertaken by a
human being. But we cannot expect that this fact placated his daughters,
who, according to a report by Thomas Warton, actually stole some of
their father's books and sold them to "the dung-hill women."[4] Milton
seems to have returned their petty hostility, grumbling to a maidservant

that since "he had made provision for his children in his life time and had
spent the greater part of his estate in providing for them,"[5] he intended
to leave his entire remaining wealth to his wife. According to his brother
Christopher he made good on this threat. As a blind man Milton had to
dictate his will orally, in front of witnesses who included Christopher. As
Christopher testified, John used the occasion to spitefully extract from his
daughters the money he had failed to squeeze out of their grandfather:

> The portion due to me from Mr. Powell, my former wife's father, I
> leave to the unkind children I had by her, having received no part
> of it; but my meaning is, they shall have no other benefit of my es-
> tate than the said portion and what I have besides done for them,
> they having been very undutiful to me.[6]

His daughters inevitably disputed the will in court and, after fraught
negotiations, eventually received some share in the pathetically small
estate of £900 left by the old moneylender. We might expect such bick-
ering over finances from a family of usurers, but perhaps we would not
have expected it from the immediate family of the greatest poet in the
English language. But if we assume that poetry and usury are opposite or
even different activities, that bespeaks only our anachronistic ignorance
of their true nature. Milton knew well that verbal and financial forms of
representation were interlinked, and he was fully aware of their implications in the sphere of personal relations, as well as in politics and religion.
Living through and participating in the birth of finance capitalism, he was
perfectly positioned to perceive its effect on every aspect of human life.
For centuries we have forgotten that usury has an impact beyond what
we narrowly label the "economy"; we have ignored its effects on people's
morality, their family ties, their politics, their sexualities. Milton wrote
early enough in the history of capital to see and describe those effects with

a clarity that should speak to us today as we witness what may be the terminal crisis of the financial system that he helped to construct.

The most intransigent intellectual problem that faced Milton and his fellow revolutionaries after their defeat arose from the fact that, during their period of political ascendancy, they had frequently and brashly based their argument on their success. Their cause must obviously be righteous, they asserted, because a benign and omnipotent God had allowed it to succeed. Cromwell was particularly prone to such bold claims, but he was far from alone. As Milton remarks in the *Second Defence*, the Parliamentary officers "have been always wont to ascribe the whole glory of their successes to the favour of the Deity, whose help they have so suppliantly implored, and so conspicuously obtained" (4.i.601). In 1649's *Eikonoklastes* Milton had made this argument himself, attributing Parliament's victories to "the powerfull and miraculous might of Gods manifest arme: For to other strength in the midst of our divisions and disorders, who can attribute our Victories?" (3:555).

Milton never believed that the defeat of a good cause casts doubt on the cause's goodness. Rather, he assumed, it casts doubt on the goodness of the cause's defeat. If a good cause is defeated, we must blame the power that permitted that outcome. We must blame God. We must either do that, or deny God's omnipotence and attribute the defeat of righteousness to a sinister, independent force. Is Milton now imagining himself in conflict with divinity, boldly challenging the omnipotence of God as he had attacked the absolute power of Charles I, perhaps even asserting that there are other deities whose powers are beyond the control of Yahweh? These issues bring us back to the identity of the spirit that Milton believed had dictated his poem to him as he slept. When, years after the poet's death, this question was raised with Betty Milton, she indignantly defended her late husband's monotheism:

[B]eing asked whether he did not often read Homer and Virgil, she understood it as an imputation upon him for stealing from those authors, and answered with eagerness that he stole from nobody but the Muse who inspired him; and being asked by a lady present who the Muse was, replied that it was God's grace, and the Holy Spirit that visited him nightly.[7]

There is a strong note of condescension in this conversation, and it seems that the widow of John Milton was not regarded with excessive respect in Restoration intellectual circles. But Betty's answer is intriguing. Her initial instinct is to describe Milton's source as a "Muse," which is of course a classical rather than a Christian concept. She qualifies this under interrogation, but in terms that raise yet further questions. The terms "God's grace" and "the Holy Spirit" refer to different aspects of the Christian Trinity. By which had Milton been inspired? Could he have been inspired, as his widow seems to imply here, by all of them?

The famous invocation that opens book one of *Paradise Lost* addresses just these questions. Milton appeals to a "heavenly Muse" (1:6), which seems to imply access to both the classical, pagan source of poetic inspiration and to the dwelling place of the Christian God. He then rapidly addresses all three aspects of the Christian Trinity, while taking care to differentiate and separate them from one another. First he calls upon the Being who "on the secret top / Of Oreb, or of Sinai, didst inspire / That shepherd. . . ." (1:6–8). The shepherd in question is Moses, who received the Ten Commandments from the Judaic God of the Old Testament. In Christianity, this is God the Father, the stern, tribal God of judgment. But Milton immediately shifts his ground: "or if Sion hill / Delight thee more, and Siloa's brook that flowed / Fast by the oracle of God; I thence invoke thy aid. . . ." In contrast to Mount Sinai, the symbol of the Law,

Mount Sion represents the heavenly Jerusalem which, for Christians, is only accessible through God the Son, the universal God of mercy and redemption. Milton presents these two aspects of the Godhead as alternative sources of inspiration, and throughout *Paradise Lost* he reminds us of his heretical opinion that the Son is a separate being from the Father.

A third mountain now looms into view, as Milton announces his intent "to soar / Above the Aonian mount" (14–15). He refers here to Mount Helicon, the haunt of the classical Muses, and this claim to surpass all pagan literature, while hardly modest, is not unexpected from a poet attempting to write a Christian epic that will supersede Homer and Virgil. It is the next lines that are truly unexpected. Milton claims that his poetry "pursues / Things unattempted yet in prose or rhyme" (1:15–16). There is a conspicuous absence of qualification here: Milton is surely stating his aspiration to surpass the Bible itself. He believes himself capable of insights that the authors of the Bible never even attempted. This raises arrogance almost to the level of blasphemy, but it follows logically enough from Milton's frequently expressed view that truth evolves, that history is a progressive, developing revelation of truth. In 1644's *Areopagitica* he had likened truth to an "ever-streaming fountain" that cannot ever cease to change, lest it "sicken into a muddy poll of conformity and tradition" (2:543). Milton does not deny that the Bible was divinely inspired, but an awful lot has happened since the Bible was written. As Milton saw it, the recent history of England was a particularly significant addendum to divine revelation, and Providence had selected him as the man to record it. He completes the roster of the Trinity with a final invocation: "And chiefly thou O Spirit, that dost prefer / Before all temples the upright heart and pure, / Instruct me . . ." (1:17–19). This is the Holy Spirit, whose temple is located by St. Paul within every human being.[8] When Milton claims that the Spirit prefers this venue to all exterior temples, he announces his final rejection of organized religion. He had seen enough of the oppression and fanaticism that can result from attempts to impose church discipline by coercion, and in his blind old age he communed with the deity only in solitude.

So it seems that the spirit whose voice Milton heard was an amalgamation of the classical Muses and all three aspects of the Christian Trinity. At the start of *Paradise Lost*'s seventh book, for the only time in his entire corpus, he gives that deity a proper name, but this very act seems to produce doubt as to its adequacy: "Descend from heaven Urania, by that name / If rightly thou art called, whose voice divine / Following, above the Olympian hill I soar . . ." (7:1–3). Urania was the classical Muse of astronomy, but Milton explicitly denies that he is alluding to her. As throughout his career, he forces the reader to look behind the literal and to understand "Urania" as a convenient figure, a symbol or trope, for some ulterior referent. As he carefully specifies: "The meaning, not the name I call" (7:5). Not only is he soaring "above the Olympian hill," or transcending the realm of the pagan Muses, he explicitly reminds Urania that she is:

> Nor of the Muses nine, nor on the top
> Of old Olympus dwell'st, but heavenly born,
> Before the hills appeared, or fountain flowed,
> Thou with eternal Wisdom didst converse,
> Wisdom thy sister, and with her didst play
> In presence of the almighty Father. (7:6–11)

Wisdom, the divine Sophia of the ancient world, is said to preexist creation in the biblical book of Proverbs (8:24), and on this basis she was frequently glossed by Christian readers as shorthand for the Holy Spirit. Milton's "Urania" is the "sister" of that Spirit, and hence not identical to it. The above lines also distinguish her clearly from "the almighty Father." There is only one element of the Trinity left; "Urania" can only refer to what Christians call the "Son" of God. Milton blurs that metaphor's gender in order to emphasize that he does not understand the "Son" as the only the historical Jesus of Nazareth, but primarily as the *logos* mentioned in John 1:1: "In the beginning was the Word, and the Word was with God, and the Word was God." Christians identify this "Word" with the "Son," but the original Greek term used, logos, can also mean "act," "mind," "thought," "truth" and "reason." Milton often comes close to identifying the Son of God with reason, the immortal "divine spark" within every human soul. By invoking "[t]he meaning, not the name" of "Urania," rather than appealing directly to the Son, Milton announces his reinterpretation of the Trinity's Second Person.

These were of course highly heretical doctrines, held only by the most radical sects such as the Quakers. The argument that the "Son" of God is Reason itself is hardly compatible with Protestant Christianity, which emphasizes the inherent and completely sinful, fallen nature of the human soul. It is entirely compatible with the thought of Plato, however, and this is one of many ways in which Milton imports pagan doctrine into what superficially seems a Christian poem. As Milton wrote, these ideas were already taking a philosophical form in the work of the so-called Cambridge Platonists, and over the century following his death they would evolve into the eminently respectable philosophy known as deism. During the French Revolution, Reason actually was worshipped with full religious rites imposed by Robespierre. Milton was ahead of his time in theology as well as in politics.

The identification of the Son with Reason also destroys the doctrine of the Trinity. The concept of the Trinity is deliberately irrational: it is logically impossible for something simultaneously to number both one and three. As Tertullian, the great second-century Patriarch, expressed his attitude to this doctrine: "I believe it because it is impossible." But Milton could never believe anything irrational, and so he boldly advances an anti-Trinitarian theology. It is confirmed by the invocation that begins book three. As we have seen, Milton there calls upon a "holy Light," which, in an intractable, tortuous formulation that surely bespeaks many years of profound contemplation, he calls "offspring of heaven first-born / Or of the eternal co-eternal beam" (3:1–2). The trouble with reading this as a reference to the Son is that, according to orthodox Christian doctrine, the Son is not the "first-born" of heaven but is just as eternal as the Father. But Milton is clearly distinguishing between the Father and the Son, when he goes on to refer to the light as "[b]right effluence of bright essence increate" (3:6). An "effluence" is an emanation from something other than itself, in the same way that a beam of light is different from the sun. And this idea that the light is a secondary, derivative power is reinforced when Milton asks whether it would be preferable to describe it as a "pure ethereal stream, / Whose fountain who shall tell?" (3:7–8). The "fountain" is the unknowable heavenly Father, but the "stream" is the Son, the continually evolving aspect of God who is revealed to us in the course of our history and biography.

So I think we can conclude that Milton believed *Paradise Lost* to be directly inspired by the "Son" of God. But this introduces yet one more question we must answer before we can approach the poem more closely: What exactly does Milton mean by the "Son" of God? The historical Jesus of Nazareth hardly features in *Paradise Lost*; rather the nature of the Son is discussed in largely abstract, theological terms. In book five the archangel Raphael tells Adam and Eve the story of how, before the creation of the universe, "the Father" gathered all his angels together to inform them that "[t]his day I have begot whom I declare / My only

Son" (5:604–3). This is Milton's most blatant and succinct expounding of the heresy known as Arianism: the doctrine that the Son was created in time by the Father. The Son, for Milton, is not an eternal but a temporal God, a God who makes himself known in and through history. Furthermore, the Father announces that his Son will hold over the angels the power of a "vicegerent" (5:609), or representative of the Father. From this point in cosmic history on, no one can approach the Father except through the Son. No one can approach truth except through the medium of representation.

Satan takes this as an insult. He "thought himself impaired" (5:665) by the fact that he could gain access to the Father only by means of his representative. He accordingly raises an army of rebellious angels, and urges them to rise up against this new "prostration vile, / Too much to one, but double how endured, / To one and to his image now proclaimed?" (5:782–4). The fact that he perceives the Son as the Father's "image" is important, for that is not a word the Father had used. The term "image" was a loaded one in Milton's England, evoking as it did the religious icons and psychological idols that the revolution had attempted to smash. Satan's use of it here bespeaks his misunderstanding of the Son's true nature. He imagines that he is being commanded to adore the Son, to worship him as an idolator worships a block of wood or stone. In reality, though, the Father's command is far more subtle. Satan and his fellow angels have been told to regard the Son not as an image but as a *sign* of the Father. The purpose of the Son is not to act as King but as "vicegerent" of the King. Satan's fall consists in his misrecognition of a sign for an image.

We have already heard of him making such an error in book two. Meeting Satan at the gate of Hell, the personified figure of "Sin" introduces herself as his daughter. Satan is initially mystified, until Sin reminds him how "at the assembly, and in sight / Of all the seraphim with thee combined / In bold conspiracy against heaven's king. . . . Out of thy head I sprung" (2:749–51, 758). Sin was born out of Satan's "conspiracy" against the begetting of the Son. The birth of Sin, and the fall of Satan's rebel angels, is the direct result of the exaltation of the Son, and of Satan's misinterpretation of that act. Most of the angels are horrified at the appearance of Sin, because they understand that she represents rebellion against the Father: "[B]ack they recoiled afraid / At first, and called me Sin, and for a sign / Portentous held me" (2:759–61). The unfallen angels can recognize a sign for what it is, but Satan has already lost this ability. As Sin describes it to Satan: "Thy self in me thy perfect image viewing / Becamest enamoured" (2:764–5). To Satan, Sin looks like an image, not like a sign. He therefore does not understand her significance; he cannot interpret her. Moreover, what he sees in her is himself; he has himself already become an "image." The begetting of the Son and the birth of Sin are mutually determining opposites. The Son announces the necessity of representation as the sole means to the Father, while Sin denies that necessity, advancing instead the idolatrous claim that representation is an end in itself, that we should concentrate our veneration on the icon, not the referent.

It is worth pausing here to reflect on the circular nature of what has just happened. God has announced the begetting of his Son, who has earned this position, we are later told, "by merit, more than birthright" (3:309). The Son's "merit" consists in his function as the Redeemer of mankind. As Milton summarizes it in the prefatory "Argument" to book three: "The Son of God freely offers himself a ransom for man: the Father accepts him, ordains his incarnation, pronounces his exaltation above all other names in heaven; commands all the angels to adore him." It is his function as the Redeemer of mankind that earns him the role of "Son" of God. But the redemption of mankind is necessary only because of their fall. The fall of mankind, as *Paradise Lost* shows us, is the result of Satan's rebellion against God: defeated in his attempt at revolution, he takes revenge by seducing Eve. Satan's rebellion against God has itself been caused by the exaltation of the Son, but that exaltation has been caused by the Son's willingness to undo the results of that rebellion. Milton has constructed a kind of theological *ouroboros*: a serpent with its tail in its mouth. Part of his purpose is to show that the spiritual and metaphorical events he describes in the poem take place in eternity and are not subject to temporal constraints. But the effect is also to emphasize the interpenetration of good and evil, the fact that sin and redemption bring each other into existence and, most disturbingly, the collusion between God and Satan.

For Milton ultimately rejects the Manichean heresy. In spite of Satan's conviction that he is heroically struggling against God, Milton makes it clear that the devil is actually working on God's behalf. The very first action that Satan takes in the poem, lifting himself out of the infernal fiery lake, is immediately ascribed to God's complaisance: "nor ever thence / Had risen or heaved his head, but that the will / And high permission of all-ruling heaven / Left him at large to his own dark designs" (1:210–13). Satan follows his own "designs," but he can do so only with God's "permission." In a monotheistic universe it cannot logically be otherwise; if heaven is "all-ruling," then it rules over Satan. This uncompromising theory is difficult to accept because it makes God responsible for the very worst things that have happened in our private and public histories: for the death of our loved ones, for the Holocaust, for the torture of children. In *The Brothers Karamazov*, Dostoevsky expresses our instinctive revulsion from such a deity through the figure of Ivan, who, after giving a harrowing account of a real-life case of child abuse, announces that, while he can accept that God is moving in mysterious, symbolic ways, and planning to bring a greater good out of an apparent evil, the visible, surface appearance of events is so morally disgusting that he wants nothing to do with such a God. As he memorably puts it, "I return my ticket" to heaven.

Milton strongly considered returning his, as the palpable sympathy with which Satan is frequently described in *Paradise Lost* clearly shows. Ultimately, however, his indeliably ingrained iconoclasm, now confirmed by the experience of blindness, prevents him from doing so. He insists that there must be (he is incapable of believing that there is not) a hidden, ulterior significance lying beneath the shallow appearances of events. The images that confront our sensory, empirical experience must be mere signs that point to metaphysical referents. We must not take things literally; things cannot be what they appear to be. We must destroy images by recognizing them as signs. In the autobiographical passage that follows his invocation of "Urania," Milton insists that his voice remains

> unchang'd
> To hoarse or mute, though fallen on evil days
> On evil days though fallen, and evil tongues
> In darkness and with dangers compass'd round,
> And solitude; yet not alone, while thou
> Visit'st my slumbers nightly, or when morn
> Purples the east. Still govern thou my song,
> Urania! And fit audience find though few.
> But drive far off the barbarous dissonance
> Of Bacchus and his revelers, the race
> Of that wild rout that tore the Thracian bard
> In Rhodope, where woods and rocks had ears

To rapture, till the savage clamour drown'd
Both harp and voice; nor could the Muse defend
Her son. So fail not thou who thee implores;
For thou art heavenly, she an empty dream. (7:24–39)

Orpheus, "the Thracian bard" and son of Calliope, the Muse of epic poetry, was torn to pieces by female worshipers of Bacchus. Milton had identified with Orpheus throughout his life, and after the Restoration, surrounded by hostile women and endangered by the victory of the Bacchic Cavaliers, he fears that his voice may be silenced in similar fashion. Finally, however, Orpheus was merely an imperfect prefiguration of Christ, whose redemptive power would prove fully successful, transcending the half-success of Orpheus's attempted liberation of Eurydice from the underworld. Milton confirms that his "Urania" is the second person of the Trinity by affirming her "heavenly" reality, in contrast to the beautiful but ultimately "empty dream" of the classical Muse. Milton believes that *Paradise Lost* is the work of the "Son" of God, and he believes that the "Son" is made manifest in the human ability to see the ulterior meanings concealed behind the surface appearances presented to us by our senses.

III

PARADISE LOST DESCRIBES the influence of the "Son" from multifarious perspectives, but brevity demands that we concentrate on just one example. Consider the nature of the "serpent" and its role in Eden. Genesis makes no reference to Satan at all; Eve is tempted by nothing more than "the serpent." This fact has given rise to numerous heretical interpretations, most notably that followed by the most formidable and tenacious heresy of all: Gnosticism. The term "Gnostic" means "Knower," and the Gnostics, much like the aged Milton, believed that human knowledge of divinity is innate, interior, to be sought within the mind rather than through the external trappings of formal liturgy or ecclesiastical organization. For the Gnostics, the "serpent" who brings knowledge of good and evil to the human couple is not their enemy but their Redeemer. The "serpent," in short, is Christ. The true enemy of the human race is the Being to whom Genesis refers as "God." This deity is evil and malicious; he has created the material world as a prison for the immortal soul, and he has denied us knowledge in order to prevent us from grasping the fact that we are imprisoned. In support of this argument, the Gnostics pointed to the fact that Adam and Eve do not die upon eating the fruit, as "God" had threatened they would, but they do attain knowledge, as the "serpent" had promised they would. "God" lies, while the "serpent" tells the truth. And quite apart from that, why would any benign deity want to deny us knowledge? Milton's own *Areopagitica* is arguably the most famous and convincing argument for the utterly unlimited, unrestrained pursuit of knowledge. In *Paradise Lost*, Satan puts the Gnostic case to Eve with devastating, remorseless logic. What can possibly be wrong, he asks, with

> knowledge of good and evil;
> Of good, how just? Of evil, if what is evil
> Be real, why not known, since easier shunned?
> God therefore cannot hurt ye, and be just;
> Not just, not God; not feared then, nor obeyed:
> Your fear it self of death removes the fear.
> Why then was this forbid? Why but to awe,
> Why but to keep ye low and ignorant,
> His worshippers. (9:697–705)

Milton refuses to flinch from a fair and thorough examination of the most powerful arguments that have ever been made against Christianity. But he is equally determined to refute them. The biblical Book of Revelation identifies the "serpent" with "Satan," and Milton follows its symbolic reading of Genesis. He explicitly refutes the Gnostics in the first sentence of the Argument prefacing book one, which blames the fall on "the serpent, or rather Satan in the serpent." To assume that the "serpent" of Genesis designates a mere animal is to read the text literally. Logically, it must fall to the Son, the viceregent of God, the Mediator through whom we must pass in order to arrive at truth, to destroy this literalistic reading. He does so in book ten, announcing His intention to judge the human pair, and also Satan, but to refrain from condemning the hapless snake: "Conviction to the serpent none belongs" (10:84). The serpent is not guilty; the guilty party is the one whom the serpent represented. On arrival in Eden, however, the Son immediately proceeds to do exactly what he has just described as unjust. He judges the serpent:

> Because thou hast done this, thou art accursed
> Above all cattle, each beast of the field;
> Upon thy belly groveling thou shalt go,
> And dust shalt eat all the days of they life.
> Between thee and the woman I will put
> Enmity, and between thine and her seed;
> Her seed shall bruise thy head, thou bruise her heel. (10:175–81)

This is of course a paraphrase of Genesis 3:14, but as throughout *Paradise Lost* Milton expands (he would have said "improves") upon the biblical text. He has already superseded Genesis by explaining why the Son condemns the

Serpent though brute, unable to transfer
The guilt on him who made him instrument
Of mischief, and polluted from the end
Of his creation; justly then accursed,
As vitiated in nature: more to know
Concerned not man (since he no further knew)
Nor altered his offence; yet God at last
To Satan first in sin his doom applied,
Though in mysterious terms, judged as then best:
And on the serpent thus his curse let fall. (10:165–74)

The first question raised by this passage is how an omnipotent deity could be "unable to transfer / The guilt" from the serpent to Satan. Milton answers that the Son is accommodating his speech to the now-fallen understanding of Adam and Eve. The fall involves a lapse into literalism, so that the human pair "no further knew" than that they had been deceived by an animal. They have lost the capacity to think "in mysterious terms," and so they assume that the Son has literally cursed the serpent. And they are confirmed in this belief by the fact that, from this point on, serpents literally do begin to crawl upon their bellies, and so to be literally trodden upon by human feet. We of course understand that crawling on their bellies is not experienced by serpents as a punishment; it is simply what they naturally do, but to Adam and Eve it appears to resemble a punishment, and their understanding is now limited to the level of appearances.

As Milton spent his life testifying, however, human understanding is not static. It develops and changes with history, and Milton believed that the acquisition of the ability to interpret symbols, to perceive the reality hidden behind surface appearances, was part of this progressive historical narrative. Following a thousand lines of further instruction, discussion and reflection, Adam reasons his way to an epiphany:

calling to mind with heed
Part of our sentence, that thy seed shall bruise
The serpent's head; piteous amends, unless
Be meant, whom I conjecture, our grand foe
Satan, who in the serpent hath contrived
Against us this deceit: to crush his head
Would be revenge indeed. (10:1,030–36)

Adam has finally learned to read the Word of God in the correct manner: symbolically, figuratively, in the manner later invited by the parables told by Jesus of Nazareth. And this is precisely the lesson that Satan fails to learn. Returning to Hell in triumph, Satan brags to his fellow devils about the success of his mission to alienate mankind from God. As he sees it, this victory has been won at very small expense:

True is, me also he hath judged, or rather
Me not, but the brute serpent in whose shape
Man I deceived: that which to me belongs,
Is enmity, which he will put between
Me and mankind; I am to bruise his heel;
His seed, when is not set, shall bruise my head:
A world who would not purchase with a bruise. (10:494–500)

Satan is a literalist, and we experience the influence of Satan whenever we are tempted to read texts or events in a literal fashion. He imagines that the surface appearance of the snake has been cursed, not its underlying meaning. Just as he adapts his mode of speech to the intellectual capacities of Adam and Eve, God responds to Satan's vaunting boasts in an appropriate fashion: He literally turns him into a snake:

His visage drawn he felt to sharp and spare,

His arms clung to his ribs, his legs entwining

Each other, till supplanted down he fell

A monstrous serpent on his belly prone. (10:511–4)

Because Satan stands for the tendency to mistake appearance for reality, it is eminently fitting that he should be, as Milton puts it, "punished in the shape he sinned" (10:516). Satan is not constrained into this form forever; indeed, he is generally free to take whatever form he pleases, but Milton drives home the central importance of his literalistic error by announcing, entirely without biblical warrant or patriarchal precedent, that "some say" (10:575) this metamorphosis will be inflicted annually, as a salutary reminder of the basic nature of the Satanic mistake.

IV

BUT WHAT DOES all this have to do with us? Throughout this book I have suggested that Milton's ideas are even more relevant to the twenty-first century than they were to the seventeenth. But have we now not strayed rather far away from the concerns of the postmodern era? Why should we care about talking snakes and fatal fruit? The answer to that question was obscure to many critics of the nineteenth and early twentieth centuries, which were historically the high-water mark of secular thought. The famous Victorian critic Sir Walter Raleigh dismissed *Paradise Lost* as "a monument to dead ideas,"[9] and the greatest literary minds of the last century's interwar years, minds of the caliber of T.S. Eliot and F.R.

Leavis, were frankly baffled, simply incapable of grasping the nature of Milton's wisdom. They thought he was writing about things that did not exist. They could not understand why such things should concern them. They imagined that such beings as God and Satan are comparable to the Yeti or the Loch Ness monster; they exist either literally or not at all. Their hermeneutic error, in short, was precisely that which *Paradise Lost* attributes to the influence of Satan.

It is a commonplace that the twenty-first century is a "post-secular" age. In every corner of the globe, religion is forcing its way back onto the center stage of politics. This development would have horrified Milton. He insisted on the separation of spiritual from civil power as a matter of deepest principle, and he would have been especially disgusted by the literalistic, fundamentalist forms that this religious revival is currently taking everywhere from Alabama to Jerusalem to Pakistan. But such tendencies are not to be countered by the petulant repetition that religion is simply false, a tissue of lies and fantasies, that emanates from secular fundamentalists like Richard Dawkins, Christopher Hitchens or Salman Rushdie. That response repeats the error that its practitioners believe they are attacking. It takes things literally.

Many readers may want to ask what is so terrible about that. Literalistic habits of interpretation are perhaps naive, but are they actually evil? Maybe most readers could agree that literalism is evil when it takes the form of religious fanaticism, and especially when it drives its adherents to physical violence, as it very often does. But why should those of us who, like Milton, follow no organized religion, those of us on whose daily lives religion does not impinge, why should *we* care about such archaisms? The most immediately obvious answer is that religion is too important to be abandoned to the fundamentalists, who will not be defeated by a smug dismissal of their entire world view but who can be

countered, even persuaded, without much difficulty by intelligent arguments based on their own terms.

But there is another, deeper reason why even atheist inhabitants of
the postmodern world must take account of Milton's ideas. To return to
a point made in the Introduction, our world is ruled by a force that everyone now recognizes as supernatural: money. Having finally abandoned its
material manifestations, money appears only in symbolic form and truly
exists only within the mind. What we get from Milton is an understanding
of that force and, even more vitally, a comprehensive explanation of why
the particular, peculiar way in which money behaves today is evil. We
receive this message in "mysterious" terms in *Paradise Lost,* but Milton
also discusses money in a vocabulary that is perfectly legible to modern
economists. For biographical reasons that we have already discussed, as
well as for complicated theoretical reasons, Milton is specifically interested in the question of usury. There is nothing evil, and certainly nothing
new, about money in itself. What is both new and evil, however, is the
widespread triumph of the belief that money can reproduce itself independently of any human intervention.

In *Paradise Lost,* as in the Bible, money is personified in the figure of
"Mammon," a Hebrew and Greek word for "money." Mammon is the
antithesis, the dialectical opposite of God, as Jesus makes unambiguously
clear in Luke 16:13, and Matthew 6:24: "No man can serve two masters:
for either he will hate the one and love the other; or else he will hold to
the one and despise the other. Ye cannot serve both God and Mammon."
To despise money is to love God; to love money is to despise God. God
and money are antitheses. Milton emphasizes this in *Paradise Lost,* where
Mammon's response to the devils' expulsion from heaven is to propose
that they use the "gems and gold" of Hell to construct a new civilization "[i]n emulation opposite to Heaven" (2:298). The phrase brilliantly

captures the nature of dialectical antithesis: Mammon's artificial paradise will both imitate and oppose the true paradise from which he has been expelled. Milton is careful to remind us that Mammon is no mere mythological creature but that he has an obvious, empirical effect on human history and society:

> By him first
> Men also, and by his suggestion taught
> Ransacked the centre, and with impious hands
> Rifled the bowels of their mother Earth
> For treasures better hid. Soon had his crew
> Opened into the hill a spacious wound
> And digged out ribs of gold. (1:684–90)

Mammon is idolatry's manifestation in the "economic" sphere. He represents the human tendency to attribute independent, creative, autonomous power to money, to believe that money is a real, substantial thing rather than a mere symbol referring to things beyond itself. He represents, in sum, the false god who reigns triumphant over the postmodern world: usury. Usury is probably as old as money itself. So are envy, anger, lust and gluttony. But every system of theology and philosophy that has addressed itself to the moral status of usury has concluded that it is unnatural, unethical, antisocial and violently destructive. Usury is regarded as a vice, a sin, by every society known to history except one: ours. Admittedly when I say "ours" I mean "mine": the liberal, secular, capitalist society of the Western world. That is of course not the kind of society that most people live in. It was, however, the kind of society in which Milton lived. The mercantile milieu of seventeenth-century Protestant Europe that produced Milton also produced the first ethical rationalizations of usury. It is an uncanny historical irony that they were produced by Salmasius, Milton's greatest polemical opponent. Along with the facts that he was himself a usurer, and the son of a usurer, and that his emotionally unhappy but intellectually productive first marriage was the direct result of his usurious activities, this placed Milton in a uniquely advantageous position to survey every aspect of the debates that raged around the subject. His personal circumstances made him into the prophet of usury: the single individual in all history best placed to tell us what it is, to describe its psychological and social effects and to predict what it is going to do.

Early modern anti-usury literature ceaselessly refers to creditors as "adversaries," and this term naturally evokes Satan, which is the Hebrew word for "adversary." Literature on all sides of the issue dwells on this trope at length, referring to usurers as devils, to debt as damnation and ceaselessly reminding the reader that, as the author of *Every Mans Right* (1646) notes, "Imprisonment [for debt] may be compared to Hell." This pattern of association informs the passage in *Paradise Lost* where Satan recalls his vain hope that rebellion against God would

in a moment quit
The debt immense of endless gratitude,
So burthensome, still paying, still to owe;
Forgetful what from him I still receiv'd,
And understood not that a grateful mind
By owing owes not, but still pays, at once
Indebted and discharg'd; what burden then? (4:51–57)

Satan had conceived of his debt to God in the same terms as the opponents of usury described moneylending. He imagined his relationship to deity in quantitative terms, so that "one step higher / Would set me highest" (4:50–51), and this led him to imagine gratitude as compound interest, a never-ending, always increasing burden exacted on a regular temporal basis. He did not understand that the difference between Creator and creature is qualitative rather than quantitative and that this alters the nature of the gratitude owed. Time, the quantitative measure of life, does not affect this debt, which pertains to the quality, the nature, of life. Satan's very existence is a loan from God, and the appropriate form of gratitude would be an acknowledgement of that fact, which would induce a permanent adjustment in his understanding of his own essence. He would then, as Milton puts it, "still" pay his debt—always be paying it, pay it through his very existence, just as he "still receiv'd" the loan of existence. Satan's status as debtor is not temporary or temporal but inherent in his essential nature. His "fall" consists in his denial of that nature, which causes him to regard God as a cruel and unjust usurer.

Satan refuses to pay his debt because he fails to understand it. He thinks usury is unfair because he misconceives it. The implicit refutation of his position parallels Salmasius's defense of usury: it is not unjust, because it is the renting of an essential thing, a qualitative use-value rather than a mere quantitative expression of value. Satan's debt to God is not sustained by excessive compound interest; it is not a temporal debt that God has unfairly extended in duration to the point that it can never be paid. The debt can never be paid because it is Satan's essential quality. The fact that Satan's debt is "endless" is not supposed to stimulate a frantic and futile effort to pay it but rather an understanding of its true nature. In fact the debt is forgiven as soon as its nature is acknowledged: it is paid by the recognition that it exists. Once it is acknowledged to be a debt, once its essential quality is grasped, it ceases to be a debt.

This critique of Satan's attitude to usury runs throughout the poem. As he tempts Eve, Satan claims that "[t]he Gods" practice usury in order to defraud the rest of creation into thinking that they have produced the universe: "The Gods are first, and that advantage use / On our belief, that all from them proceeds" (9:718–9). He suggests, like the opponents of usury, that this divine "use" is actually barren and unproductive. But the Son has already praised the Father for his genuinely productive usury, which uses even Satan's own activities for creative ends: "his evil / Thou usest, and from thence creat'st more good" (7:615–6). This description of usury as the production of good out of evil is given a more aggressive tone in Milton's last work, when the hero of *Samson Agonistes* figures usury as warfare: "I us'd hostility, and took their spoil / To pay my underminers in their coin" (1,203–4). After the Fall, the human couple immediately adopt Satan's erroneous, quantitative view of usury as a hostile, destructive numerical progression:

> There stood
> A Grove hard by, sprung up with this their change,
> His will who reigns above, to aggravate
> Their penance, laden with fair Fruit, like that
> Which grew in Paradise, the bait of Eve
> Us'd by the Tempter: on that prospect strange
> Their earnest eyes they fix'd, imagining
> For one forbidden Tree a multitude
> Now ris'n, to work them further woe or shame. (10:547–55)

Milton thus indicates that the conception of usury as magical and malignant reproduction is a consequence of the Fall. In *De Usuris*, Salmasius had claimed that the benignity of usury is sensed instinctively on a subjective level: that, as Conrad Moehlman puts it, "[i]nterest ethically is the gratitude experienced by the borrower towards his benefactor."[10] Satan conspicuously neglects to pay this kind of interest, which was recognized as "verbal usury" in the Talmudic and Patristic traditions.

Verbal usury occurs when the usurious relationship is allowed to bleed into normal social intercourse; it can consist in merely greeting one's creditor on the street if one had not previously been accustomed to do so. Maimonides describes it as "non-economic gratuities," non-financial benefits that accrue to the usurer.

But verbal usury can also involve the exploitation of linguistic ambiguity for economic gain. Marc Shell has described it as "an illegal . . . supplement to verbal meaning by use of such methods as punning and flattering."[11] The Talmudic scholar Hillel pronounced, "A man may say to his fellow, 'Weed with me and I'll weed with you,' or 'Hoe with me and I'll hoe with you,' but he may not say to him 'Weed with me and I'll hoe with you,' or 'Hoe with me and I'll weed with you.'"[12] Because hoeing and weeding are qualitatively different activities; they can only be rendered equivalent by being expressed in terms of a third element. This can be either financial or, as in the case of the above bargain, verbal. According to Hillel, this kind of exchange can never be equitable and must always involve usury, because the physical actions of weeding and hoeing, being qualitatively distinct, can never be precisely equated through the medium of a common denominator. It is exactly such a translation of qualitatively distinct actions into quantitative equivalence that Eve proposes to Adam in *Paradise Lost*:

> Let us divide our labours—thou where choice
> Leads thee, or where most needs, whether to wind
> The woodbine round this arbour, or direct
> The clasping ivy where to climb; while I,
> In yonder spring of roses intermix'd
> With myrtle, find what to redress till noon (9:214–9)

Eve already conceives of human activity as "labour," a thing that can be made equivalent to other things of the same species, as when she fears lest "th'hour of supper comes unearn'd" (9:225). It is not supper itself that she imagines must be earned through labor, but its hour. She has acquired the proletarian habit of conceiving life in quantitative terms, as chunks of measurable time that can be exchanged for one another. Although this speech occurs before the Fall, by making the division of labor the occasion for Satan's successful seduction of Eve, Milton indicates that this attitude to human life is intrinsically postlapsarian and alienated in nature. He had already drawn the connection between the concept of "labor" and usury in *Comus*, when the tempter employs it to convince the Lady that it is time to rest:

> Why should you be so cruel to yourself,
> And to those dainty limbs which nature lent
> For gentle usage and soft delicacy?
> But you invert the covenants of her trust,
> And harshly deal like an ill borrower
> With that which you received on other terms,
> Scorning the unexempt condition
> By which all mortal frailty must subsist,
> Refreshment after toil, ease after pain. (680–68)

Comus's depiction of nature as a usurer recalls the seducer in Shakespeare's Sonnets, who informs the object of his desire that "Nature . . . gives nothing but doth lend" (78). In reality, of course, it is Comus himself who "invert[s] the covenants" of nature. In spite of his protestations, he actually thinks of usury as illegitimate reproduction, as is revealed by his deployment of financial imagery to persuade the Lady to circulate her sexual favors: "Beauty is Nature's coin, must not be hoarded,

/ But must be current" (738–9). Like Comus and Satan, Eve misunderstands the nature of usury. Her conviction that the "hour of supper" can be "earned" by equivalent hours of labor shows that she thinks of time as a commodity, and the fact that it appeared to sell time was a well-established argument against usury. In 1564 a memorandum to the Royal Commission on Exchanges noted that "[e]xchange might be truly termed by the odious name of buyenge and sellinge of money for tyme, otherwise called usurye."[13] Since money was fungible and destroyed in use, the borrower could not be paying for both the money and its use, for that would be to buy the same thing twice. Rather, the borrower purchased a certain amount of time, during which he was the owner of the money. All usury was a Faustian bargain, blasphemously commodifying what could never be owned, let alone sold, by any human being.

V

MILTON'S POWER AS a poet, and his penetrating insight as a philosopher, is produced by the deep contradictions in which he lived, and in particular by the labyrinthine moral complexities raised by his involvement in usury. Those confident enough to cast the first stone can call him a hypocrite. But his hypocrisy, if that is what it was, encouraged an unflinching self-examination, a rigorous interrogation of the conscience that, although by no means unusual in the milieu of seventeenth-century Puritanism, allowed a mind as daring as Milton's to reach conclusions whose utility is only now becoming clear, more than three centuries after his death. As we have seen, Milton's age conceived of usury as a basically sexual sin. They called it a "sodomy in nature," because it made the naturally barren substance of money reproduce, while sexual sodomy prevented the naturally fertile act of sexual intercourse from bearing fruit. Usury and

sodomy were mirror images, so that it would be unsurprising to find that
a practicing usurer would also be a practicing sodomite. Milton was certainly accused of homosexual indulgences, and he had the reputation of
a sexual libertine. There are several passages in *Paradise Lost* that appear
to support this reputation. He insists, against many earlier theologians,
that sexual intercourse is inherently good and that it must have been practiced by Adam and Eve before the Fall. After their day's work the couple
retire to their bower:

> nor turned I ween
> Adam from his fair spouse, not Eve the rites
> Mysterious of connubial love refused:
> Whatever hypocrites austerely talk
> Of purity and place and innocence,
> Defaming as impure what God declares
> Pure, and commands to some, leaves free to all.
> Or maker bids increase, who bids abstain
> But our destroyer, foe to God and man? (4:741–9)

This sounds like straightforward advocacy of free love. But in fact it
is not the expression but the restriction of sex that makes it holy, as the
immediately following lines make clear: "Hail wedded love, mysertious
law, true source / Of human offspring, sole propriety / In Paradise of all
things common else" (4:750–2). So it is the fact that love is "wedded,"
legalized, a matter of property—unlike anything else in Paradise—that
makes it sacred and that makes it definitively human. But what does
Milton mean by "wedded"? Obviously Adam and Eve are not "wedded"
in our sense of the word; they have not participated in any formal religious or civil ceremony. It seems that Milton considers them "wedded"
simply because their rational capacities are in harmony. The implication

is that any couple whose rational faculties are harmonious, who enjoy what Milton called in his divorce tracts "fit conversation," are already "wedded," and so presumably no legal ceremony is necessary for them to consummate their bliss. Milton is arguing for the permissibility, even the preferentiality, of extramarital sex. He continues: "By thee adulterous lust was driven from men / Among the bestial herds to range, by thee / Founded in reason. . . ." (4:753–5) Reason is the definitive characteristic of a human being, and it is therefore naturally the foundation of love between a man and a woman. Milton had argued this point at length in the divorce tracts, where he criticizes the Anglicans for allowing divorce for adultery but not for psychological incompatibility, thus putting the appetites of the body above the aspirations of the soul. Here he makes a yet more radical point, claiming that the elevation of love between a man and a woman above the physical plane, its exaltation to the status of "reason," has made it the basis on which "Relations dear, and all the charities / Of father, son, and brother first were known" (4:756–7).

If we do not pay close attention we will miss what Milton is saying here. He is not saying that the love between a man and a woman is the foundation on which all other kinds of love are constructed. He is saying that the elevation of the love between a man and a woman from the sexual to the rational plane makes it that foundation. He is making the Platonic argument that spiritual love is superior to physical. This argument was (and is) often employed to advocate the ethical primacy of male homosexuality. Sexual relations between men and women are necessary for the propagation of the species, but sexual relations between men can have no such purpose. They can thus be entered into for purely spiritual reasons, rather than out of a desire to propagate, and as such they are morally superior to heterosexual love. After the Fall, Adam's sexual responses are purely to Eve's body, not to her soul, and they have a notably enervating effect on his morality, unremittingly working "to inflame my sense / With ardor to enjoy thee" (9:1,031–2). Eve's physical beauty, in short, has become a problem for Adam rather than a blessing.

Many modern feminists would argue that the male response to the female body remains a centrally important problem in contemporary society, and Milton would have heartily agreed with this position. Although frequently accused of disliking women, Milton was no more a misogynist than he was a libertine. On the contrary, the divorce tracts show him to be among the most progressive feminists of his age. Effeminacy is the problem for him, not the female gender. Similarly, it is masculinity rather than mere membership of the male gender that is admirable. This reasoning may still sound rather boorish to us, but that impression dissolves once we grasp what Milton means by these terms. By "masculinity" he emphatically does not mean the modes of behavior that we know as "machismo." He mocks machismo in his earliest college exercises when he turns the tables on the ruffians who nicknamed him "The Lady," scorning their pathetic pride in their prowess in the bordello. He does so again in *Paradise Lost*, when he scoffs at the physical, martial heroism praised by the pagan epics. What he means by "masculinity" is *virtu*, the Stoic ability not to be affected by the coquettish vagaries of Fortuna. Clearly these are what our age knows as "gendered" terms, but equally clearly they are metaphorical and not to be literally applied to actual men and women.

Similarly, by "effeminacy," Milton does not intend the characteristics that we associate with the term. For him it designates primarily a loss of control over the appetites and passions. Adam's conversation with Raphael reaches a verdict on sexuality that anticipates the theories of modern feminists with uncanny precision. Adam complains that God has made Eve too beautiful, because his sensual enjoyment of her elevates his passion above his reason:

here passion first I felt,

Commotion strange! in all enjoyments else

Superiour and unmoved; here only weak

Against the charm of Beauty's powerful glance.

Or Nature failed in me, and left some part

Not proof enough such object to sustain;

Or, from my side subducting, took perhaps

More than enough; at least on her bestowed

Too much of ornament. (8:510–8)

But Raphael responds that the fault lies not in Eve herself but in Adam's reaction to her: "Accuse not Nature, she hath done her part; / Do thou but thine" (8:541–2). The "part" of duty that belongs to Adam is precisely to resist the temptation offered by Eve's beauty. Adam requires repeated instruction on this point. In book eleven, on being shown the course of future history by the angel Michael, he remarks on the frequency with which men appear to be seduced away from righteousness by women: "[T]he tenor of man's woe / Holds on the same, from woman to begin" (11:632–3). But like Raphael, Michael angrily contradicts him: "[F]rom man's effeminate slackness it begins" (11:634). The term "slackness" has an interesting history (like many other English words, it has preserved its seventeenth-century sense in modern Jamaica); here it designates a negligent lack of vigilance in the face of sexual temptation. This, rather than any qualities inherent in the female body, is the true cause of humankind's repeated historical misfortunes.

Remarkably, these arguments found in poems written in Milton's sixties closely parallel the controversies explored in his first teenage verses: the Elegies that he wrote to his friend Diodati at the age of eighteen, and the sonnets he devoted to the girl he called "Aemilia." These early

poems develop from portraying Cupid as forcefully assaulting the adolescent sensibility with his penetrating arrows to the understanding that,
properly used, the objects that tempt us also produce our virtue, which
consists in resistance to temptation. The young Milton adopted the same
initial position as Adam, assuming that the erotic force he experiences on
sight of Eve is something that is being done to him, rather than something
he is doing to himself. He imagines himself being penetrated by Cupid's
arrows or, at the more literal level of the sonnets, being shot with bolts
darted from the pretty girl's eyes. But his sexual education involves learning that the reverse is the case: his desires, almost irresistible as they are,
come from within. They are a part of him, an element of what he is. And
above all, they are an aspect of his being that he must learn to subdue and
control, to master, before he can attain personal, political or sexual liberation. The consequences of failing to control sexual passion are described
in terrible detail in the capstone of Milton's career, *Samson Agonistes*.

CONCLUSION:
THE LIMBS OF OSIRIS

I

PARADISE LOST IS not a popularly accessible work, even by the standards of the seventeenth century, but it performed reasonably well in the marketplace, selling 1,300 copies over the eighteen months following its publication in August 1667, although no second edition was deemed necessary until 1674. It would have amazed Milton's contemporaries, though not Milton himself, to learn that in the twenty-first century the poem sells more copies in a day than the original edition did in a year. He always knew he was writing for the future. For the present, he spent his sixties bringing to completion various literary projects that he had been forced to postpone during the heat of his revolutionary years. He published a student guide to Latin grammar and a pedagogical *Art of Logic.* He translated for posterity his Latin letters of state, employed a student to transcribe a lengthy, highly heretical treatise on theology known as *Of Christian Doctrine*, and completed his *History of Britain* up to the

Norman conquest. In 1673 he brought out a new, augmented edition of his 1645 *Poems* and was even allowed to publish a brief argument for universal toleration of Protestants entitled *Of True Religion.* In 1674, the year of his death, he produced the second edition of *Paradise Lost,* which he expanded from ten books to twelve by breaking up the longest books into smaller segments. His years of retirement were busy and productive.

They also brought forth two original works that, while lacking the inspirational splendor of *Paradise Lost,* should certainly be ranked among the highest achievements of any English poet. *Paradise Regained* and *Samson Agonistes* were published together in a single edition in 1671. The former work is not, as the title might seem to imply, a sequel to *Paradise Lost* but rather a gloss explaining how the earlier poem ought to be interpreted. In a series of conversations between Satan and the Son of God, in his human incarnation as Jesus of Nazareth, Milton fleshes out the sparse biblical account of Christ's temptation by Satan in the wilderness. The devil muses on the all-important issue, announcing his intent to discover

> In what degree or meaning thou art called
> The Son of God, which bears no single sense;
> The Son of God I also am, or was,
> And if I was, I am; relation stands;
> All men are Sons of God; yet thee I thought
> In some respect far higher so declared. (4:516–21)

But as the absurdly futile nature of the temptations he offers clearly indicates, Satan is inherently incapable of grasping the true nature of the Son. In fact this very incapacity constitutes Satan's own essential nature. The Son gives us the ability to approach the Father through the medium of representation, while Satan embodies the tempting tendency to focus on representation itself, to the exclusion of what is represented. At one stage Satan suggests that Jesus might use his power to liberate humanity from the brutal tyranny of the Roman Empire. Christ responds by noting that the people's real enslavement is not political but psychological. It is fostered by many cunning ideological manouvers, and especially through humanity's enervating addiction to visual spectacles:

first ambitious grown
Of triumph that insulting vanity;
Then cruel by their sports to blood enured
Of fighting beasts, and men to beasts exposed,
Luxurious by their wealth, and greedier still,
And from the daily scene effeminate.
What wise and valiant man would seek to free
These thus degenerate, by themselves enslaved,
Or could of inward slaves make outward free? (4:137–45)

The morally destructive nature of fetishized visual spectacles has been observed by thinkers ranging from the second-century African Christian Tertullian in *De Spectaculis* to the twentieth-century French Marxist Guy Debord in *The Society of the Spectacle*. It is brought home to us today on a daily basis in the self-destruction of "celebrities": human beings who have made themselves, or who have been made by force, into walking, talking (if not exactly living) human spectacles. Milton took the licentious culture of Restoration society as clear evidence of the causal relationship between interior and exterior forms of slavery. As he put it in *Paradise Lost*:

Reason in man obscured, or not obeyed,
Immediately inordinate desires,
And upstart passions, catch the government

From reason; and to servitude reduce
Man, till then free. Therefore, since he permits
Within himself unworthy powers to reign
Over free reason, God in judgment just,
Subjects him from without to violent lords
Who oft as undeservedly enthrall
His outward freedom. Tyranny must be;
Though to the Tyrant thereby no excuse. (12:86–96)

If tyranny is both inevitable and inexcusable, how should the just, internally free man respond to it? This is the question that Milton addresses in his final work, the bleak, Beckettian drama *Samson Agonistes*, whose autobiographical overtones are bold and unambiguous. Its relevance to the twenty-first century is equally obvious. The action takes place in Gaza, where the blinded and defeated Samson has been jailed, and the modern resonance of presenting Gaza as a place of imprisonment and torture hardly requires amplification. The would-be liberator of God's chosen people has been enslaved, condemned to a life of "servile toil" (5), and the drama involves his progressively more successful attempts to perceive the underlying meaning of his situation. Like Milton's, Samson's most grievous complaint concerns his blindness, which he bemoans as having excluded him from the "beam" of heavenly "light." As in *Paradise Lost*, Milton identifies this image with the "Word," or "Son," of God:

O first created Beam and thou great Word,
Let there be light, and light was over all;
Why am I thus bereav'd thy prime decree? (83–85)

The "Son," we recall, represents the capacity to discover the true meaning behind the apparent surfaces of events, and at first it seems that Samson has indeed lost that ability along with his physical sight. His initial response to his situation is simple despair, and he indignantly rejects the various compensations offered by the figures who visit him. His father, Manoa, assures him that his freedom can be bought from the Philistine lords; his martial opponent Harapha tempts him to purge his guilt through violence; his wife Delilah offers him a life of sensual pleasure. All these characters have biographical resonance for Milton, but this is particularly clear in the case of Delilah. Like Milton's first wife, whose family was Royalist, Delilah was a member of a hostile "tribe," and this alone should have dissuaded Samson from his attachment. But he recalls how her physical beauty exerted on him a force more tyrannical than his present chains, and blinded him to the true significance of his situation, to far more deleterious effect than his current, literal blindness:

> foul effeminacy held me yok'd
> Her Bond-slave; O indignity, O blot
> To Honour and Religion! servil mind
> Rewarded well with servil punishment!
> The base degree to which I now am fall'n,
> These rags, this grinding, is not yet so base
> As was my former servitude, ignoble,
> Unmanly, ignominious, infamous,
> True slavery, and that blindness worse then this,
> That saw not how degenerately I serv'd. (410–19)

Whatever temptation is offered to him, Samson's response remains constant. He refuses any immediate or obvious comfort, by insisting that his predicament is a part of a wider historical narrative that has been designed by God. He repeats this point whenever it appears that he is about to accept some more literal form of succor: "[L]et me not rashly call in doubt / Divine Prediction" (43–44); "I must not quarrel with the will / Of highest dispensation, which herein / Hap'ly had ends above my reach to know" (60–62). Although he willingly, almost masochistically, accepts the blame for his personal transgressions, Samson does not appear to connect them to the seemingly perpetual enslavement of the Israelite nation. This he attributes to the general human preference for slavery over freedom: "what more oft in Nations grown corrupt, / And by their vices brought to servitude, / Then to love Bondage more than Liberty" (268–70). When he is eventually prompted to take vengeance, Samson does not do so on behalf of the Israelites. He does it against the Philistines. His destruction of the temple is a purely negative, hostile act, designed as pure iconoclasm and lacking any constructive aspect whatsoever. The sin of the Philistines that, in Samson's blind eyes, justifies their indiscriminate slaughter is their worship of a god different from his own. He is summoned to perform at a festival where

> *Dagon* shall be magnifi'd, and God,
> Besides whom is no God, compar'd with Idols,
> Disglorifi'd, blasphem'd, and had in scorn
> By th' Idolatrous rout amidst thir wine. (440–3)

This news inaugurates Samson's internal revival, for he is certain that, no matter how complete his personal defeat and humiliation may be, the true God will never be vanquished by idols: "Dagon must stoop, and shall e're long receive / Such a discomfit, as shall quite despoil him / Of all these boasted Trophies won on me" (468–70). Manoa heartily agrees, and the audience is invited to assent when he declares "these words / I as a Prophecy receive" (472–3).

A prophecy is exactly what they are. Earlier in the drama the Philistine warrior Harapha had charged Samson with being "a Mutherer, a Revolter and a Robber" (1,180) on the grounds that he rebelled against legally constituted authority: "Is not thy Nation subject to our Lords?" (1,182). He notes that Israel's own magistrates acknowledge their submission to Philistine authority, and like Charles I at his trial, he demands to know by what authority Samson can justify his rebellion. On whose behalf was he fighting, whom does he represent? The English regicides had shown a fatal uncertainty on this point, and Milton is determined that Samson should not repeat their mistake. He unambiguously announces that his cause is God's and that he need represent no other constituency to justify his actions: "I was no private but a person rais'd / With strength sufficient and command from Heav'n / To free my Country" (1,211–3). He does not hesitate to announce that the means by which this cause should be prosecuted is physical violence: "My Nation was subjected to your Lords. / It was the force of Conquest; force with force / Is well ejected when the Conquer'd can" (1,205–7). We recall here Milton's declaration in *The Tenure of Kings and Magistrates* that

> it is Lawfull, and hath been held so through all Ages, for any, who have the Power, to call to account a Tyrant, or wicked King, and after due conviction, to depose, and put him to death; if the ordinary Magistrate have neglected, or deny'd to doe it. (3:189)

"Lawfull" it may be, but it is certainly not legal for "any, who have the Power" to assassinate their ruler in spite of the refusal of "the ordinary Magistrate" to do so. It is in fact an act that the modern world knows as "terrorism." In the first *Defence of the English People* Milton went even further, announcing that "it is right for a people to do away with a tyrant

either before or after trial, in whatever way they can" (3:469). Such thinking is justified by an appeal to a law that is unearthly, supernatural and
thus finally unknowable except by the person who experiences its impera-
tives. "A dreadful way thou took'st to thy revenge" (1,591), as Manoa
accurately reflects on hearing the news that his son has pulled down the
Philistines' temple on their heads and on his own, crushing the political and religious leadership of his enemies to death along with himself.
Although Samson's father is naturally distressed at hearing of his son's
demise, the Chorus appears to express Milton's own view of the event
when it describes it as a "dearly-bought revenge, yet glorious!" (1,660).
In order to celebrate this judgment with due felicity, the Chorus divides
into two, and their joyous description confirms Samson's own conviction
that this horrific act of indiscriminate violence was ordained of God. As
one Semi-chorus expresses it:

> While their hearts were jocund and sublime,
> Drunk with Idolatry, drunk with Wine,
> And fat regorg'd of Bulls and Goats,
> Chaunting thir Idol, and preferring
> Before our living Dread who dwells
> In Silo his bright Sanctuary:
> Among them he a spirit of phrenzy sent,
> Who hurt thir minds,
> And urg'd them on with mad desire
> To call in hast for thir destroyer. (1,669–78)

In fact, when the Chorus finally reunites it is to announce that
Samson's murderous act was nothing less than the revelation of the long-
hidden God himself:

Oft he seems to hide his face,

But unexpectedly returns

And to his faithful Champion hath in place

Bore witness gloriously; whence *Gaza* mourns. (1,749–52)

In our own day, when increasingly radical and potent "non-state actors" are eagerly circumventing the laws of "the ordinary Magistrate" in the name of what they believe to be the higher law of divinity, Milton's advocacy of political and religious terrorism has inevitably attracted a great deal of criticism. Most famously, the well-known English critic John Carey wrote a piece for the *Times Literary Supplement* on the first anniversary of the attack on the World Trade Center on September 11, 2001. It was entitled "A Work in Praise of Terrorism?" and it pointed out that Milton's Samson "is, in effect, a suicide bomber." Like the perpetrators of the attack on New York, Carey points out, "Samson sacrifices himself to achieve his ends. Like them he destroys many innocent victims, whose lives, hopes and loves are all unknown to him personally." Milton's unabashed glorification of his hero's action is, in Carey's view, nothing less than "an incitement to terrorism," and the distinguished Miltonist even wonders whether *Samson Agonistes* deserves to be "withdrawn from schools and colleges and, indeed, banned more generally."[1]

So much for the notion that Milton's work is "a monument to dead ideas." Milton's prose and poetry are just as dangerous and inflammatory, perhaps even more so, in the twenty-first century than they were in the seventeenth. It seems undeniable that he does, under certain circumstances, advocate acts of violence that we would call "terrorism." But it would be a woefully simplistic reader who concluded from *The Tenure* of *Kings and Magistrates* or *Samson Agonistes* that Milton believes that any stray lunatic has the right to destroy any group of people he may take it into his head to resent. On the contrary, Milton's corpus painstakingly explores, and severely restricts, the circumstances under which terroristic acts are permissible. Terrorism can be countenanced only against those who practice, and who force others to practice, the most heinous sin of all, the sin out of which all other sins arise: the worship of Dagon, or, to put it in more general terms, idolatry. It is the heavy responsibility of each individual student of Milton to decide for himself or herself who are the idolaters of the twenty-first century. A heavy responsibility, but not exactly a difficult task.

II

HAVING BEEN GRANTED sufficient time to complete his life's literary work, Milton lived happily enough in his modest London house at Bunhill Fields, puttering around in his garden, dotting the occasional *i* and crossing the odd *t* in his remaining projects, tended to by his loving young wife, visited regularly by his friends, and even receiving a steady stream of admiring tourists. On July 20, 1674, his brother Christopher found him "not well" and heard him dictate the will that would be squabbled over in court for years to come. On November 8, in the middle of the night, John Milton died of kidney failure, as Cyriack Skinner reports it "in a fit of the gout, but with so little pain or emotion that the time of his expiring was not perceived by those in the room."[2] He was buried near his father in St. Giles, Cripplegate, on November 12, and Skinner found it appropriate that, like the Patriachs of Israel, Milton had finally been "gather'd to his people." But this gathering was to be roughly dispersed. On August 4, 1790, according to a contemporary report in *The*

Gentleman's Magazine, following a "merry-meeting" involving some minor church officials and their friends, the poet's body was disinterred:

> They cut open the leaden coffin, from the head to the breast, and found the corpse done up in its shroud; on disturbing which, the ribs fell. They knocked out the teeth, cut off the hair, six inches long, which had been combed and tied together, and after pulling the bones about, left the whole a prey to the grave-digger, who made money by showing it till Thursday four o'clock, when the ground was closed.[3]

The scene is replete with ironies. The body of the lifelong usurer is itself commodified, cruelly exploited for commercial gain in a world more ruthlessly capitalist than even Milton could have imagined. The revenge that Charles II had exacted on the bodies of Milton's friends Cromwell, Bradshaw and Ireton, which the King had disinterred and hanged, drawn and quartered, is belatedly visited upon their yet more radical colleague. The unflinching advocate of political violence is given a posthumous taste of his own medicine. But Milton, of course, would have cared not a fig for the fate of his earthly remains, which, if anything, would serve to remind witnesses that his soul was long departed for more auspicious climes. The prospect of his bones, hair and teeth being peddled on the streets of London would doubtless also have reminded him of the moving passage he had composed, over three decades before his death, in *Areopagitica*:

> Truth indeed came once into the world with her divine Master, and was a perfect shape most glorious to look on; but when ascended, and his apostles after him were laid asleep, then straight arose a wicked race of deceivers, who, as that story goes of the Egyptian Typhon, who with his conspirators, how they dealt with the good

Osiris, took the virgin Truth, hewed her lovely form into a thousand pieces, and scattered them to the four winds. From that time
ever since, the sad friends of truth, such as durst appear, imitating
the careful search that is made for the mangled body of Osiris,
went up and down gathering up limb and limb still as they could
find them. We have not yet found them all, Lords and Commons,
nor ever shall we do, till her Master's second coming. (2:549)

Are we beginning to find them now? In this book I've pointed out
that Milton attempted to make prophetic pronouncements regarding
what later ages would conceive as widely separate spheres of experience—
money, monarchy, marriage, monogamy, masculinity—and that the difference between his mind and the minds of his later readers is that he
did not think of them as separate. He is the last great English thinker to
complete his work before the "dissociation of sensibility" that divided the
human mind into discrete, delineated areas of interest and expertise. But
there seem to be signs, gathering number and strength as the twenty-first
century advances, that the buried connections between sex and money,
images and morality, the personal and the political, are once again forcing themselves into the forefront of people's consciousness. The ethical
status of usury, the power that rules the world, is once again under serious debate, and the moral, psychological implications of market-driven
celebrity culture are increasingly recongized as distinctly dubious.

Above all, there is a new *ethics of representation* in the air, a rebirth
of the knowledge, so obvious and familiar to Milton and his contemporaries, that the way things are represented, the way signs relate to
referents, the question of whether images are independent, autonomous
entities, are issues that affect every part of our psychological, sexual and
social lives. Since Milton's day money has, gradually at first, then with

greater rapidity and boldness, revealed itself to be nothing more than a self-reproducing image, while simultaneously seizing control of the entire world's human and material resources. Milton was able to live, and to write, because he understood and successfully exploited the nature of usury. This understanding was, for him, the source of immensely painful yet extraordinarily productive internal contradictions. He resolved them by dedicating his life to exploring and explaining the nature of usury and to warning posterity of its powers and intentions. Perhaps we have finally reached a stage in history when we are capable of heeding that warning.

NOTES

EPIGRAPHS

1 "Quotations from Milton's poetry." William Blake, *Milton: A Poem* (Princeton UP, 1988).

2 Philip K. Dick, *VALIS* (New York: Vintage Books, 1991).

INTRODUCTION:
PROPHETIC STRAIN

1 From Merritt Y. Hughes, ed., *John Milton: Complete Poems and Major Prose* (New York: Prentice Hall, 1957). Lines of poetry without a source given are from this work, hereafter.

2 Sonnet XII, lines 1–4.

3 William Wordsworth, "London, 1802," in *The Collected Poems* (Ware, Hertfordshire: Wordsworth Editions, 1994).

4 John Milton, *An Apology against a Pamphlet* (1641), in *Complete Prose Works of John Milton*, ed. Don M. Wolfe, 8 vols. (Yale UP, 1953), 1:890. Subsequent references to Milton's prose will be to this text, hereafter.

1

THE FRUIT OF USURY

1 William Shakespeare, *Hamlet*, in *The Riverside Shakespeare*, eds. G. Blakemore Evans et al. (Boston: Houghton Mifflin, 1974), 1:3.75.

2 Richard Stock, *A Learned and Very Usefull Commentary upon the Whole Prophesie of Malachy*, prepared by Samuel Torshell (London: Daniel Frere and William Wells, 1641), 224. I am grateful to Matthew Jordan of John Moores University, Liverpool, for this reference.

3 Ernest Brennecke, *John Milton the Elder and His Music* (New York: Columbia UP, 1938), x.

4 Retrieved on 10/05/2009 from Chadwyck-Healey, Early English Books Online, http://eebo.chadwyck.com.ezproxy1.lib.asu.edu.

5 Thomas Dekker, *News from Hell* (1606), in *The Non-Dramatic Works of Thomas Dekker*, vol. II, ed. Alexander Grosart (The Huth Library, 1885), 137.

6 For the association of usury with sodomy, see David Hawkes, "Sodomy, Usury, and the Narrative of Shakespeare's Sonnets," *Renaissance Studies* 14:3, 344–361.

7 Miles Mosse, *The Arraignment and Conviction of Usurie* (1595), 110.

8 Edmund Leach, *A Supply to a Draught of an Act or System Proposed* (London: n.p., 1623); William Bagwell, *The Merchant Distressed His Observations When He Was a Prisoner for Debt in London in the Yeare of our Lord 1637* (London: T.H., 1644).

9 Phillip Stubbes, *The Anatomie of Abuses*, ed. Margaret Jane Kidnie (Arizona Center for Medieval and Renaissance Studies, 2002), first published 1583.

10 Cit. J. Milton French, *Milton in Chancery: New Chapters in the Lives of the Poet and His Father* (New York: The Modern Language Association of America, 1939), 11. Subsequent references will be to this edition.

11 Aristotle, *Politics*, Book 1, Chapter 3, trans. H. Rackham (Loeb Classical Library, 1950, 1998), 51.

12 Cit. Susan L. Buckley, *Teachings on Usury in Judaism, Christianity and Islam* (Lewiston, NY: The Edwin Mellon Press, 2000), 116.

13 Don M. Wolfe, Introduction to *CPW*, 1:61n12.

14 Cit. J. Milton French, ed., *The Life Records of John Milton*, vol. I (New Brunswick, NJ: Rutgers UP, 1949), 83. Subsequent references will be to this edition.

15 French, *Milton in Chancery*, 36.

16 John Stow, *A Survey of London. Reprinted from the Text of 1603*, ed. Charles Lethbridge Kingsford. 2 vols. (Oxford: Clarendon, 1908). Reprint: Elibron Classics, 2001, 1.346.

17 Barbara Lewalski. *The Life of John Milton: A Critical Biography* (Oxford: Blackwells, 2002).

18 John Shawcross, *John Milton: The Self and The World* (Lexington: U of Kentucky P, 2001), 59.

19 John Wilmot, Earl of Rochester, *The Complete Poems* (Yale UP, 2002), 77.

20 Cit. Christopher Hill, *Milton and the English Revolution* (New York: Viking Press, 1978), 109.

21 Nigel Smith, *Is Milton Better than Shakespeare?* (Harvard UP, 2008), 6, emphasis in the original.

22 Cit. Roy Flannagan, ed., *The Riverside Milton* (Boston: Houghton Mifflin, 1998), 224.

23 A.N. Wilson, *The Life of John Milton* (Oxford UP, 1983), 16. Subsequent references will be to this edition.

24 Sir John Suckling, "Against Fruition," in William Carew Hazlitt, ed., *The Poems, Plays and Other Remains of Sir John Suckling* (Kessinger Publishing, 2006), 1–6.

25 Cit. William Riley Parker, *Milton: A Biography*, 2 vols. (Oxford: Clarendon Press, 1968), 2:187. Subsequent references will be to this edition.

26 Anthony A. Wood, from *Fasti Oxonienses*, cit. Roy Flannagan, ed., *The Riverside Milton* (Boston: Houghton Mifflin, 1998), 95.

2

TYRANT SPELLS

1 Cit. Todd Butler, *Imagination and Politics in Early Modern England* (Burlington, VT: Ashgate Press, 2008), 7.

2 Cit. *CPW* 1:337.

3 Cit. Anna Beer, *John Milton: Poet, Pamphleteer and Patriot* (London: Bloomsbury, 2008), 56.

4　John Keats, "Ode to Psyche" in John Barnard, ed., *The Complete Poems* (New York: Penguin, 1977), 38–9.

5　William Shakespeare, Sonnet IV, in John Kerrigan, ed., *Shakespeare's Sonnets* (London: Penguin, 1999), 3–4.

3

SAMSON SYBARITICUS

1　Lucan, *Pharsalia* 3:705–8, retrieved from http://omacl.org/Pharsalia /book3.html.

2　Cit. Lewalski, 89.

3　Ibid., 75.

4　Cit. Hughes, 638.

5　Cit. Lewalski, 99.

6　Cit. David Masson, *The Life of John Milton*, 6 vols. (London: 1859), 5:135.

7　Cit. Masson, 5:133.

8　Ibid., 5:144.

9　Cit. Wolfe, Introduction, *CPW* 1:64.

10　Cit. Masson, 5:123.

11　Cit. Wolfe, Introduction, *CPW* 1:55.

12　Tertullian, *De Spectaculis*, cit. Edward Gibbon, *The History of the Decline and Fall of the Roman Empire*, J.B. Bury, ed., 12 vols. (New York: Fred de Fau and Co., 1906), 2.15.

13　*An Apology Against a Pamphlet* (1642), *CPW* 1:871. The reference here is to Bishop Hall's youthful claim to be the first writer of satire in England: "I first adventure, follow me who list / And be the second English satirist." Joseph Hall, *Virgidemiarum* (1597). Milton enthusiastically took up this challenge.

14　John Milton, *Areopagitica and Other Prose Works* (Whitefish, MT: Kessinger Publishing, 2004), 136.

15　Cit. *CPW* 1:883–4.

16　Cit. Masson, 313.

17　Ibid., 343.

4

REVOLUTION AND ROMANCE

1. This was a commonplace sentiment among the revolutionaries. Oliver Cromwell's letters and speeches constantly stress the insignificance of his own personal efforts: "I could not, riding alone about my business, but smile out to God in praises, in assurance of victory, because God would, by things that are not, bring to naught things that are. Of which I had great assurance and God did it." Cit. Charles H. Firth, *Oliver Cromwell and the Rule of the Puritans in England* (New York: G.P. Putnam, 1906), 127.

2. Cit. Hughes, 1,029.

3. Ibid., 1,024.

4. Cit. Masson, 3:38.

5. The Book of Tobit, 12:20.

6. See Gordon Hall Gerould, *The Grateful Dead: The History of a Folk Story* (Chicago: U of Illinois P, 2000), originally published by the Folklore Society, London, 1908.

7. Paul Haupt, "Tobit's Blindness and Sara's Hysteria," *Proceedings of the American Philosophical Society*, vol. 60, no. 2 (1921), 71–95.

8. John Milton, *The Prose Works* (London: William Ball, 1838), 147.

9. Several novels have been devoted to Milton's marriage and sex life, most notably Robert Graves's *Wife to Mr. Milton* and Peter Ackroyd's *Milton in America*. Both of these treatments present him, quite falsely in my view, as a frigid and puritanical misogynist.

10. Cit. Hugh Maclean, ed., *Ben Jonson and the Cavalier Poets* (New York: W.W. Norton, 1975), lines 29–32.

11. Cit. Masson, 3:35.

12. Cit. Hughes, 1,022.

13. John Milton, *Selected Prose*, ed. C.A. Patrides (U of Missouri P, 1985), 179.

14. John Milton, *The Prose Works*, ed. Charles Symmons (7 vols) (London: T. Bensely, 1806), 354.

15. Matthew 19:9.

16. Cit. Masson, 50–1.

17 Cit. Lewalski, 179.

18 Cit. Annabel Patterson, "Milton, Marriage and Divorce" in Thomas N. Corns, ed., *A Companion to Milton* (Oxford: Blackwells, 2003), 279–94, quotation from 288.

19 Cit. Parker, 264.

20 Cit. Masson, 287.

21 Thomas Edwards, *Gangraena* (London: R. Smith, 1646).

22 Cit. Katherine Gillespie, *Domesticity and Dissent in the Seventeenth Century: English Women's Writing and the Public Sphere* (Cambridge UP, 2004), 122.

23 Cit. Parker, 290.

24 Cit. Lewalski, 182.

25 Cit. Masson, 291.

26 "On the Same," lines 9–12.

27 *An Answer to a Book, intituled The Doctrine and Discipline of Divorce* (London, 1644), 6, reprinted in William Riley Parker, *Milton's Contemporary Reputation* (Columbus, Ohio, 1960), 170–217.

28 Cit. Masson, 277.

5

WAR ON TWO FRONTS

1 Cit. Christopher Hill, *Century of Revolution, 1603–1714* (New York: W.W. Norton, 1982), 107.

2 Cit. Antonia Fraser, *Cromwell: The Lord Protector* (New York: Grove Press, 1973), 302.

3 Isocrates, *Areopagiticus*, trans. George Norlin (Harvard UP, 1980), 7.37. Subsequent references are to this edition.

4 Cit. Fraser, 347.

5 Cit. Masson, 3:46.

6 Cit. Lewalski, 184.

7 Ibid., 185.

8 Ibid., 207.

9   Cit. Masson, 289.

10 Cit. Lewalski, 181.

11 Cit. J. Phillip Wogman, *Christian Ethics: A Historical Introduction* (Westminster: John Knox Press, 1993), 143.

12 Cit. W.C. Abbott, ed., *The Writings and Speeches of Oliver Cromwell* (Oxford: Clarendon Press, 1988), 3:41.

13 Andrew Marvell, "An Horatian Ode Upon Cromwell's Return From Ireland," in Nigel Smith, ed., *The Poems of Andrew Marvell* (London: Longman, 2006), 49–52. Subsequent references to Marvell are to this edition.

14 Milton was far from alone in this. In a Fast Sermon preached in 1645, Hugh Peter remarked: "Methinks I see Germany lifting up her lumpish shoulder, and the thin-cheeked Palatinate looking out, a prisoner of hope . . . Indeed, methinks all Protestant Europe seems to get new colour in her cheeks" (cit. Fraser, 408).

6
KILLING NO MURDER

1   Phillip Henry, *Diaries and Letters*, ed. Matthew Lee (London: Kegan Paul, 1882), 12.

2   W. Carlos Martyn, *Life and Times of Milton* (New York: American Tract Society, 1866), 12.

3   E.g., Romans 7:14.

4   Cit. Fraser, 302.

5   Ibid., 300.

6   Ibid., 299.

7   Cit. Parker, 354.

8   Cit. Lewalski, 246–7.

9   William Riley Parker, *Milton: A Biography* (Oxford UP, second edition 1996), 355.

10 *Eikon Basilike*, or *The King's Book*, ed. Edward Almack, (London: A. Moring Ltd., 1904). Retrieved 10/05/09 from http://anglicanhistory.org/charlesleikon /4.html.

11 Ibid.

12 Ibid.

13 Sir Thomas Browne, *Religio Medici*, ed. R.H. Robbins (Oxford UP, 1972), 64.

14 Thomas Hobbes, *Leviathan*, ed. J.C.A. Gaskin (Oxford UP, 1996), 114.

7

UXORIOUS USURERS

1 Sir Robert Filmer, *Quaestio quodlibetica* (1653), 17.

2 Max Weber, *Economy and Society*, vol. I, eds. Gunther Roth and Claus Wittich (Berkeley: University of California P), 190.

3 Max Weber, *The Sociology of Religion*, trans. Ephraim Fischoff (Boston: Beacon Press, 1993), 220.

4 Eugen von Böhm-Bawerk, *Capital and Interest: A Critical History of Economical Theory*, trans. William A. Smart (London: Macmillan and Co., 1890), 1:448. Retrieved from http://www.econlib.org/library/BohmBawerk/bbCI1.html.

5 Cit. Buckley, 116.

6 Cit. *CPMP*.

7 Cit. Böhm-Bawerk, 1:448. He quotes Salmasius in Latin. I am indebted to Leslie MacCoull of the Arizona Center for Medieval and Renaissance Studies for generously providing an English translation in private correspondence.

8 Karl Marx, *Capital: A Critique of Political Economy*, vol. I, trans. Ernest Mandel (Vintage Books: London, 1977), 125–6.

9 William Shakespeare, *The Sonnets*, ed. John Kerrigan (Penguin Books: London, 1986), 86.

10 Paul Johnson, *A History of the Jews* (London: Orion Books, 1987), 7.

11 Cit. Charles H. Firth, *Oliver Cromwell and the Rule of the Puritans in England* (London: Pomona Press, 2006, orig. 1900), 218.

12 Cit. Fraser, 283.

13 Elizabeth Storey Donno, ed. *Andrew Marvell: The Complete Poems* (London: Penguin Classics, 1977), 101–104.

14 Cit. Lewalski, 256.

15 Cit. Blair Worden, *Literature and Politics in Cromwellian England: John Milton, Andrew Marvell, Marchamont Nedham* (Oxford UP, 2008), 202.

16 Cit. Worden, 22.

17 Wilson, 3.

18 Cit. Parker, 398.

19 Cit. Darbishire, 71.

20 Ibid., 5–6.

21 Ibid., 29.

22 Cit. Parker, 579.

23 Ibid., 472.

24 Ibid., 463.

25 Ibid., 478.

26 Cit. Fraser, 475.

27 Pierre du Molin, *The Cry of the Royal Blood* (1652).

28 Cit. Parker, 454.

29 Cit. Fraser, 421.

30 Thomas Salmon, *Chronological Historian* (London, 1723), 106.

31 Cit. Beer, 232.

32 Cit. Parker, 548–9.

33 Ibid., 621.

8
BLIND MAN'S BLUFF

1 John Milton, *Paradise Lost*, ed. David Hawkes (New York: Barnes & Noble, 2004), 1:26. All quotations are from this edition.

2 Cit. Parker, 586.

3 Cit. Darbishire, 77–8.

4 Cit. Parker, 586.

5 Cit. Lewalski, 459.

6 Cit. Parker, 647.

7 French, *The Life Records*, 2:222.

8 1 Corinthians 6:19.

9 Sir Walter Raleigh, *Milton* (London, 1900), 88.

10 Conrad Henry Moehlman, "The Christianization of Interest," *Church History* (1934), 13.

11 Marc Shell, *Money, Language and Thought: Literary and Philosophic Economies from the Medieval to the Modern Era* (Johns Hopkins UP, 1993), 49.

12 Cit. Vincent J. Cornel, "In the Shadow of Deuteronomy: Approaches to Interest in Judaism and Christianity," in *Interest in Islamic Economics: Understanding Riba*, ed. Abdulkader Thomas (London: Routledge, 2006), 13–25, quotation from 16.

13 Cit. John M. Houkes, ed., *An Annotated Bibliography on the History of Usury and Interest* (Lewiston, NY: The Edwin Mellon Press, 2004), 195.

CONCLUSION:

THE LIMBS OF OSIRIS

1 John Carey, "A Work in Praise Of Terrorism?" *Times Literary Supplement*, September 6, 2002, 15–16.

2 French, *The Life Records*, 5:351–2.

3 Cit. Carol Barton, "'Ill Fare the hands That Heaved the Stones': John Milton, A Preliminary Thanatography," *Milton Studies* 43 (2004), 198–242. The identity of the desecrated body was immediately disputed, but having carefully examined all the available evidence, Barton argues convincingly that it was indeed that of the poet.

INDEX

Elegies: I, 42, 49, 52, 77; IV, 38; V, 44–
45, 67–68; VII, 45–46, 65, 66
Eliot, T.S., 12, 308
Elizabeth I, 55
Enclosure, 25–26
English Revolution: cause of defeat of,
19, 293; conservatives' view of, 13;
degeneration of, 271; effects of, 121,
172; military conflicts in, 142–43,
162, 171, 205; origin of, 57
Epithaphium Damonis, 264
Essex, Earl of, 162
Evil. *See* Good and evil

F
Fairfax, Sir Thomas, 205, 210, 269–70
Fall, the, 7, 186–87, 301, 303–8, 314, 316
Featley, Daniel, 164
Fifth Monarchists, 211, 221
Filmer, Robert, 239–40
Financial value, as image, 17
Fish, Stanley, 182
French Revolution, 283, 297

G
Galileo, 98
Gardiner, Sir Thomas, 192
Gauden, John, 226
Genesis, 303–5
Geoffrey of Monmouth, 86
Gill, Alexander, 75
Glorious Revolution, 283
Gnosticism, 304–5
God: as evil being, 285, 289–90, 304;
in *Paradise Lost,* 284–85, 290, 301;
as reason, 186–87; Son of, 297–301,
303, 305–6; as Trinity, 297–98
Good and evil, 183–85, 289–90
Grotius, Hugo, 98
Gunpowder Plot, 59

H
Hall, Bishop Joseph, 109–10, 121, 122,
123, 124–25, 131, 160
Hartlib, Samuel, 191, 192
Haupt, Paul, 136
Hegel, Georg Wilhelm Friedrich, 220
Heinsius, Nicolaas, 100
Hell, Christian depictions of, 120
Henrietta Maria, 56, 77
Heroism, nature of, 130–31
Hillel, 315
History of Britain, 206, 248, 323–24
Hobbes, Thomas, 235
Hobson, Captain, 190
Holstein, Lucas, 100
Homosexuality, 41–42, 44, 99, 103,
137, 319
"How Soon Hath Time," 89

I
Iconoclasm: English Revolution and,
193; of Milton, 6–8, 11–12, 18, 220,
286; today, 18; true, 16
Idolatry: abolishment of, 7, 18; in
capitalist society, 8–9; definition
of, 11; magic and, 14; poetry vs.,
21; religious, 6–8, 57, 58, 114;
significance of, to Milton, 11; slavery
and, 6, 7, 115, 120. *See also* Images
"Il Penseroso," 70–73
Images: iconoclasm and, 16, 18; ideas vs.,
43; modern issues surrounding, 334–
35; in poetry, 21; in politics, 228–30,
233, 249–50; power of, 16, 18; ubiquity
of, 16; usury and, 240. *See also* Idolatry
Ireton, Henry, 333
Isocrates, 178

J
James I, 55, 59, 60, 61

Printed in the United States
by Baker & Taylor Publisher Services